Praise for Mallory O'Meara

"O'Meara achieves her goal. Thanks to her persistent efforts, *The Lady from the Black Lagoon* pulls Milicent Patrick and her considerable accomplishments out of the murky swamp of overlooked history and back into the light."

　　—*New York Times Book Review* on *The Lady from the Black Lagoon*

"Engaging and compelling.... A fierce and often very funny guide to the distaff side of geekdom."

　　　　—*Los Angeles Times* on *The Lady from the Black Lagoon*

"Chatty, impassioned...O'Meara is a dogged researcher and a fierce partisan."

　　　　—**NPR's** *Fresh Air* on *The Lady from the Black Lagoon*

"An incisive criticism of the erasure of women in Hollywood."

　　　　　　—*Bustle* on *The Lady from the Black Lagoon*

"An insightful, entertaining feminist history."

　　　　　　　—*USA TODAY* on *Girly Drinks*

"Thorough, and thoroughly entertaining... Provoking both thought and laughter, this serves as bracing refreshment from a master textual mixologist."

　　　　—*Publishers Weekly*, **starred review**, on *Girly Drinks*

"An exhaustively detailed yet breezy history set against the arc of overall women's rights around the globe."

　　　　　—*Kansas City Star* on *Girly Drinks*

"This book feels like having cocktails with some of the most fascinating—and dangerous—women in history. Cheers!"

　　　　　　—*The Guardian* on *Girly Drinks*

Also by Mallory O'Meara

The Lady from the Black Lagoon

Girly Drinks

Girls Make Movies

DAUGHTER OF DARING

The **TRICK-RIDING,**
TRAIN-LEAPING, ROAD-RACING
life of
HELEN GIBSON
Hollywood's First *STUNTWOMAN*

MALLORY O'MEARA

HANOVER
SQUARE
PRESS

**HANOVER
SQUARE
PRESS™**

ISBN-13: 978-1-335-00793-3

Daughter of Daring

Hanover Square Press
22 Adelaide St. West, 41st Floor
Toronto, Ontario M5H 4E3, Canada
HanoverSqPress.com

Printed in U.S.A.

for everyone who is still trying

DAUGHTER OF DARING

"I owe my greatest success to women."

—Frances Marion

"If you ask me, Hollywood needs a little of the old-time craziness."

—Mary Pickford

"What? You never heard of Helen Gibson?
The girl who laughs in the face of the most perilous feats that can be devised for her?"

—*Motion Picture Magazine*, 1917

Table of Contents

Author's Note

This is a book about Helen Gibson.

Like many who enter the world of Hollywood, she found herself taking a new name. In fact, over the course of her remarkable life, she went by several.

In this book, she'll always be Helen. Rose was the name that was given to her. But Helen was the name she made.

Introduction

This book began, as many things in my life do, with me being pissed off.

In the spring of 2021, I was writing my third book, *Girls Make Movies*, a nonfiction book for young girls about filmmaking. I'm someone who deeply, passionately, dorkily believes in the power of history, so as I was typing up paragraphs about what a grip does and how you get a job as a sound designer, I peppered them with bits of women's history in the movie industry. You know, the first ever woman to win an Oscar for this thing; the first woman to do that other thing. My life as a twelve-year-old movie nerd would have drastically changed had I known how much female filmmaking history there is, and I wanted to give girls today the experience that I didn't get to have.

When I got to the chapter about stunt work, I realized that, despite having worked on films that required stunts, I didn't know much about the history of women in the field. Soon, I fell into an internet rabbit hole.

My task, besides not getting distracted by an article about something weird and obscure on Wikipedia, was to find who the first stunt woman was. I thought that it had to be during the 1980s, when the modern action movie craze began. In my head were thoughts of Linda Hamilton fighting the Terminator, Sigourney Weaver crushing the Alien queen, and Sandahl Bergman swinging a sword alongside Conan the Barbarian. Truly, it was an awesome montage. I filed it away as inspiration for when I went to lift weights later that day.

So, imagine my surprise when I found an article listing the first stuntwoman as someone who worked even earlier than the 1980s. Much earlier.

It was the first time I saw the face of Helen Gibson.

White and pale with dark hair, her huge, defiant eyes almost dared me to write about her. The article next to her black-and-white photo claimed (it *is* Wikipedia) that she worked during the *1910*s. That seemed wrong. That seemed preposterous. That seemed...fascinating.

An hour later, I was in an absolute tizzy and wrote a frantic email to my agent, asking if it was okay if I put together a proposal to write about her. Then, I went to the library.

While I read through stacks of books on women's film history, my whole world turned upside down.

I started researching to learn more about Helen, but the historical context around Helen's life drew me in deeper. Because as exciting as it is that there was a stunt woman working in film in the 1910s and 1920s, it was far more exciting to find out that, although she was the first, Helen was one of many.

My jaw actually dropped when I read that in those early days of film, there were a *lot* of women making movies. Directing them, writing them, starring in them. The more I read, the more I made noises that certainly do not belong in a public library.

Having worked in film for nearly a decade, I was vaguely aware that there were a lot of women who worked in the industry in the early twentieth century. But I was operating off the 2021 idea of "a lot." In 2021, several years "post" #MeToo, a mere 12 percent of the top hundred films of the year were directed by women.[1] Despite a storm of ugly men on Twitter screaming that female filmmakers in Hollywood were "taking over," women accounted for only 25 percent of those working in key behind-the-scenes jobs, such as writers, editors, and cinematographers, in the two hundred fifty top grossing films of the year. Women in the United States, just so you know, make up a little over 50 percent of the population.

Compared to the barren years of the early 2000s, the 1990s, the 1980s, and well the 1970s, the 1960s, and you know, the 1950s and the 1940s, too, that does seem like quite a lot. You can count the number of working female directors in each of those decades on one or two hands. You can also bet your bucket of popcorn that most of those working female directors were white.

One of the questions I have gotten asked the most in the wake of the release of my first book, *The Lady from the Black Lagoon: Hollywood Monsters and the Lost Legacy of Milicent Patrick*, a biography of the life and career of the artist who designed the Creature from the Black Lagoon, is "Things have been hard for women in film for a long time, but they are getting better now, right? Now that #MeToo happened?" As if outrage on Twitter is a magic wand. Well, those depressing statistics are your answer.

To some degree, there's progress, sure. But there's definitely not as much progress as I'd like. Seeing a woman get hired to direct a big-budget movie or win an Oscar always feels like a victory. It usually *is* a victory. One is a hundred percent improvement from none.

But it's still one. One woman floating in a sea of dudes, like the world's creepiest water park ride.

These numbers are both an improvement and a frustrating drop in the bucket. Of course, if you point this out, you're a

---

1   From the Center for the Study of Women in Television and Film.

downer, a feminist killjoy, a drag. When people ask if things are better, they're usually thinking that there's more awareness. Articles, people yelling on Twitter, hashtags, that sort of thing. However, hashtags aren't jobs. Trending doesn't pay the bills. Like many things in the world today, there is an increased awareness, but not an equivalent amount of change. There's still a long way to go.

When talking about progress, people usually look to the future.

This book looks to the past.

I was stunned to discover, hunched over those slightly musty library books, that when film historians say that there were a lot of women working during the early days of film, they really meant *a lot*. A lot as in nearly as many women as men were making films.

Before the mid-1930s, there were women making movies about abortions! There were out lesbian directors, making movies about open marriages! Many of the top action stars were women. Women ruled at the box office and films were made with female audiences in mind.

How did this happen? How did women's opportunities in Hollywood *decline* over time? How was it possible that there were more women making movies in America *before* it was illegal to discriminate based on gender?

See, I was born in 1990. When I was growing up, I was taught the rickety fantasy that America was a postfeminist, post-racial society. We were told that the country was past sexism, discrimination, racism, past all that bad stuff. I got to vote for a female presidential candidate. I saw the White House lit up in a rainbow when the Marriage Equality Act was victorious. I believed that social progress was linear and things were on the up and up.

What an idiot, right?

Here in 2023, after the Trump administration, the #MeToo movement, the January 6 terrorist attacks, the rescinding of *Roe v. Wade*, and honestly, take your pick of everything that's happened since 2016, I could see clearly how progress is not a line. It is a pendulum that swings wildly back and forth.

If gender parity in the film industry was possible over a hundred years ago, when many still believed that women's brains were lighter and smaller, it could be possible again.

The thing about a lot of history books is that they're usually written about history's main character, the non-marginalized dude. If you're lucky, you'll get a little sidebar or a paragraph with a smidge of women's history or Black history (rarely both).

For much of my writing career, I've had to sift through heaps of written history for scraps. I once wrote an article about female film monsters that included Biollante, a large plant who fights Godzilla and is only considered female because she was made from the cells of a dead girl. You know, those kinds of scraps. Jesus Christ, that shit is exhausting.

But this period of Hollywood? Oh, this was not a time of scraps.

I, of course, wanted to know everything about this incredible period of film history. I wanted to know how to replicate it and make it better. How could an environment be fostered that allowed every type of woman, regardless of race, sexual orientation, or physical ability, to make art? That allowed all those women to make a living off of that art? Most of all, I was ravenous to know about these women. How did these women shape the history of cinema?

There has been a recent push, in the wake of #MeToo, to get more women working in the film industry. More female directors, yes, but also writers, cinematographers, producers, all the way down the line. No one is more thrilled and relieved and excited about that than I am. However, none of these women sprang out of holes in the ground in the 2010s. Women have a *legacy* in film. A legacy that stretches as far back as the invention of cinema itself.

Smack dab in the middle of it was Helen Gibson.

From the earliest days of Hollywood, the rise of female film-makers and their subsequent fall, the rise of the system that booted them out, and *its* subsequent fall—Helen saw and influenced the whole damn thing.

A tally of her accomplishments, many of them uncredited, is as long as a CVS receipt. She was a stuntwoman, an actor, a producer, a background actor, a trick rider, and she even had her own production company. Helen Gibson saw her name up in lights.

Now, Hollywood didn't give all that to Helen—she made herself a star. But Hollywood did take everything away. The story of her life is the perfect lens through which to view the rise and fall, and rise again, of women in film.

So, let's go back. Let's travel to Hollywood's true golden age, to a time when women ruled America's film industry. Let's meet "the most daring woman in Hollywood."

She's ready to give you a thrill.

Helen Gibson stood on the roof of the train depot and felt the rumbling in her bones. Thousands of tons of steel and iron barreled toward her. Great gusts of hot, dusty air billowed up her long skirt and through her long curls. Helen was twenty-three years old and she was about to make history.

Precious seconds had already gone by. She needed to leap onto that train.

No one was watching for her safety. She had no cushion to land on, no rigging, no green screen, not even any padding. Just the thin leather of her low-heeled boots and the starched white cotton of her dress to protect her from death. Everything in this moment hinged on Helen. Her skill, her sense of timing, her daring.

The moment she landed on that roof would unlock a whole world full of glamor and triumph. It would change everything. She stood on the very edge, muscles braced, hair whipping around her face.

She jumped.

Act One

Dashing-Daring HELEN GIBSON in
"RIDING WILD"

2 REELS   2 REELS

THE MOVING PICTURE WEEKLY, MARCH 1, 1919,
VOLUME 8, NO.2.

1

The Invention of Hollywood

"Have you ever stood close to the tracks when a great train tore past with about ten cars behind it? The suction of the draft it made almost pulled you off your feet, didn't it? And you had an impression of supreme, irresistible power... Can you imagine yourself on terms of familiarity with such a mighty mass of mechanism?... Controlling its gigantic bulk and terrific speed, making the whole immense thing obey you as if it were no more formidable than a little Ford car?... Of course you couldn't, if you are a normal person. And really, one would have to be excessively abnormal to do such things. Well, then Helen Gibson must be a real anomaly..."
—"The Girl that Tames Trains," *Moving Picture Weekly*, June 1917

Underneath the great mythology of Helen Gibson, stories that claimed she was conquering trains and breaking broncos from a young age, there was just a stubborn little girl from Cleveland.

She was born as Rose Wenger on August 27, 1892, in Ohio. Eventually, she became the middle child of five girls (one of whom sadly passed away in childhood). Her parents were both

European immigrants; her father, Fred (Gottfried), was from Switzerland and her mother, Annie (Augeste), was from Germany. Annie was a stay-at-home mom, and despite publicity claims made by film studios later in Helen's career, Fred was not a railroad engineer.

He did not bring her for rides on his engine, she was not taught how to operate a telegraph, and she was definitely not familiar with air brakes or steam gauges. All that came much later, and Helen became acquainted with them on her own. Fred, on the contrary, worked at the local nut and bolt factory.[2]

Helen grew up fewer than two miles from the banks of Lake Erie, in a city that was on the verge of a boom. Cleveland in 1892 was a happening place. (Depending on who you ask, it still is.) Perfectly placed as a transportation hub between the East Coast and the Midwest, it was about to emerge as a major American industrial city. By the time Helen left Cleveland in 1910, it was the sixth largest city in the country.

Despite all this hustle and boom, from a young age, Helen was a girl who wanted a little *more*. She never quite fit into the box that she was born into. This was the Victorian age, an era when the domain of women was the home. Women were not meant to be seen, let alone heard. They were expected to stay inside, embroider things, and try very hard not to think too much or upset themselves. Maybe every now and then they could look out the window, as a treat.

Don't worry, this isn't a book that looks down on traditionally feminine (and really cool) pursuits like needlework. This is, however, a book that advocates for choice, something that most women in the United States had little of in 1892.

Today, we know that everything is girl stuff. Unfortunately,

---

2 On his 1900 census form, instead of "fastener manufacturer," as his employer Lamson and Sessions referred to themselves, he put his occupation as "nut maker," which initially made me think that perhaps I had been poring over historical documents for far too long and had started to misread things.

when Helen was born, there was a very clear delineation between girl stuff and other stuff, like pants and civil rights. Helen didn't *want* to do girl stuff, though. She wanted to be out of the house and run around and play in the mud. From an early age, the pale little girl with big dark eyes and soft dark hair could not be contained.

Fortunately, Helen was lucky enough to be born into a family that encouraged her and all her mud-covered ways. She was nudged by her father to fill the role of the son he wanted and couldn't seem to get. Helen was, in her own words, a tomboy. Living a thirty-minute walk from one of the Great Lakes and a twenty-minute walk from the Cuyahoga River afforded young Helen lots of opportunities for swimming, climbing trees, hitting things with sticks—you know, all the good stuff. She spent her childhood, not as a delicate lady-in-training, but as a filthy, shrieking, scampering force of nature. Leaping out of trees on the banks of Lake Erie, the wind flying through her dress, Helen wanted adventure. In a society that insisted women, especially young women, remain passive, Helen was as active as she could get.

On the even more fortunate side of things, that society was slowly beginning to change. In the late 1800s, American women were finally starting to leave the house and enter the workforce.

It started slowly. The jobs offered to women were usually what was considered to be feminine work. Poorly paid housecleaning positions or menial, repetitive jobs on a factory line. There was one line of work however, that even though it was unstable and unreliable, offered more money and more adventure.

Entertainment was one of the few industries where a girl could find significant excitement and a bigger life. And of course, the entertainment industry of the late nineteenth century looked quite different than it does today. Theater, vaudeville, and music were really the only options. Even the first major radio broadcast wasn't until 1920. Newspapers, books, and gramophone records were about as close as it got to mass media.

See, when Helen Gibson was a little girl, she did not dream of Hollywood. Mostly because in the late 1800s, Hollywood did not exist.

The first thing that you have to understand about Hollywood is that the term refers to several different things. Hollywood is a busy boulevard, a neighborhood in the Southern California city of Los Angeles, and, depending on how familiar you are with the entertainment world, either the entire American film industry or specifically the major studio system in the United States. To confuse things further, lots of Hollywood events happen on Hollywood, which goes through Hollywood.

If you walk through Hollywood today, you'll find a pretty lovely neighborhood, as long as you don't take Hollywood, which is a slightly overwhelming thoroughfare filled to the brim with tourists and people trying to sell things to tourists. The only problem is that no one walks in Los Angeles,[3] so you'll actually be in a car. If you drive north, away from the lit-up signs for restaurants, theaters, shops, and tourist attractions, you'll start winding through the Hollywood Hills and eventually wind up at the Hollywood sign. It's here that you'll catch a glimpse of the Hollywood of old. From your vantage point, you can look down at the glittering city and start to see the glamor and excitement that still draws thousands and thousands of hopefuls every year. You'll feel the warm Southern California night air and understand.

But, of course, it wasn't always this way.

Long before movie stars were walking red carpets, before the film industry arrived to turn the area on its head, before

---

3   Unless they're going for a hike, a baffling mania that's gripped Los Angeles society for many years.

Hollywood was even a neighborhood, it was simply one rich family's ranch.

Underneath the traffic-packed freeways and buildings full of overpriced apartments, Hollywood is about five square miles of land tucked into the eastern slopes of the Santa Monica Mountains. Originally, it was the home of the Shoshone tribe and it's easy to see why they chose it. Even in winter, Hollywood never freezes. It's mostly protected from the hot desert winds to the east, and enjoys the breeze off the Pacific Ocean to the west. East Coasters love to scoff at Los Angeles, but they always mysteriously show up to visit during the winter.

When the Shoshone lived there, the area was mostly scrubland. Nary a single taco truck to be found. The mighty Southern Californian sun shone down upon miles of hard-packed dirt, and patches of cacti and sunflowers. On the edge of the mountains, deep, shady canyons were filled with trees and sage.

In the late 1700s, the Spanish arrived to establish missions (religious communities who sought to absorb native people into the Spanish colonial empire) and things began to change rapidly (and badly) for the native tribes of the area. By 1781, the Spanish had established El Pueblo de Nuestra Señora la Reina de los Ángeles (the Town of Our Lady the Queen of the Angels), which was shortened to Pueblo de los Ángeles. It was the second town created during the Spanish colonization of what is now California and it was entirely dependent on native labor. Pueblo de los Ángeles started out as a small settlement of only forty-four people, but it quickly grew as more settlers (and Spanish soldiers) arrived. Whenever you get stuck in traffic on the 405, you can blame the eighteenth-century Spanish missionaries.

Once Mexico's War of Independence from Spain ended in 1821, things started developing even more quickly. Most of the economy (and social life) of the area revolved around the ranchos, huge areas of land that were mainly dedicated to the raising of livestock (many of which enslaved the native populations of the area). After the Spanish were booted out, land previously used by the missions was redistributed to the ranchos. Within six years of the end of the war, Pueblo de los Ángeles was the largest, most bustling town in the whole territory.

Okay, stick with me.

Soon came the war between the United States and Mexico, the peace treaty for which was signed in 1848. After the signing, California officially became a US territory. And boom, just like that, Los Angeles was an American city. The first American mail arrived in what is now Los Angeles in May, 1848.

Three years later, Congress passed a law requiring all those with Spanish or Mexican land grants to get them confirmed by the federal government. Many of the land owners who did not speak English were unable to do this, and without confirmation, they lost their claim to the land. This lost land was then conveniently snapped up by white farmers and land developers. Funny how that always works!

The little area to the north of Los Angeles that is now Hollywood, or the western half of it anyway, was part of one of the ranchos, Rancho La Brea. This is Spanish for "The Tar Ranch"[4] as the land was pitted with great swamps of tar. It sounds like a big problem, but later on, white settlers and farmers would use that tar to waterproof their roofs.

Today, we think of Southern California as a hotspot for the entertainment industry. When California was in her early days of statehood, she was still considered a hotspot, just of a less glamorous sort. In 1860, the first California farmer sent a shipment of wheat to Europe, which sent up the bat signal for the other farmers of America to travel to the new state and try their hands (and plows) there. Eight years later, the first Californian

---

4   Which means that calling them La Brea Tar Pits is saying "The Tar Tar Pits," which I believe is the name of a rejected Star Wars character.

human-made harbor was created in San Pedro, near modern-day Long Beach. Southern California's first real estate boom had begun. Just add harbor.

Despite what old-timey cowboy movies will tell you about the people of the Wild West, California has always been a multicultural society. Massive steamboats loaded with immigrant farm workers would puff their way down from San Francisco. The people that embarked were looking for a new life, and many of them were Chinese. In fact, most of the produce grown in what is now the neighborhood of Hollywood was farmed by Chinese hands.

The year-round warmth of Southern California made it a fantastic place for agriculture and almost immediately, farmers began cultivating gigantic crops, enough to ship up north and provide the rest of California with fruits, vegetables, and wool. That's right. Before Los Angeles was full of traffic, it was full of sheep.

During this time, the area of downtown Los Angeles was filled with citrus groves. It is mind boggling to think of a place that constantly reeks of urine and car exhaust being perfumed by the gentle scent of lemon and orange blossoms. But this was when scurvy was a big public concern, and not just for pirates. Lemons sold for a dollar a piece and were quite a lucrative product to farm.

The famous intersection of Hollywood and Vine originally featured nothing more than dirt. Vine Street was so named because of the twenty-five thousand grape vines planted there. Hollywood Boulevard began its storied existence as little more than a narrow, dusty track.

Soon, however, the lemons and sheep had to skedaddle.

One of the many eager real estate developers to arrive in Los Angeles was a man named Harvey Wilcox. He showed up in 1883, opened a real estate office, and quickly began to purchase property so he could subdivide it. A few years later, he bought one hundred and twenty acres along the slope of the Santa Monica Mountains for one hundred and fifty dollars an acre. The area was rich with apricot and fig groves, and Harvey built a ranch there for him and his wife, Daeida.

Now, the legend goes that Daeida was traveling from Southern California by train to visit her hometown of Hicksville, Ohio. While she was on the train, she struck up a conversation with a fellow passenger. After Daeida described her ranch, this woman told Daeida all about her own summer home, a place she called Hollywood. On the way back home to California, Daeida couldn't stop thinking about that name. She loved it. And, despite no holly growing anywhere nearby, when she returned to the ranch, she told Harvey that their home would too be named Hollywood.

Soon, Harvey began to subdivide the land. He sketched out a big rectangular grid and lined it with streets. Those streets were then filled with feathery pepper trees to create shade and entice prospective buyers. Finally, on February 1, 1887, Harvey went down to the county recorder and filed a map of his subdivision, emblazoned with the name his wife picked out. Hollywood was officially born, just a few years before Helen Gibson was.

Unfortunately for Hollywood—well, unfortunately for Harvey—1887 was the year that Southern California's first big real estate bubble burst. The period of frenzied buying was over for a while, but development continued steadily. Other communities began to grow nearby, including what is now Beverly Hills, Westwood, and West Hollywood. In September of that year, the first train ran in Hollywood.[5] A decade later, the

---

5   This was owned and operated by the Los Angeles Ostrich Farm Company. Yes, you read that right. It was a line that connected the city to Dr. C.J. Sketchley's Ostrich Farm, located in what is now Griffith Park, to the east of Hollywood. The farm was enormously popular. It served dual functions of a great way to farm ostrich feathers for ladies' fashions and a very successful tourist destination where people could marvel at the creatures. Ostriches were available for feeding, petting, and even riding, although I cannot tell you how successful the last activity was. Extensions were soon built to what is now Santa Monica and Burbank. We can all thank ostriches for both the creation of Griffith Park and helping bring public transportation to Los Angeles.

United States government recognized the town by opening a post office in the Sackett Hotel. Hollywood was here to stay.

Then came all the other things that make a town a town: a newspaper in 1900 (the *Hollywood Sentinel*), street numbers in 1904, and a public library in 1906. By now, Hollywood was an idyllic place to live. If you walked down Hollywood Boulevard, which was now a country road, you'd see quaint cottages and gardens, fields rich with vegetable crops, and vibrant orchards. You'd smell heady blossoms and lemon trees. You'd hear birds singing and deer rustling around in the trees. Before the film industry arrived to bring chaos, Hollywood was a lovely, quiet little town to call home.

But the film industry certainly did arrive, and it certainly did bring chaos.

While all of this was happening a couple thousand miles away, Helen was growing up in Cleveland.

It was a fortuitous time to be a teenage girl looking for a different kind of life. At the turn of the century, the United States was undergoing a massive social transformation. The late 1800s were ruled by Victorian sensibilities that had women cast in the role of "angels of the home," which is a nice way of saying "please stay inside where we can keep an eye on you." Women were discouraged from almost any public activity that didn't involve domestic errands and children, which ruled out having jobs, drinks, financial independence, you know, that sort of thing.

When the 1900s began, however, American society started to change. Women stepped out into the world. Helen, having evolved from a rambunctious, dirt-covered child into a still rambunctious, but slightly cleaner teenager, was one of them.

Welcome to the rise of the New Woman.

"New Woman" was a term that sprang up in the late 1800s to describe women who were more active participants in society. No more passive ladies here. The New Woman was independent, opinionated, educated, and of course, infuriating.[6] She was most influenced by the suffragette movement of the time, and could be seen out and about, exercising autonomy over her body and demanding rights.

She also might be riding a bicycle, which became an important tool in the New Woman's feminist agenda. Bicycles offered hugely increased social mobility. They gave women (at least the ones who could afford them, which Helen could not) the ability to easily travel outside the home, and this fueled the fire that burned away a lot of Victorian societal traditions. Bicycles also influenced women's fashions to become more practical, since elaborate Victorian dresses were unsafe to pedal in. Bikes aren't just environmentally friendly, they're also feminist.[7] Please remember that when you are irritated while driving behind a cyclist.

Even if they could not afford to buy a bicycle, lower-class women weren't left out of access to affordable transportation. Newfangled electric trolleys and streetcar systems were popping up in cities all over the country, and the fare was only a few cents. Soon, the male-dominated public sphere was filled with interlopers.

And where did they go?

Some met with women's social clubs, many of which became rich sources of feminist thought and wellsprings of activism. Although they were called social clubs, their aim went beyond simply hanging out. These organizations were dedicated to improving society, and they supported causes such as education and library creation, and worked to end issues like child labor. Even though the common image of the New Women was white,

---

6   And usually white and upper-class.

7   Many physicians in the early 1900s were against women riding bicycles because they thought the seats would give the riders orgasms and cause these women to become "oversexed." Bikes truly are feminist.

there was a huge wave of Black women's clubs, with legendary thinkers like Ida B. Wells who encouraged their growth. In fact, by 1910, there were more Black women's clubs than white women's clubs.

These clubs often had their own headquarters, which meant the attendees were meeting in public, a new and exciting experience in an age where previously the only public place women could reliably gather was church.

Others—like Helen—didn't have time for shopping or socializing. They had to go to work.

In 1880, only 10 percent of women performed paid labor.[8] By 1910, it was as high as 30 percent in cities. During these years, the birth rate began to lower, and more and more women (40 percent in rural areas and 60 percent in cities) worked for at least a few years before they got married.

Helen's oldest sister got a job at a cigar factory in town, and around 1907, when she was about fifteen years old, Helen went to join her. At this time, usually only upper-class girls had the opportunity to receive more than an elementary education. Nut makers' daughters were typically not among them.

The two Wenger girls worked at the factory as "floor ladies," which meant they ran around the factory floor, doing odd jobs and errands. Neither the hours nor the pay were great—the average women's wage at a Midwestern cigar factory at the time was around three dollars a week, about ninety-five dollars a week today—but at least Helen was out of the house, earning money. Though she was just a teenager, Helen found herself, in this sense at least, a part of this progressive movement of American women.

But it wasn't all work. There were a number of brand-new entertainments available to the public during this time, including amusement parks and music halls. These establishments raced

---

8   Unpaid labor, of course, includes household management, childcare, cooking, etc.

to accommodate this new type of customer. Businesses didn't care about feminism, but they sure cared about profits. They were eager to welcome the New Woman through their doors to spend her money. It is a truth universally acknowledged, that a single woman in possession of a new paycheck, must be in want of a way to blow it.

The invention and spread of electric street lights further encouraged the New Woman by expanding the hours that she felt safe being out of the house. Women were more likely to stay out late at the music hall if the streets were well lit when they were walking or biking home.

More than the music hall or amusement park however, one particular business welcomed female customers more than any other. This same one that would completely change the course of Helen's life.

Enter the movie theater.

In the first years of the twentieth century, America's burgeoning film industry was not actually based in the West; most of the big film companies were located in New York and New Jersey. These companies shot films all over the East Coast, and even in Midwestern hubs like Chicago, but their business headquarters were usually in New York City.

In 1907, Colonel Willam Selig, head of film studio Selig Polyscope Company, was planning a shoot in Chicago for *The Count of Monte Cristo*. Unfortunately, if you've ever been to Chicago, you know that the weather doesn't always cooperate with your plans. A storm forced him to find an alternate, drier location for his shoot. Selig sent a group consisting of the director Francis Boggs, a cameraman, and six actors to the Southwest to look for a suitable place.

The crew went all the way to Southern California and ended up shooting the needed scenes on the sunny, warm expanse of the Santa Monica Beach. Like many who travel to Los Angeles, he

fell in love with the weather and most of all, the famous Southern California sunshine. As director David Lynch says in his book
Catching the Big Fish, "The light is energizing and inspiring. Even
with smog, there's something about that light that's not harsh, but
bright and smooth. It fills me with the feeling that all possibili-
ties are available. I don't know why. It's different from the light
in other places."

Boggs knew an opportunity when he saw one. He rented a
building in Los Angeles and converted it to a miniature film
studio. The space was filled with dressing rooms and an office,
and then Boggs built a forty-square-foot stage right next to it.

He went back to Chicago for his next project, but then returned to Los Angeles in 1909 to make *In the Sultan's Power*, the
first ever film to be shot totally in California.

Selig agreed with Boggs, Los Angeles was the ideal place
to make films. Not only was the light perfect and the weather
mostly dry, but the landscape has the unique perk of offering
many different types of locations. Whether you need beaches,
mountains, deserts, forests, canyons, urban hubs, or farmland,
Los Angeles has got it. Selig decided to decamp from Chicago
and move his base of operations to Southern California.

The rest of the American filmmaking world was not far behind him. Soon enough, half a dozen different film companies
decamped from the East Coast and set up shop in and around Los
Angeles. The New York Motion Picture Company, Biograph,
Essanay Company, and Kalem Film Company were all settled
and shooting in the area within the next few years. Hollywood
got its first film studio when the Nestor Film Company moved
there from Bayonne, New Jersey, in 1911. It was headed up by
a man named David Horsley, who rented out a local tavern for
thirty dollars a month and converted it into offices, dressing
rooms, and storage space for props and cameras.

The freshly settled filmmakers were thrilled with Los Angeles. Suddenly, they could shoot all year round! There was no

snow to worry about, even in January, and rain or cloudy skies were rare.

Hollywood residents did not share their excitement, however. Almost immediately, there was friction between the locals and their new neighbors. The arrival of the film industry caused the infrastructure chaos that had been brewing to finally erupt.

The year before, in February 1910, there was a vote for Hollywood to become a district of Los Angeles. With the quickly rising population, Hollywood couldn't handle the ever-growing list of maintenance issues. It was simply too much shit to handle for one little town's infrastructure.[9] Becoming a part of Los Angeles would give Hollywood the support it needed to continue to develop. The vote passed and Hollywood was a small pastoral town no longer.

In 1911, the same year Nestor Film Company came to Hollywood, the cozy little town dotted with fruit trees and country roads was annexed into the hungry maw of Los Angeles. Its official boundaries were (and still are) the Los Angeles River[10] to the east, Melrose Avenue to the south, the mountains to the north, and Doheny Drive to the west.

While some towns in the area, such as Burbank, Glendale, and Santa Monica, stayed independent, Beverly Hills and Culver City eventually joined Hollywood as districts of Los Angeles. The city provided these new districts with better infrastructure, and these districts helped Los Angeles to grow into a major American metropolis. In 1900, Los Angeles was the thirty-sixth largest city in the United States. In the next census in 1910, it had leapt over other cities like Minneapolis and Kansas City to become seventeenth. After gobbling up Hollywood, Beverly Hills, and Culver City, in 1920, Los Angeles had finally cracked the top

---

9   I mean this literally. Sewage was one of the biggest problems.

10   Nowadays, thanks to years and years of drought, "river" is a very generous word for it.

ten. By then, it had left San Francisco in the dust as the biggest city in California.

Despite the fact that it was now part of a city, Hollywood tried to cling to its small-town origins. Soon after the annexation, the Hollywood Board of Trustees was formed and started passing ordinances that attempted to keep the fun and partying to a minimum. Liquor was not allowed to be sold at *all*, no matter the time or the day of the week, unless you were getting a prescription from a pharmacist. You were not allowed to bicycle (or tricycle) on the sidewalk, or ride your horse too fast. Billiard rooms, shooting galleries, and pool rooms had strict hours and were closed on Sundays. Hollywood battled any attempt to introduce vice into town, whether it was gambling, drinking, or sports. Even bowling, a notoriously sinful game, was forbidden on the Lord's day.

In an attempt to retain the lovely neighborhood scent of blossoms and fruit, the board also forbade smelly businesses such as slaughterhouses, tanneries, oil refineries, and glue or soap factories. Little did they know that an even stinkier trade had already infiltrated their neighborhood.

When film companies first started trickling into Southern California, they actually avoided Hollywood. The residents made it pretty clear that they did not approve of movies and the weird people who made them. Although today the American film industry is arguably the largest entertainment business in the entire world, at its start, movies were a low-class enterprise. They were cheap, sordid amusements for poor people. Consequently, Hollywood's citizens were afraid that the film industry would lower their property values[11] and turn their cozy little suburb into shady squalor. Rentable buildings were plastered with "NO MOVIES" signs.

Hollywood was even slow to get a movie theater, especially

---

11   Hilarious.

compared to the rest of the country. Los Angeles got its first theater in 1902, but Hollywood didn't get one until 1910. The upper-class residents largely avoided going to the movies because of the association with immorality and idleness. It didn't help that Hollywood's theater was literally called The Idle Hour (renamed to The Iris Theater a few years later, possibly for marketing purposes). It was simply a storefront that had been cleared out and filled with chairs that had a projector in the back and a screen in the front.

The thing is, the stuffy Hollywood residents were not totally wrong. Movie companies did attract a rougher crowd, as they began to hire transient workers. Film crews often interfered with traffic flow. Also the residents were certainly right to be concerned about the smell of the movie industry. At the time, the only available disposal method for film was burning, which produced an acrid stench that quickly overpowered Hollywood's orchards and gardens. To top it off, most of the scenes filmed at Nestor Film Company were shot outside. No one was particularly concerned with being quiet, seeing as sound had not been incorporated into film technology yet.

To the dismay of their neighbors, Nestor quickly discovered that with year-round good weather they could churn out movies. Film companies back East were stunned at the output of the crews shooting in Southern California. Within months of Nestor setting up shop, fifteen other film companies began shooting in the area, too, which made Hollywood residents even more unhappy.

Besides the prodigious output of the burgeoning Los Angeles film scene, companies in New York and New Jersey were already keen to find a new place, preferably as far from the East Coast as possible. In 1908, a group of producers licensed by Thomas Edison formed something called the Motion Picture Patents Company, which was nicknamed "The Trust." It was a group of all the major American film companies at the time, and included Selig, Vitagraph, and Edison's own[12] company. The Trust had a monopoly on the film industry on the East Coast, which meant that smaller, independent companies had a difficult time getting equipment and distribution for their films. Many started to make their own bootleg versions of film cameras and had to shoot movies in secret.

The Trust loved to sue these indies and bog them down in lawsuits. Eventually, they were forced to stop making films, or flee the area altogether. Los Angeles, far away from the reach of the Trust, was the perfect place to relocate.

If those independent filmmakers had been able to hang on a bit longer, the landscape of the United States film industry might look quite different today. The Trust deteriorated in 1915 after being broken up by the federal court. Edison, that monopolizing jerk, lost a considerable amount of money and ended up selling his film company. But by then, the filmmaker exodus from New York to Los Angeles was already well under way. Many of the indies Edison chased away were thriving in California.

Over in Hollywood, the crew at Nestor were cranking out movies. On a twelve hundred–dollar weekly budget from their offices on the East Coast, the company was required to shoot *three* films. Two of those films were required to be a Western and a comedy. They were short films, since feature-length films were not in demand yet. Nearly all the movies being made in America were only two to twenty minutes in length. But still, it was quite a workload for one week.

Every night, the writers went home to churn out new scripts.

---

12 "Own" is a bit generous. Much of Thomas Edison's contributions to the film world are exaggerated. Even the Vitascope, an early type of film projector associated with Edison, was not actually his invention. It was the creation of two other male inventors, Thomas Armat and Charles Francis Jenkins. They agreed to let Edison take the credit and call the Vitascope his "latest marvel" in exchange for a portion of the profits.

All the actors were required to bring their own costumes, the staff of craftspeople brought their own tools, and everyone on set, from the stars to the writers, had to help dress the set with props and decor. Gigantic sheets of muslin cloth were hung up around the scene to diffuse the bright sunshine.

And what was the first film made in Hollywood's first studio? A short Western called *The Law of the Range*, written by Alexandra Fahrney.

That's right. Women were working in Hollywood at the very beginning. In fact, it was a woman who invented narrative film in the first place.

See, film did not start out as an art form. It was an applied science, created in the incredibly male-dominated world of 1800s machinery and electronics.[13] The first film displays were only seconds or minutes in length and featured simple footage, such as a train going along a track. Movies were considered more as technological marvels than art forms.

Initially, displays of motion pictures generated great excitement in audiences. The world had never seen anything like it. But after a few years, people started to get bored watching sixty second loops of a horse galloping along a track. Technological marvels can become technological snores once you've seen them a few times. Film's popularity began to wane.

Until one French woman had an idea.

In 1885, Alice Guy-Blaché was working as a secretary for the Gaumont Film Company in France, which made photography equipment. At the time, film companies around the world were racing to figure out how to best project film, and Gaumont was one of them. They eventually developed their own camera that

---

13   Filmmaking in the early, early days was a skill usually acquired in a technician's shop, a place where women were rarely welcome. The earliest film cameras had to be cranked by hand at the exact correct frame per second or the movie would look extremely wonky.

took moving pictures, but the men who ran the company could not, for the life of them, figure out what to do with it. They couldn't see any practical use for the camera and considered it fit to be nothing but a children's toy.

Guy-Blaché asked for permission to use the camera, and seeing no reason to say no, her bosses let her. She wanted to use it to create short "plays" that might entice customers to buy the camera. After gathering some props, costumes, and borrowing quite a few babies, Guy-Blaché shot what is considered to be the first narrative film in history, *The Cabbage-Patch Fairy*.[14]

At only about a minute long, *The Cabbage-Patch Fairy* launched cinema as we know it. Previously bored audiences were interested again. They wanted to see a story, not just moving images. Soon, other filmmakers were making their own "short plays" and the film industry was born.

Thanks to director Alice Guy-Blanché,[15] motion pictures had now moved from the world of technology to the world of art.[16] It was here that something magical was about to happen.

All the pieces of the modern movie industry were finally falling into place. Narrative movies were being made, the film industry was flocking to Southern California, and Hollywood was becoming a hub for filmmakers. Movie history was converging on this one sprawling, sunny city. All we need now is Helen.

---

14   It was based on a fable concerning a fairy who finds babies in a cabbage patch which shockingly seems to have no connection to Cabbage Patch Dolls.

15   She was sometimes called a "directrice" which is somehow even sillier than the word "comedienne."

16   Guy-Blaché would go on to have a briefly successful career as one of film history's most influential directors. Considered the first female director, she should actually be considered the first director, full stop. She would eventually direct, write, or produce over three hundred films in all sorts of genres, such as fantasy, comedy, romance, and science fiction, including 1912's *In The Year 2000*, about a world where women rule.

★ ★ ★

Working at the cigar factory was quickly getting old for Helen. There was not a lot of opportunity for advancement there, or excitement, unless you counted someone getting injured in one of the machines. Luckily, excitement was exactly what she was about to get.

In the summer of 1909, at sixteen years old, Helen decided to visit Luna Park with a friend of hers from the cigar factory. Luna Park was a trolley park, which was sort of an early form of amusement park at the end of a trolley line.[17] Passengers could get off the line to picnic, see a concert, dance in the dance hall, or, if they were brave enough, try out some roller coasters or bumper cars.

That particular day, a "Wild West" show was visiting Luna Park, complete with cowboys and horse riding performances. Watching the riders from the sidelines, Helen was completely entranced.

After it ended, Helen and her friend approached one of the performers and asked if it was possible to join the show. The cowboy told the girls that there weren't any openings in this particular tour, but if the two were serious, they could find a copy of *Billboard* magazine and flip to the back. In the help wanted ads, he said, were loads of listings for Wild West shows.

They thanked the man, and the first chance they got, the girls bought a copy of *Billboard*. Among the listings, they found one for the Miller Brothers 101 Ranch, over one thousand miles away in Ponca City, Oklahoma. This specific ranch was looking for girls who wanted to learn how to ride.

Helen took down the address and wrote to the ranch. Weeks later, she was stunned to find that they had written her back. She and her friend were instructed to report at the Miller Brothers 101 Ranch the following spring, in 1910.

---

17   This was the second in an international chain, the first being the iconic Coney Island Luna Park.

After months of saving every penny they could from the cigar factory, these two bold girls were off to Oklahoma, and, though Helen didn't know it yet, the silver screen.

2

The Wild West

Wild West shows were gigantic, steaming piles of bull (well, in this case, horse) shit, and yet they were not just wildly popular entertainment, but billed as valuable education for the entire family. As many things do in America, the concept all started with one insecure man.

William F. Cody dreamt of being an actor. Unfortunately for him (and the Native populations of the United States), he was stuck working as a buffalo hunting guide. In the late 1800s in America, killing buffalo was en vogue. For white people, it served a dual purpose: help annihilate Native populations and serve as a fun sport for the rich. Cody was especially skilled at hunting and killing buffalo, which is where he got his nickname: Buffalo Bill.

While he took tycoons on their blood-soaked adventures, Buffalo Bill loved to spin tall tales of his daring deeds on the American plains. His clients shared these stories and soon the press wanted to talk to him. Newspapers printed his flights of fancy. Plays were commissioned to bring them to life, starring the man himself, of course. Finally, Buffalo Bill was living his dream and capering across the stage, dazzling audiences with his over-the-top fabrications of life on the frontier.

Eventually, Buffalo Bill put himself out of a job. Buffalo populations, decimated from mass hunting, were in critical decline. With no more buffalo to present to rich killers, in 1876, Buffalo Bill decided to enlist in the military, which at the time was embroiled in the Plains Wars (aka genocide). He even brought along his silky stage costume to fight in. You can't make this stuff up.

At one point during their campaign in Wyoming, Buffalo Bill's company fought a rather small, inconsequential skirmish in which Buffalo Bill, dressed in his flamboyant finery, killed two Native men. Doing what he did best, he immediately began to exaggerate the fight and claimed (falsely) that one of the men was a chief. The newspapers picked up the story, and a few months later Buffalo Bill left the military for good to make his triumphant return to the stage. He began to do reenactments of his so-called battle to completely packed audiences.

Buffalo Bill continued to develop the show and in 1882, was contracted by a group of ranchers in the town of North Platte, Nebraska, to arrange a traveling version of it for a massive Fourth of July celebration. He agreed to come, and greatly expanded the stage show with cowboy demonstrations, riding and roping displays, and the big finale, a mock stagecoach attack by a group of Native actors. The crowd went wild.

Within a year, Buffalo Bill's Wild West Show was born.[18]

The show was an immediate success. Americans were ravenous for stories of the West, and the courageous heroes that conquered it. Manifest destiny was one of America's earliest myths about itself, that American men *had* to be strong because they dominated the Wild West. It's important to remember that Wild West shows also rose in tandem with the New Woman. What

---

18   For more information about how Buffalo Bill and his ridiculous show deeply shaped the American psyche, please check out Ijeoma Oluo's incredible book, *Mediocre*.

better to soothe the minds of men shaking in their boots over growing female independence than inflating how courageous they still were?

Crowds ate up this white male supremacist illusion and reveled in the glory of their own power and righteousness. Soon, Buffalo Bill's Wild West Show was the most popular show in the country and the man behind it all was one of the richest, best known entertainers in the world.[19]

The incredible success of the show swiftly spawned imitators. It was at one of these that Helen arrived in the spring of 1910, small suitcase and friend in tow.

The Millers 101 Ranch, so named because of its one hundred and one thousand acres, was a hit even before the days of the Wild West show. Owned by three brothers, Joseph, Zack, and George, it was founded in 1892. The ranch included cattle herds for both beef and dairy, hogs, poultry, fruit orchards, a meat packing plant, and oil drilling. It was all a bit overwhelming for a city girl from Cleveland. Wandering the grounds, she saw miles of alfalfa, wheat, and corn fields, as well as ponies, mules, peacocks, camels, buffalo, and the reason Helen was there: horses.

There were rodeo grounds on the ranch, and in 1904, roundup competitions started being held there, in which riders showed their skills at roping and "bronco busting" to thousands of spectators. It was a perfect fit. The gigantic ranch had the space and the infrastructure to support huge crowds, and the cowboys were already on hand.

Once the Miller brothers got word of what Buffalo Bill was doing, they wanted in. In 1906, after adding some theatrical and, um, "educational" elements to their rodeo competitions, their Oklahoma ranch hosted the biggest Wild West show in the history of the southwestern United States. Fifty thousand came to

---

19 Because the show was presented as educational reenactments, many of Buffalo Bill's wild stories were taken as fact and woven into the ugly tapestry of American history.

watch, and two thousand performers took part in the program. There were two hundred workers on staff just to take care of administrative work. Visitors—many of whom camped out on the grounds—witnessed trick riding, roping displays, and racing of all kinds. There were even turtle races. Alma Miller, one of the founders' daughters, called the 101 Ranch, "the wonder spot and show place of Oklahoma."

The show was so popular that the Miller brothers kept it going year-round and it soon attracted affluent visitors, like John Ringling, John D. Rockefeller, Nancy Astor, Warren G. Harding, and William Randolph Hearst. A year into the enterprise, President Theodore Roosevelt invited the Miller brothers to bring a small part of their show to Washington, DC, and put on a cattle display. It was such a big hit that other requests started rolling in, and the Miller brothers began to take the whole shebang on the road.

With rodeos running at the ranch and a now traveling show, the Miller brothers needed as many riders as they could get. They needed so many, in fact, that they were willing to provide training to anyone who wanted to join, even if they had never been on a horse in their lives. The 101 Ranch recruited heavily in magazines and newspapers, which was how two young women from Cleveland with absolutely no experience got an invitation.

Cowgirls performed similar feats to men at Wild West shows and rodeos (which were almost identical, only rodeos usually didn't advertise themselves as being educational). These women sure didn't ride sidesaddle. They roped cattle while precariously balanced on horses galloping at top speed, shot targets on horseback, and swung down from the saddle to pick up a handkerchief on the ground. This last feat was something Helen was already practicing after her first few weeks of training. As she told a film magazine in 1968, "When veteran riders told me I could get kicked in the head, I paid no heed. Such things might happen to others, but could never happen to me, I believed." Although Helen was still a teenager, she already displayed the fearlessness and confidence in herself that would shine through her entire career.

The world of ranching, and consequently the rodeo, was largely a male one. This meant that, at first, it was difficult for women to break into the industry. The talent for rodeos was pulled from the working cowboy roster of whatever ranch created the particular show. Many riders in the traveling 101 Ranch Show were also employees of the ranch itself and had to regularly return to Oklahoma to work. As Alma Miller recalled, a cowboy might be "subduing a bucking bronco in front of the public one day and branding calves at the ranch a week later." So, if rodeos were recruiting from an all-male talent pool and not holding tryouts, there weren't many opportunities for women to get their boots in the door.

Even still, cowgirl talent was out there. Many women worked on ranches (mainly wives and daughters) and roped steers, worked with cattle, and sometimes even became ranch owners themselves. Finally, in 1885, a woman named Annie Oakley joined Buffalo Bill's show and threw open the door for female riders.

A deadeye markswoman, Oakley can be considered the first cowgirl celebrity. Known as "Little Sure Shot," she eventually became the world's most famous Wild West show entertainer. In fact, Oakley developed into such a Western legend that she nearly stole the show from Buffalo Bill himself.[20] Thanks to her, within a couple of years there were dozens more women working Buffalo Bill's show. Some of them made costumes, some helped behind the scenes on the show, while others were performers. And just like the show itself was swiftly imitated, all the other Wild West shows began actively recruiting female riders and soon had their own daring cowgirls and trick shooters. These women began to catch media attention for being novel additions to Wild West shows.

---

20 Something that, considering Buffalo Bill's history, would have been all too appropriate.

Show managers didn't want the women competing in *every-thing*, however. Cowgirls were discouraged from riding buck-ing broncos, one of the rodeo activities that caused the most injuries. At the 101 Ranch, a small percentage of bronco rid-ers were sent to the hospital every day, sometimes a dozen at a time. It was not unheard of for a rider to die from "broncing." Because of the danger involved, bronco riding was a big draw and would attract hordes of people eager to see the breath-taking feat. Some women, however, demanded that they too get the chance to get flattened like a pancake by an angry horse.

In 1901, a future cowgirl legend named Prairie Rose Hen-derson tried to enter a bronco riding contest in Cheyenne, Wyoming. Henderson was the daughter of a local rancher and an expert rider. The rodeo managers told her that no women were allowed to compete, and Henderson asked to see the official rulebook. After proving that there was no writ-ten rule that stated such, Henderson was allowed to enter the competition.[21]

The incident sparked a sensation in the newspapers, and soon many other rodeos and Wild West shows featured cowgirl bronco riding. Although they weren't widely called cowgirls until Presi-dent Theodore Roosevelt, who was clearly a big rodeo fan, used the term to describe steer roping champion Lucille Mulhall. The term had been used a few times before, but the president sealed the deal and brought national attention to these rope-slinging women. Cowgirls they were, and cowgirls they are.

The gender dynamics of the rodeo were being shaped by the same societal shifts that were shaping the country at large. What constituted "appropriate female behavior" was changing. Cowgirls benefited from a movement that inspired women to

---

21 Prairie Rose Henderson's story is a strange one. After years as a champion rider, she rode off into a blizzard one winter night and was never seen again. Her skeleton was discovered nearly a decade later in the Green Mountain region of Wyoming, and was only identified because it still sported her silver rodeo championship belt buckle.

become more active and move out of the domestic sphere. Riding a bucking bronco was about as far from the Victorian ideal of submissive, domestic womanhood as you could get. A great way to escape the conservative ideals of rural towns was to get on a horse and join a rodeo. Becoming a cowgirl offered a rare life of thrills for women. Which was exactly what Helen Gibson found at the 101 Ranch.

Helen didn't want to be on stage, she didn't sing, she didn't write, she didn't dance, and she didn't tell jokes. One thing she did like to do, however, was play rough. As soon as she arrived in the early spring of 1910, she was immediately enrolled in a riding course. She took to it like a duck to water. Her childhood as a "tomboy" and years of running along the shores of Lake Erie had prepared her for the rough and tumble lifestyle of a cowgirl. Instructors taught her not just riding, but also roping and herding.

Quickly, the managers of the Wild West show realized that Helen was a talent. Even though she was only seventeen years old, the 101 Ranch offered her a contract as a performing rider.

Unfortunately, Helen's friend did not have the same innate equestrian skills. She didn't, as Helen said, "make the grade" and soon returned to her family in Cleveland. Helen, however, was about to see her life drastically change.

Now that she had basic training under her belt, Helen was ready to join the 101 touring show on a whopping countrywide tour.

Before she set out, however, Helen needed a wardrobe makeover. The sensible, plain dresses and blouses that she wore to the factory in Cleveland would not cut it on the open range. Time for an episode of *Steer Eye*.

Cowgirls were in an interesting situation in 1910, somehow both upholding and pushing expectations for women. They needed riding outfits that looked feminine, but also accommodated the activities they were trying to do. Years before, in 1904, cowgirl Bertha Kaepernick made the papers when she rode a bronco while sporting a complicated Victorian-style updo, corset, and long skirts. Clearly that wasn't ideal. It's hard enough to stay on top of a bucking horse without several yards of fabric billowing around your legs.

And of course, cowgirls weren't allowed to wear cowboy clothes. Even with the shifting gender norms, women were still not encouraged to wear pants, especially not denim jeans.[22] Bronc riding was one thing, but having pockets was still a bridge too far. Being called "mannish" or a "masculine woman" was a deep insult during this time period. When they were first breaking into the rodeo industry, cowgirls sported huge hair bows, frilly skirts, and tightly laced corsets. How the bows survived after a day of rodeo riding is anyone's guess.

In order to keep pushing the envelope on what they were allowed to do, women needed to still look like what women were supposed to look like, so they didn't cause too much of a shock. It was almost a disguise. Childlike styles were quite popular for exactly this reason. The wide sailor collar, for example, was common to see. Women thought that by dressing like little girls, they'd look less threatening. Oh, don't mind me, just shooting a playing card out of midair on horseback, nothing to worry about here!

Luckily for Helen, soon women started to design cowgirl gear that was a little more practical. By the time Helen hopped on a horse, bloomers made from satin or corduroy and sturdy jodhpurs were becoming popular. They allowed a much greater freedom of movement, not to mention that they were much safer to ride in. Before long, cowgirls and Wild West show costumers were creating beautiful riding outfits. Some shows even judged female riders on their costumes. No companies made clothes for cowgirls, so everything had to be handmade. The clothes were flashy, but they never flashed any skin. Because cowgirls were pushing so many boundaries already, it was important that they did not appear immodest.

---

22 Which, yes, were around at this time, and had been available for miners, farmers, and cowboys since the mid–1800s.

What riders wore was important, since the costumes helped amplify the mythology surrounding the Wild West. A lot of fringed leather was featured, in either skirt, vest, or jacket form. There were wide cowboy hats, beaded belts, leather gauntlets, neck scarves, and brightly colored silk stockings or sashes. The show wasn't about historical accuracy, it was about dazzling an audience.

Helen generally preferred a pair of jodhpurs or a split skirt (sort of a proto version of culottes), with a tight-fitting blouse and a wide brimmed hat to keep the sun out of her eyes.

Helen sitting proud and pretty during a 101 Ranch Brothers show.

So, with her new skills and new costume, Helen set out in April of 1910 on her first Wild West show tour. It was, quite literally, her first rodeo.

Even though her friend had to return to Cleveland, Helen wasn't the only female rider. The Miller Brothers 101 show featured quite a few cowgirl stars, including Florence Le Due, Alice Lee, Lottie Aldridge, Babe Willets, and Mabel Klein. Most of the women in the show were the daughters or sisters of local ranch families, but some were like Helen and had been recruited from afar. Even the city girls picked up the basics, just from training on the ranch, and Helen soon felt comfortable working with horses, cows, and donkeys.

Including Helen and her fellow cowgirls, the entire company of riders, hands, cooks, costumers, etc., was around a thousand strong. There were Native performers from nearly a dozen different tribes, a cavalry unit all the way from Russia, a big band, and around six hundred different animals, such as horses, oxen, mules, ponies, and buffalo, along with more exotic species like elephants and camels. Some of them, like long-horned steers and buffalo, were supplied from the ranch. Others, like the elephants, were purchased specifically for the traveling show.

To fit all these various people and creatures, several tents were packed and set up at each location. There was an absolutely massive arena tent, measuring three hundred and ninety feet wide by five hundred and fifty feet long, about twice the size of a football field. Under this tent, Helen performed, galloping through the dusty, stuffy air to rolling waves of cheers and applause. Alongside, three large horse tents were set up, and a cook tent, as well.

But what was Helen doing under the big top? What feats did she and her female colleagues perform? If you were a little girl watching the show in 1910, it looked like they were working magic.

Vaulting, jumping, standing up in the saddle, riding bucking broncos—the tricks only got more elaborate and incredible as the show went on. Cowgirls also did steer riding, an event where female riders were known to shine. Steer riding is similar to calf roping, although you can imagine it's a bit more difficult to rope a huge, grumpy steer than a little calf. In this event, the cowgirl is mounted on a horse and must rope the steer—only the horns, mind you—pull him up off his feet, and tie him up. It's not an easy event, but it was actually a favorite of many riders because every contestant, no matter their gender, was on equal footing. Cowgirls were given no special equipment or help, so it was a pure contest of skill. All a girl needed was finesse with rope and an intelligent horse, and she could compete on the same terms as the boys.

The area where female riders had the real advantage was trick riding. Trick riding is essentially performing stunts on horseback, and Helen excelled at it. (You'll see later how much this rodeo experience helped her in Hollywood, in more ways than one.)

Before each event, all the riders were required to submit a list of around ten tricks to the judges. The arena director might call upon a rider to perform her tricks multiple times, so she had to be prepared. Each rider was judged on her skill, grace, ease, speed, trick difficulty, and the number of straps her horse was outfitted with. The higher the number of straps, the lower the score.

During the early 1900s, tricks generally fell into one of three categories. There was top work, which included standing in the saddle and staying on top of the horse. There were vaults, which required the rider to hit the ground with her feet and jump back up to the saddle. Finally, there were drags, also known as strap work. Cowgirls would attach specifically designed straps and holds onto their saddles so that they could hang off the sides or even the back of a horse, usually while the animal was at a full gallop around the arena. (Hence why a judge would give a rider more points for doing this with fewer straps.)

The big finale of a trick rider's performance was passing under the belly or the neck of the horse. Because cowgirls were usually smaller and more flexible than the cowboys were (but not always), they were generally better at trick riding. This event was the big crowd favorite, which meant that talented female riders quickly generated hordes of fans. Trick riding was Helen's favorite event and it was the one she was best at.

In August of that year, Helen turned eighteen years old. You can imagine how exhilarated she was feeling. It is so rare that the thing we love to do is what we are best at, rarer still to get the chance to make a life out of that thing.[23] Rough-and-tumble Helen was on her own for the first time in her life, flying on top of a galloping horse for a living. Her uniform was dirt on her boots and the wind in her hair.

Just a decade earlier, this life wouldn't have been possible for her. Two decades earlier, she might not even have been able to find a job at that cigar factory in Cleveland. The times were rapidly changing for women in America, the cowgirl was a symbol for that, sometimes literally. In a few years, suffragette and lawyer Inez Miholland would lead the very first women's suffrage parade in Washington, DC, on horseback. Cowgirls were everything suffragettes wanted for American women. They were strong, independent, and under all the dust, undeniably feminine.

MOTION PICTURE NEWS, JULY 8, 1916, PAGE 83.

Helen grinning in the saddle.

---

23   Shout out to everyone else who is best at "reading on the couch."

Besides a reliable bra,[24] the best thing a trick rider could have was a good horse. Helen's days at the Miller Brothers 101 Ranch fostered a long-term love of horses. She spent so much time relying on horses for both her safety and her livelihood that she developed strong bonds to her favorites. (Same with the bras.)

A good horse was a phenomenal help to a rider, making every trick—even the most difficult ones—look easy and graceful. In trick riding, a good horse meant one that had a smooth gait and control over his or her nerves. More than anything, the horse could not be easily distracted. A momentary distraction could lead to a ruined trick, or worse, a ruined rider. Cowgirls ran the risk of being dragged or stepped on during a trick, which usually didn't turn out well for either party involved.

Another popular event was the relay race, which required a bit more space than the others. It wasn't a relay for multiple riders, but rather a relay with multiple horses. Each rider had three horses for the event. She walked them to the starting line, and when signaled, she'd hop on the first horse and ride the track. Once she got back to the starting line, she'd then hop on the second, and so on. The race itself was not as exciting as the changing of the horses was. Depending on what was allowed at this particular show or rodeo, the rider stopped her horse behind the next horse in line, vaulted out of her current saddle and directly onto the next horse (who would ideally already have started running), and off she would go around the track again. This was known as "pony expressing."

Other women's events included trick roping, flat races, and a personal favorite of your author's, steer undecorating. A ribbon was tied around a steer's flank and had to be removed by the rider. It seems like there should have been a prize for the person who had to decorate the steer in the first place.

Along with the trick riders and bucking broncos, featured

---

24 Which did exist in an early form in 1910. And thank God, because you know those riders needed the girls strapped in tight.

performances included steer wrestling,[25] an exhibition of the Pony Express to show audiences how mail was carried during the frontier days, stagecoach "raid" shows, and Native tribal dances and ceremonies.

In the 1920s, many shows had trains to transport them from location to location, but when Helen was riding with the 101 Ranch show, everyone quite literally had to hoof it. If the show stopped off in a big city, many of the performers got to stay in hotel rooms, but otherwise, the whole company camped. Many female performers during this time were wives and mothers, and in a very unusual move for the time period, passed off their children to stay with grandmothers or friends until the season was over.

With the 1910 tour schedule, there was quite a lot of hoofing it. Once the season commenced on April 18 with a show in Missouri, Helen and her one thousand or so colleagues galloped through twenty-eight different states. The 101 Ranch company usually stopped at multiple cities in a state. Unfortunately, the show skipped Cleveland on Helen's inaugural tour, which meant that her family and friends back home didn't get a chance to see her new set of skills.

Their arrival in a city was heralded by a boisterous parade down Main Street, with performers on horseback, ponies, and various other animals. This got the public, especially kids, excited to attend the show the next day. There were typically two shows a day, one in the morning, one in the afternoon, six days a week.

It's exhausting just typing all of that out, but for Helen, still technically a teenager, the schedule was a thrill. This was a time when few lower-class young women were afforded the luxury of travel. The company had Sundays off, which gave Helen

---

25 Also known as "bulldogging," which was invented by Bill Pickett, a Black cowboy. Despite the pervasiveness of white cowboys in Wild West shows, the first cowboys were mostly Mexican and Black riders.

time to sightsee, meet new people, and generally have the time of her life.

The show often swung back through states two or three times, and the entire run took almost seven months, ending in West Point, Mississippi, on November 19.[26] Instead of being burnt-out, Helen "could hardly wait" until the next season started. She told *Film Review Magazine* in 1968 that "the season ended all too soon. I was sorry when I had to go home..."

She spent the winter of 1910 back in Cleveland with her family, no doubt the object of envy for all her friends still at the cigar factory. Helen never spoke about her family's reaction to her career on horseback, but judging from the fact that they welcomed her back, it seems like the Wengers were accepting of their cowgirl daughter. At least, what remained of the family. Historians believe that Helen's father, Fred, died on August 21 that year, a few days before her eighteenth birthday.[27]

It's tough to know what Helen's relationship with her family was like. She never, ever spoke about them publicly, neither her parents, nor her sisters. Was she looking for an excuse to take off because she didn't connect with her family? Did the wild turn her life took make visiting often too difficult? It seems that Helen kept in touch occasionally over the years. All we know for certain was that Helen was chomping at the bit to leave home and she never returned.

Helen—athletic, strong, well traveled, independent, *financially* independent—was becoming a New Woman.

As soon as the Miller Brothers 101 Ranch began preparations for the new season in March of 1911, Helen arrived back

---

26 I don't know for sure, but besides the winter, this might have been to give the company time to get back home to their families for Thanksgiving. Which, given the nature of the show, is hilarious.

27 Ohio death records show that *a* Fred Wenger of Cleveland died on this date. It seems quite likely that this was Helen's father, but we can't be totally sure.

in Oklahoma, ready to shake off the winter and learn some new tricks.

The tour kicked off in Massachusetts on April 4. It only encompassed twenty-two states that year, but the company traveled much farther west than usual.

On the way, they stopped off in Cleveland for two days, June 26 and 27. Helen's grand homecoming sparked her first feature in the press. The *Cleveland Plain Dealer* ran a small piece in the Sunday paper that focused on her, titled "Cleveland Girl Rides Steer Daily at Wild West Show." It was accompanied by a picture of Helen hanging off the side of a steer, wearing one of her wide-brimmed hats, very wide-legged loose pants, a long-sleeved blouse, and a thin scarf. Most noticeable, however, is the huge grin she has stretched from ear to ear.

Rose Wenger, former Cleveland girl, arrived in the city today with the 101 Ranch Show outfit and will demonstrate tomorrow and Tuesday just what a Cleveland girl can do.

Miss Wenger found long ago that the dodging of automobiles and street cars on the Cleveland highways was far too tame, so she went to Oklahoma...

It's clear that already, merely a year into her career, Helen was a *former* Cleveland girl. At just eighteen, those around her recognized that Helen was on the way to something bigger.

They couldn't begin to guess just how much.

Once the 101 Ranch Show made its way up and down the East Coast and through the Midwest, they headed west through Texas, New Mexico, Arizona, and all the way to California. Finally, after seven months on the road, the show ended near the beach in Venice on November 19.

Just as the entire outfit was preparing to tromp back across the country toward the snow and ice, everyone was thrilled when the managers were approached with another option. A film producer named Thomas H. Ince, who was working with the New York Motion Picture Company, showed up and offered to hire the entire show, from the performers to the cooks. He wanted background riders and actors for the Western movies he was producing, and having an entire Wild West show at his disposal would be quite convenient for him. The offer was $2,500 a week, which is equal to about $78,425 today (2022). The performers would be paid $8 a week, about $250 today, which, considering that many in the show didn't work over the winter season, was a pretty damn good deal. The answer was a resounding yes.

It was time for Helen to head to Hollywood.

3

The City of Girls

While Helen's life was undergoing a significant transformation over at the 101 Miller Brothers Ranch, the American film industry was going through its own over in Los Angeles. In fact, the entire country was.

The early 1910s were a time of incredible change in the United States,[28] and sometimes, a time of incredible tumult. America was now the richest nation in the entire world. This was an era of massive business expansion (fueled mostly by an immigrant workforce). This explosion of business meant that many Americans (you can probably guess which ones) were enjoying a higher standard of living, such as having electricity in their homes and owning cars...even though the speed limit in most cities was only ten or twelve miles per hour.

To keep up with it all, many activists and politicians were pushing progressive reforms and regulations to protect the poor,

---

28   There were only forty-six of them at the time. New Mexico and Arizona weren't added until 1912.

workers, women—essentially anyone who wasn't puffing on
a big cigar and driving a car to work. Helen arrived in Los
Angeles in 1911, the same year as the infamous Triangle Shirt-
waist Fire, where many workers in a women's clothing factory
were trapped inside during a fire because of abysmal working
conditions that included the exits being locked. Headlines read
"Over 100 Girls Leap from Upper Windows." To escape a life
on the factory line, many women in the early 1910s did exactly
what Helen did: they went west.

In the late 1800s and early 1900s, there was a great western
migration in America. Those traveling to the West Coast were
looking for new job opportunities, housing opportunities, any
kind of opportunity this "new" land could offer. By and large,
these migrants were male, for a number of reasons. Traveling as
a lone woman was not the safest thing at the time, and most of
the new jobs available, such as railroad workers, were meant for
men. This meant that most of the western boomtowns, towns
that underwent swift growth, were typically male-dominated
communities. These cities and towns were usually chock-full of
single young men out looking for their fortunes. Portland and
Seattle, for example, both started out as boomtowns.

There was one exception, however. In the early decades of the
twentieth century, Los Angeles was the only city in the American West with more women than men. At the dawn of Hollywood, it was a city of girls.

There was a lot to draw them out there. Besides the enticing
weather, there were many more employment opportunities in
Los Angeles than other western cities. Its economic foundation
was built on real estate and tourism, so there were many "pink-
collar" jobs—clerical work and service jobs that usually went
to women. More women in Southern California worked outside the home than anywhere else in the western United States.

Work was available for older women, as well. In a time where
many pink-collar jobs were only open to those twenty-five or

younger, Los Angeles had a high number of women working after that age, and one in five of them was divorced or widowed, to boot.

There were also a lot of legal perks for those who headed to the Golden State. California was one of the states that passed suffrage early, and in 1911, allowed women to serve on juries and passed legislation that established a maximum eight-hour work day.

All these factors proved to be a powerful lure for the scores of New Women who, as Hilary A. Hallett says in her book *Go West, Young Women!*, were in "full flight of feminine norms." Any woman looking for a different sort of life than what was normally on offer had a better chance of finding it in Los Angeles.[29] The most alluring factor, though? Southern California's brand-new industry: motion pictures.

Now remember, films had just recently passed from the realm of technology (although that wasn't a word yet) and into the realm of art. There were few, if any, laws governing the creation or distribution of motion pictures. The world of finance and big business wasn't paying much attention to the burgeoning movie industry. Many weren't quite sure what exactly to do with it. Movies were new and novel, but they weren't considered competition for *serious* entertainment like theater. Just an interesting curiosity gaining popularity among the lower class.

After the excitement of seeing a moving picture wore off in the late 1800s and rich people got bored with films, it was the lower classes who took up the torch of cinema. Exhibitioners

29 Another special thing about Los Angeles was that it had more residents from other nations than any other city on the West Coast. Black people, Mexican people, Asian people, European people—this diverse population of immigrants became the foundation of the city's economic structure, working all the "unskilled" jobs that drove Los Angeles's rapid expansion. BIPOC women occupied the bottom of the barrel when it came to the Los Angeles job market for a long time, but they, despite discrimination from bosses and social services, helped build the city as it is today.

realized that even though the upper classes stopped showing up, if they priced the tickets cheaply, the lower classes were happy to come out and be entertained for a short while. Poor people could rarely afford tickets to see a play, but they could afford a few cents to see a motion picture.

In the early 1900s, films were projected in vaudeville theaters or, the precursor to the modern cinema, the nickelodeon. So named because of the five-cent entrance fee, nickelodeons were usually storefronts that had been converted into indoor film exhibition spaces. With poor ventilation and uncomfortable wooden seats, they weren't exactly luxurious. They were essentially just a room with chairs, like when the substitute teacher sets up a movie to play for the classroom. There was no air conditioning, no plush, reclining seats, and no cup holders. Nickelodeons usually didn't even have refreshments, not even overpriced popcorn. With people crammed in, the room was stuffy and a little bit (and during the summer, quite a bit) smelly. But the cheap tickets attracted crowds and going to a nickelodeon to see a few movies became a popular pastime of the lower classes. Soon, nickelodeons were being built all over the country and film was becoming available to the masses.

Big business never pays attention to anything poor people do, unless they're trying to unionize, so in the first decade of the twentieth century, film was not on the radar as something that would become financially or culturally significant.

What did that mean for early filmmakers? Freedom.

Without oversight, there was an incredible amount of creative freedom during the first era of motion pictures. There was no corporate presence breathing down anyone's necks and there were no strict delineations about who should do what, when, and how. Of course, this often meant there was a lot of blundering around and screwing up, but most importantly, it also meant that the door to the industry was unguarded.

Anyone who could get or make a film camera could start

making movies. The new camera models didn't need as much specialized training, and film degrees didn't exist yet. A woman didn't need advanced education to work as a director or a screenwriter. It seems wild to think about today, but when film first started in America, it was a very accessible industry for women.

In the early 1900s, actresses were the top billed (and paid) stars of the stage, and that trend continued in motion pictures. Even though actors were uncredited at this point, motion pictures with female stars became the most popular, and those stars were paid accordingly.

With this uniquely female-friendly industry blossoming in this uniquely female-friendly city, many women, especially those from rural areas who had fewer options, migrated to Los Angeles. Why not hop on a train to the West Coast? Truly, what did they have to lose?

They came in droves.

In 1900, the population of Hollywood was five hundred. In 1909, it was four thousand and rapidly growing. Scenes were being shot all over town, every day of the week. Homes were used for domestic dramas, comedies were shot inside stores and on the streets. Even banks were used on Sundays for big heist scenes.

Actors, directors, designers, all sorts of industry people were constantly scurrying around town. Frances Marion, a supreme talent who would go on to become the most successful screenwriter of the age (not the most successful *female* screenwriter, just the most successful screenwriter) said in her memoir that while the sets looked like "a series of nondescript barns and sheds... when the man in charge opened the gate, you felt as if you had looked through an opaque rock candy Easter egg into a multicolored vista beyond. This impression was due to the skeletons of various buildings which served as backgrounds for scenes, the bustle and excitement of actors in polychromatic costumes, their brightly painted faces..." We see the remnants of these days in stuttering black-and-white, but Hollywood was a riot of color and motion.

Film didn't just offer women jobs in the 1910s. It had a perk that almost no other industry offered: advancement. Because of the freedom and lack of structure, film didn't have the same hierarchy that other industries had. Everyone participated in multiple ways. Even the biggest star of the day, Mary Pickford, wrote scripts, did her own makeup, decorated and designed sets, worked the camera, and set up lighting, all before she got in front of the camera to do her scenes.

With so many people on set helping out with each department, everyone got to learn. The film industry was growing and evolving at an almost exponential rate, and all the different titles for various skills and responsibilities were still being established. By 1909, women were working nearly every possible job in film. They were writers, directors, producers, film cutters, editors, musicians, retouchers, set designers, publicists, casting directors, department managers, title writers, molders, plasterers, etc. A woman could start working at a film company as an assistant and work her way up to being an editor, a writer, even a director. If you wanted to do something, and you were good at it, you got to do it.

In the early days of American film, women were, as groundbreaking film scholar Karen Ward Mahar says, "the norm, not the exception." In fact, there were more women working in film during this time than any other time in film history, and that's including modern day, right now. There was more gender equality in the film industry *before films even had sound*.

According to the Center for the Study of Women in Television and Film, as of 2020, women in the American film industry make up only 17 percent of screenwriters. But between 1900 and 1925, female screenwriters outnumbered male screenwriters *10 to 1*. Let's repeat that, let's shout it from the rooftops, let's put a neon sign in Times Square. *A hundred years ago, female screenwriters outnumbered male screenwriters 10 to 1.* How can a single fact be so absolutely amazing and so absolutely infuriating at the same time?

Today, I still feel like throwing a goddamn parade when a woman gets nominated for the Best Original Screenplay Oscar. In a now infamous 2018 interview, a notable male film CEO struggled to name any female filmmakers. Yet, in the days before *the fucking polio vaccine*, you couldn't throw a camera lens in Hollywood without hitting a female screenwriter.

Besides writing, many women held key positions in productions, including directing and producing.[30] The very definition of these roles[31] is being in charge, either of the vision of the film in the case of the director, or the production in the case of the producer. Both roles make important decisions, give orders, and literally call the shots—all of which was completely and totally at odds with the expectations previously held for women.

Now, Los Angeles wasn't a radical feminist utopia. Women in Hollywood still very much had to deal with sexism on a regular basis and work around men who were, let's say, sensitive to being told what to do by a woman. Female directors were careful to remain in control of their emotions, even when all they wanted to do was scream. Mary Pickford, who became known as America's Sweetheart and was the film industry's biggest star for many years,[32] constantly clashed with D.W. Griffith, one of America's most influential early filmmakers and noted director of racist films. Griffith often told Pickford that she was too fat to be in front of the camera, but also regularly attempted to get

---

30   Much of this was unknown until historian and author Ally Acker wrote *Reel Women: Pioneers of the Cinema* in 1993. It was the first ever major work on the subject and is still an invaluable resource for women's film history.

31   During this time, the terms "director" and "producer" were sometimes used interchangeably. Sometimes, directors were even called "picturers."

32   And would go on to become a founding member of the Academy of Motion Pictures Arts and Sciences.

her to go out on a date with him. Funny how it always works out like that!

All of this mostly applied to white female filmmakers. Many early American films told racist stories about Native, Black, and Asian people. Often, filmmakers chose to cast white actors in red, yellow, or blackface instead of casting BIPOC actors. In particular, early Hollywood was enamored by Chinese culture and stories. Instead of honoring them in any way, many of these films perpetuated nasty stereotypes about Chinese people, portraying them as exotic foreigners, submissive peons, or cackling villains.

Fortunately, that isn't the whole picture of early Hollywood. There were incredible Asian and Black filmmakers working during this time. The first Black movie studio was founded in 1916.[33] It was called the Lincoln Motion Picture Company and it is known as the first producer of films for Black audiences. Although it only lasted for five films, the Lincoln Motion Picture Company was extremely influential and, based on speculation from film historians, more successful than most of the white-owned studios at the time.

Historian Jenny Cho says in her book, *Chinese in Hollywood*: "As early as 1916, there was a desire among Asian Americans to create realistic films about their experiences." In the late 1910s, Marion Wong wanted to make films by and about Chinese Americans, and especially tell stories from the perspective of the bicultural. She founded the Mandarin Film Company and in 1916, when she was only *twenty-one*, she directed *The Curse of Quon Gwon*. It is the earliest known Chinese American film, by a director of any gender.

---

33 During this time, Black people in Los Angeles mostly lived in an area called the Furlong Tract, named after James Furlong, a wealthy landowner who sold property to Black residents. The central avenue of this area was a huge, bustling hub with hotels, restaurants, and clubs. Historian Donald Bogle calls it a "glittering avenue of social and commercial activities" in his book, *Bright Boulevards, Bold Dreams: The Story of Black Hollywood*.

★ ★ ★

Female filmmakers were shaping American films, but so were female audiences. Theater-going women were the ones responsible for the growth of the entire industry.

It all started because of those lower-class people who kept going to see motion pictures when the rich people got bored. This gave the movies a reputation as low-class entertainment. As film grew in popularity and more theaters opened up across the country, exhibitors wanted to attract a higher class, and more importantly, higher-paying clientele. But how to do so?

Get the ladies in there.

Theater owners thought if they could get women in the seats, it would class up the joint. If the delicate sex, especially of the middle- or upper-class variety, was at the movies, it meant that it was a respectable place to be. White women were canaries in the respectability coal mine. "Playing to the ladies" was thought to purge the movies of any low-class association, a juice cleanse for an entire industry. At the turn of the century, women couldn't have pockets, equal pay, or rights, but by god, they could have the movie theater.

Not only would the presence of these more well-to-do women make the movies seem classy, but they'd have an effect on the men in the audience, as well. The guys would be more apt to act polite if there were ladies afoot. Plus, these women would hopefully influence their communities, as well, convincing their husbands, friends, and neighbors to give the theater a try.

Even though this is annoying because it was yet another responsibility laid on the weary shoulders of American women, it was also exciting during an age where society did not value women's opinions on basically anything, except household items like soap and towels. Society certainly didn't want women to weigh in on anything important, like politics or culture. Now film, which would soon develop into the most influential cultural medium *in the world*, was actively seeking, practically begging women to give their stamp of approval to it.

To help the image shift, film trade publications even began to characterize film itself as female. In cartoons and illustrations in newspapers and magazines, the motion picture industry was portrayed as a beautiful, white woman. A pure and wholesome ambassador for decent, proper entertainment.

The embodiment of motion pictures, in all her feminine glory. And her uh, husband, Mr. Baseball. Entertainment Gothic.

Movie theaters were courting female audiences at the perfect time. With the invention of home labor-saving machines in the late 1880s, such as the washing machine, which gave women (who could afford them) more freedom to leave the house, and the rise of department and grocery stores around the same time, which gave women more encouragement to leave the house to go shopping, there were unprecedented amounts of women in the public sphere. This gave female shoppers more economic power than ever before. What better way for wives and mothers to pass the time between shopping and a lunch date than popping into the theater to see a movie?

All theaters had to do was convince them.

First, exhibitors all over the country made sure to hold discounted matinee screenings during the late morning and early afternoon, exactly the time that women were out about town doing their shopping. Some theaters even created blocks of afternoon programming specifically for women.

Second, they made major upgrades to their interiors. Part of the reason why nickelodeons had a bad reputation is because frankly, they were sort of gross. The chairs were dingy, the floors were dirty, and everything was a little stinky. It feels a bit suspect to sit in the dark with a bunch of strangers in a space like that.

Ripping all of that out and replacing it with clean, plush seating, floors thick with carpeting, sparkling bathrooms, and a well-lit, decorated lobby did more to change middle-class women's minds about theaters than almost anything else. Theaters also majorly upgraded their customer service, hiring neatly uniformed ushers and friendly staff to see to anything the audience needed.

Once similar in ambience to saloons, movie theaters now advertised their elegance and luxury. To justify the cost of renovating the theaters, many owners implored filmmakers and distributors for longer films with higher production value that they could charge more in admission to see. So, you can thank female audiences for feature films...and the comfortable seats you watch them in.

Third, theater owners quite literally lured women in. Many theaters gave out—even mailed out—free "ladies tickets" hoping that once women stepped foot inside and saw the changes for themselves, they would return again and again. Some savvy owners set up small daycares near the lobby for mothers to drop their children off while they watched the films. This proved to be a successful strategy and a long line of baby carriages could often be seen snaking around the block outside the local theater.

Giveaways also worked quite well, and they were much more exciting than the novelty popcorn buckets we get today. Household items like dinner sets and cookware were used, as well as dresses and other pieces of clothing. One surprisingly effective giveaway prize was hams. Yes, whole hams, one per lady. It is believed the intention was for women to pick up their hams after the film was over and bring them home to feed their families, showing off just how family-friendly and wholesome theaters were. But there was nothing stopping a lady from getting her ham early and bringing it into the theater for a snack. This was the time before popcorn[34] and candy concessions, after all.

Industry magazines gave out tips to theater owners[35] on attracting female customers. *Motion Picture News* advised that to "cater to the feminine trade" theaters should keep an ample supply of feminine necessaries like hairpins in the lobby. It also recommended keeping women in mind when they printed their programs because "when a woman looks over an advance program and sees the name of a picture that appeals to her, she is sure to arrange with a neighbor or a relative" to see it because "once you get the ladies talking about your methods, the gossip will spread." Appealing to women would ensure that theater owners "reap profits." The same magazine, in a later article, declared that "Women are the biggest boost-

---

34 Popcorn wouldn't be introduced as a movie theater snack for another couple of decades. Sadly, movie theaters no longer offer hams.

35 Some of whom were women themselves. At the time, many theaters were family businesses that saw women working as musicians (to accompany the films, which were still silent), ushers, ticket sellers, even managers and owners. Opening one required very little startup money, which made it much more accessible for women.

ers a theatre can have and it behooves every exhibitor to cater particularly to them."

All of these strategies—including, maybe even especially, the hams—were wildly successful at getting women to give going to the movies a try. By the end of World War I, it is estimated that 75 percent of the butts in theater seats were women's.

But it wasn't the comfortable seats, the friendly ushers, or the giveaways that got them to come back. It was something that most theater owners did not even consider.

Going to the movies was, for just a little while, an escape.

Despite all the advancements in women's rights during the early decades of the twentieth century, it was still not the best time to be a woman.[36] Before World War I, many women worked seven days a week, ten-to fourteen-hour days. Even if women were lucky enough to be middle class and white, they were still living in a society that mostly disregarded them. Women could not yet vote, and few of them were able to travel, or feel much agency over their lives. The most choice middle-class housewives and mothers got during their daily lives was choosing what was for dinner. Sitting in a dark theater, faces illuminated by the silver flicker of the huge screen in front of them, these women could be temporarily transported to an entirely different life, even a different world.

Most Americans can remember their first film. Not the very first one, of course, but the first one that hit you, the first one that transported you. The first one you wanted to watch again and again, likely to the chagrin of whatever adult you were living with. Maybe you identified with the main character, maybe you wanted to *be* the main character. Either way, the experience hooked you.

Now, imagine not having that experience until you were in your twenties, thirties, forties, or even fifties. In the 1910s, thanks to a big push to get more women in theaters, a new phenomenon emerged: the "movie-struck girl."

---

36 I strongly suspect that we still have not yet reached that era. If you have a time machine and have gone ahead to check it out, let me know.

MOTION PICTURE MAGAZINE, MARCH 1914, PAGE 136.

"WHERE ARE YOU GOING, MY PRETTY MAID?"
"I'M GOING TO THE MOVIES, SIR," SHE SAID.

1914 cartoon featuring a woman on the way to the movies.

Women thronged to the movies. From teens to older women, female audiences could not get enough of the theater.

Soon, motion pictures began to compete in popularity with vaudeville and actual stage theater. And just like theater had figured out decades earlier, the financial success of a film often hinged on how well it catered to a female audience.

A cartoon in an early cinema fan magazine depicted the change coming over young American girls. Titled "But This Wasn't Our Marjorie!," the cartoon consists of a drawing of a young woman with a handful of coins, and the caption says,

See-saw, Marjorie Daw,
Sold her bed and lay upon straw;
She said that she'd much rather sleep upon hay
Than not see the Picture Plays once every day.

Magazines like *Motion Picture Classic, Motion Picture News, Motion Picture Magazine,* and *Moving Picture World* (you're probably noticing a theme here) focused on the glamorous aspects of the film industry to attract female readers. Soft-focus photos of film stars filled the pages, along with articles about style and fashion. Some started columns specifically dedicated to doling out beauty hints. Imagine getting skincare tips from *Entertainment Weekly*! In the back of the magazines, and strewn throughout the pages were innumerable ads for beauty products, corsets, jewelry, baby food. One ad for a "vacuum hand massager" proclaimed that "To Be Beautiful Is Woman's Duty."

As these magazines all but implied that women would be arrested if they didn't make themselves look pretty, they also loved to mock them for it. Cartoons showed women ruining film projections with their gigantic elaborate hats[37] (hats that, no doubt, that same magazine advertised), overdressing at the theater, being too chatty, and generally irritating other theatergoers.

READY FOR THE MOVIES

MOTION PICTURE MAGAZINE, NOVEMBER 1914.

1914 cartoon featuring a group of stone cold foxes overdressed for a night at the movies.

---

37 Which, to be fair, probably was annoying. Some theaters began posting signs that read "Ladies, please remove your hats." Eventually, most of them began to project film cards that contained a list of rules, such as no talking during the movie.

Although it was the refined, well-to-do women that theaters worked to lure in, the love of cinema never left the lower classes. Working-class women loved to stop in at the movies after their shifts for some cheap, relaxing entertainment that didn't involve them having to talk to any men. Plus, anything that the upper-class women were doing, the lower-class women wanted to emulate, if they could afford it. And at a nickel or a dime a movie (the equivalent of about three dollars today), they usually could.

In 1910, illiteracy rates for those over fourteen years of age were about 3 percent for white people, 13 percent for immigrants, and 30 percent for Black people. This means that there were millions in America[38] who could not read and therefore, could not find escape and entertainment in novels or short stories. Radios would not become widespread for another decade. For many young women, going to the movies was the only way they could get lost in a story.

These theatergoers were usually factory workers, immigrants, and other types of women who society liked to pretend didn't exist. But they kept coming back for the same reasons the upper-crust ladies did; they were entranced by what they saw on the screen, and how it made them feel.

The world jumps at the chance to laugh and belittle the things loved by a female—especially a younger female—audience, and then reap the benefits. A perfect example of this is The Beatles, whose rise to absolutely extraordinary worldwide fame was built on the backs of millions of screaming, fainting girls. Joe Brandt, who was the general manager of Universal Studios from 1912 to 1919, said, "Because of the millions of movie-struck girls in America, the moving pictures flourish. A very large percentage of our business unquestionably comes from those young women, who eagerly flock to see every new film."

The most fascinating thing about early film fan magazines, other than the ads for things like "vacuum hand massagers,"

---

38   The United States population at this time was about 92,228,496.

was that most photos of film stars were of women, not of men. These magazines were not like the glossy copies of *Teen Beat* that used to make some of us feel bad about ourselves in the 1990s, showcasing pictures of male heartthrobs. Most movie-struck girls were not going to the theater so they could swoon over the leading men, they were going because they identified with and rooted for the women.[39]

That was the only downside (in the eyes of the male executives and managers who worked at the studios, anyway) to the phenomenon of the movie-struck girl. They began to *really* identify with their heroes on screen, enough to travel to Hollywood en masse to join them on the silver screen.

Luckily for Helen, she beat them there.

By the time Helen arrived in Los Angeles in November of 1911, it was starting to look more like the bustling city it is today. There were no taco trucks, or CBD stores, or plastic surgery clinics, but it certainly was a quiet country town no longer. Now there were over five thousand people living in Hollywood, most of them those shady filmmaking types. The neighborhood council did continue to try to keep a handle on things, requiring that Hollywood Boulevard shut down at 10:30 p.m.[40] and banned the use of liquor and tobacco at the studios (although studios seldom enforced this).

The rest of Los Angeles was growing at the same rate. The film industry was beginning to attract tourists as well as industry workers, and soon the city was filled with hotels, restau-

---

39 Although I'm quite certain that some of the women looking through those magazines *were* swooning over and not just rooting for the actresses, and honestly, hell yeah.

40 Even over one hundred years later, Los Angeles continues to be a city that goes to bed fairly early. Visiting New Yorkers are always baffled to find things shutting down around 10:00 p.m.

rants, and stores selling the latest fashions.[41] Real estate prices
were exploding again as LA, and in particular Hollywood, became a name that was recognized around the country. Nearby
neighborhoods were soon renamed to capitalize on the fame,
and soon there was North, East, West, and South Hollywood[42]
in addition to Hollywood itself.

By now, the original residents of Hollywood were forced to
admit that no, the film industry had not hurt their property
values. Still, they were unhappy about the big studio buildings
being built among all the beautiful homes. Film companies were
pouring into the city or rapidly being formed. Vitagraph[43] moved
to Los Angeles and the next spring, Carl Laemmle would found
the Universal Film Manufacturing Company, which became
the much snappier Universal Studios. Some studio buildings
were small and looked like a regular house, while others were
massive, consisting of offices, warehouses, and shooting stages.

Even with all the expansion and construction, Los Angeles's
infrastructure struggled to keep up with the swell of people,
buildings, and traffic. The roads were so rough that Cecil B.
DeMille had to ride a horse from his rented house to the studio.

Filmmakers and studios were still figuring out the best and
most efficient (two *very* different things in any creative industry) way to make movies and get them out into the world. Most
were sticking to the tried and true formula of at least one comedy and one Western per week. By this time, films were usually
five to twenty minutes long, although features were becoming
more and more popular with audiences.

As you can tell by the success of the Wild West shows, Amer-

---

41   Los Angeles's most famous street for shopping, Rodeo Drive, would not be
     filled with luxury stores until the 1960s. During this time it was, however, in
     the process of being developed into a subdivision from land that was previ-
     ously used to grow lima beans.

42   Names that are still used today.

43   Over a decade later, they would sell to a man named Harry Warner and become
     Warner Brothers Studios.

icans were hungry for stories of cowboys, train robberies, and life on the frontier. While the film industry was first starting in America, some of these stories were still happening in real life. The last big American train robbery was in 1901, by the infamous Butch Cassidy and his longtime accomplice Harry Longabaugh, also known as the Sundance Kid. The film *The Great Train Robbery*, made by Edwin S. Porter, was made just two years later, in 1903.

Clocking in at a mere eleven minutes, *The Great Train Robbery* was not the first Western that was ever made, but it became incredibly popular and had a gigantic influence on the development of the genre. The film can be considered the country's first blockbuster film and almost immediately inspired a multitude of imitators. *The Great Train Robbery* put Westerns on the map and established them as a core type of American film for the next eighty years.

The content of these films was a cinematic extension of the stories being told in Wild West shows. The plot was usually a struggle between the forces of "good" (white, American) and the forces of "evil" (anyone else). Just like the Wild West shows, they drastically rewrote history in a shitty way, reinforcing the American myth that white settlers had a divine right to the land and an inherent superiority over any "uncivilized" people. The cowboy, "taming" the West and galloping in to save the day, is a distinctly American creation.

As historian Richard Aquila says in his book, *The Sagebrush Trail*, "Throughout history, people have turned to an idealized or nostalgic past to cope with stress or rapid social, cultural, and political change." What Westerns were doing was hitting a nerve for many wistful white Americans, especially the male ones. There was a lot of anxiety about shifting from a mainly agricultural country to a modern, industrial one, not to mention the shift to a country where women were allowed, even encouraged, to leave the house. It was cathartic for many men to watch a film where the good guy (who looked like them) triumphed with his "traditional values." While this is frustrating, you can at least laugh at the fact that these films were called oaters, or horse operas.

Over the next six decades, almost a third of all films made in the United States were Westerns. They were known as the meat and potatoes of the industry because they were usually cheap to make, reliably enjoyed by audiences, and regularly purchased by theater owners. Even European filmmakers tried to get in on the game in the early 1900s, but there was no substitute for the American West and they could not match American filmmakers' "authenticity." (Hilarious.)

At first, like most films made in the United States, Westerns were shot in New York, New Jersey, or Chicago. But once the industry began to decamp en masse to Southern California, Western filmmakers were more than happy to use the wide open spaces available near Los Angeles, where it was so much cheaper and faster to shoot.

In the 1910s, to keep the genre alive, and to respond to theater owners' pleas for longer, more elaborate films (so they could pay for nicer theaters for female audiences, remember), studios started making grander Westerns with better writing, more advanced filmmaking techniques, and more overall production value. But even these new, improved Westerns mainly followed a specific formula. Staples included tense shootouts, train robberies, exciting chases, beautiful western scenery, and the good guys beating the bad guys. More than anything, it included horses. They were called horse operas, after all. Which is where Helen came in.

With hundreds of Westerns being shot in the Los Angeles area every year, there was a spectacular demand for horses and riders. Big shootout, chase, and battle scenes needed a massive amount of background actors. And not just male actors, either. Cowgirls appeared in Westerns as early as 1910.

So, you can imagine burgeoning filmmaker Thomas H. Ince's

excitement when an entire Wild West show rolled into town. He would eventually go on to make around eight hundred films, many of them Westerns, but in 1911, he had only been working in the industry for about a year.

The Miller brothers, seeing the popularity of Western films, were eager to get into movie production and happily collaborated with Ince. They eventually bought property near Malibu that Ince built his first film studio on. It was called the Miller 101 Bison Ranch Studio and, it's believed, was the first of its kind. Ince created a studio that was all-inclusive, with shooting stages, production offices, film laboratories, prop houses, dressing rooms, and more. Hundreds of actors and crew members worked there, and to feed them all, the Miller brothers claimed that they invented the sack lunch. The story goes that one of the brothers had the idea to get hundreds of paper bags and put identical amounts of fruit, sandwiches, and cakes in each one and line them up on a table.[44]

Catering methods aside, at that point, Ince was shooting most of his films in an area called Topanga Canyon. Nestled into the Santa Monica Mountains to the northwest of Hollywood, nowadays Topanga Canyon is known as a great place to go for a gorgeous drive and brunch. But in 1911, it was a popular spot to shoot because of the incredible scenery. Tracts of open grassland are nestled between stands of towering live oak trees. A hike to the top of the canyon is rewarded with a stunning view of the Pacific Ocean.

After being hired by Ince, Helen and her fellow performers boarded down in Venice, where the animals from the show were stabled. Every day, they all rode their horses to set, a journey of about seven miles that would take a little over an hour. Waking up to the sparkling expanse of the Pacific Ocean and riding

---

44 This is a highly suspicious claim. If some stressed-out mom didn't think of this idea before these guys did, I'll eat my keyboard. They *might* have been the first to feed a giant film crew like this.

along the beach to work every day was a far cry from making cigars in a factory. Between all the beauty and the excitement, Helen immediately fell in love with Los Angeles.

Life on set is chaotic in today's world, with heaps of safety measures, security, and technology to make communication easy. Back in the 1910s, filmmaking really put the wild in the "Wild West." But even with horses running around, piles of flammable film canisters, and no digital spreadsheets in sight, making a movie was (and is) *fun*. Amid all the panic and pandemonium of trying to get a shot, trying to catch the light, trying to co-ordinate many people—and also in this case, large animals—to all work on different aspects of the exact same scene in front of the camera at the right time, filmmaking is truly magic. There's a reason why so many people are and want to be filmmakers, professionally or otherwise. Even during the most stressful moments, movie sets are charged with energy. You're all working together to make something, something that started out as imaginary and soon will exist for the whole world to see.

Filmmaking, no matter if you're a director, producer, actor, camerawoman or what, can also be grueling work. When you're shooting, the days are long and sometimes, the nights are, too. Trying to make things look and sound good, and more importantly, look and sound the way the director wants them to, while staying on budget and on time, can make you feel like tearing your hair out.

And yet.

It's a thrilling feeling, one that many people become hooked on from the very first day they step foot on set. Helen was one of those people.

What Ince hired the riders from the Millers Brothers 101 Ranch show to do was to work as background actors.[45] Background actors are all the actors in a scene that are not the leads

---

45 These used to be called "extras," but today the term is thought to be a bit demeaning and is no longer used.

and are not supporting. Usually this means that they have no lines or direct interaction with the main actors, and stay in the background. A couple walking down the sidewalk, customers in line at a coffee shop, picnickers in a park, etc.

For Helen and her fellow 101 riders, this could mean anything from trotting on a horse in the background of a Western town scene to being a part of a stampede in a battle scene. Most of the Western films that Ince produced and/or directed at the end of 1911 and into 1912 were ten to twenty minutes long and involved some hero, usually a sheriff or cowboy, who rescues a town/lady/etc. from villains, usually a Native tribe. Ince often put white actors in race makeup for these roles, despite the fact that he hired the Native performers who were part of the 101 Ranch show.

At the time, Ince worked mainly with two actors, a teenaged girl from New York City named Ethel Grandin, and Ann Little, a young woman who was actually born on a ranch and had some Western authenticity. They usually played the lead or leads in the films Helen was background in. Ince, even though he got her started in film, did not take particular notice of Helen.

Soon, someone else would.

The Miller Brothers 101 Ranch Show wintered in Southern California at the end of 1911. In the spring, the brothers decided that it was time to pack up the show and hit the road back to Oklahoma. The spring season would begin as it usually did in April. Helen, however, decided to quit the show and stay behind.

Even after only two seasons, the world of the Wild West show didn't have much else to offer her. Helen had traveled all over the country. She was a talented trick rider, and the only advancement was to become a featured star, like Annie Oakley was in Buffalo Bill's show. Already, the most desirable endgame for trick riders was to make it in Hollywood. Some of her fellow 101 Ranch alumni, like the eventual Western film legend Tom Mix, had already done it. The hardest part of the film industry wasn't getting to Los Angeles, it was getting a start in the movies, which Helen had just done.

She was only nineteen years old; unmarried, childless, without a single obligation in the world, and had just broken into an industry that had just begun its takeover of American pop culture. Helen would have had to be comatose to miss the electric atmosphere of possibility buzzing in the warm Southern California air. But she was very much awake. Helen wanted to stay and see what this city had in store for her.

Turns out, her instincts were correct. She was soon approached by a man named Pat Hartigan, an actor who had started directing his own films the year before. He worked with the Kalem Film Company, which had started in New York in 1907 and was part of the early wave of film companies to decamp to Southern California. Kalem originally planned the California studio to be a winter facility for shooting Westerns, but it quickly became apparent that the smart move would be to shoot there all year round.

Hartigan wanted to bring Helen to get test photographed. This was different from a live audition, where she would be trying out for a specific role. Actors were test photographed to see how they would look on camera. Since this was still the era of silent film, Helen didn't have to learn any lines. She had to emote to the lens, essentially making a silent audition tape. Studio executives and producers watched the footage, or looked at photographs, and decided who should be cast in their upcoming films.

What the folks at Kalem saw of Helen impressed them and she was hired. It was time for her to show the world what she could do.

Act Two

4

The Movie Star

By 1912, women had been coming to Hollywood[46] to make and act in films for years. Now it was time for them to take over, starting with the world's very first movie star.

It might be a little tough to imagine in today's celebrity-obsessed culture, but when the film industry was in its beginning stages, nobody knew who the actors were. Actors were not given any on-screen credit; they were simply anonymous.

This was a purposeful omission. The Edison Trust (that group of New York–based film moguls who chased independent film-makers away) believed that naming actors on screen and publicly crediting them for their work would lead to their asking for more money.

The thing is, the Edison Trust wasn't wrong. They just didn't realize they were ignoring a goldmine right under their noses.

In 1906, a white actor named Florence Lawrence began work-

---

46   At this point in time, Hollywood was already synonymous with "the American film industry, concentrated in Los Angeles."

ing for Edison's film production company. She was beautiful, with bow lips and waves of curly, ash-blond hair. Like her colleagues, Lawrence went uncredited in all the films she appeared in for Edison, despite having a wildly catchy name.

Soon, she left Edison and went on to work for D.W. Griffith's company, Biograph. Lawrence was a great actor, with an expressive face that audiences adored. She quickly developed a fan base, even though the public did not know her name. Her fans started calling her the "Biograph Girl." By 1909, Lawrence had appeared in over fifty films, all anonymously.

Griffith eventually fired her for having the audacity to consider starring in movies with other companies, and Carl Laemmle of Universal Studios quickly scooped her up. Laemmle saw Lawrence's talent and considered her to be the industry's greatest actress.

In early 1910, Laemmle orchestrated a publicity stunt to finally reveal the name of the Biograph Girl. He convinced Lawrence to make a public appearance, something actors did not really do at the time. She agreed to debut in St. Louis on March 25 when her new film, *The Broken Oath*, premiered at the Grand Opera House.

When Lawrence's train pulled into the Union Station that day, she had no idea what she was in for. A huge, frenzied crowd of adoring fans was waiting. The moment Lawrence's high heels hit the platform, they went wild. People lunged at her. Hands began to grab at Lawrence and before she could be escorted out, the fans had yanked all the buttons off of her coat.

Laemmle now had proof of something he had only guessed at: the power of stars and movie fandom.

Lawrence herself thought the entire situation was a little strange and a bit confusing. She didn't understand why fans would care so deeply about people who they didn't know and had only seen on screen.[47] What Lawrence did understand was that it gave her a lot more leverage than she had before. She was a suffragette, and believed in more rights for women. Lawrence didn't know it then, but Laemmle's idea would soon make women the most powerful players in Hollywood. That year, as the first (it's believed) actor to be given on-screen credit, Florence Lawrence kicked off something called the star system.

At D.W. Griffith's company, she was making $25 (about $783 today) a week. Now she was making $500 a week at Universal (about $15,700 today). Even though Laemmle was paying Lawrence what was considered to be an astronomical salary, he was making it back hand over fist. Devoted fans rushed to see every film that she was in.

Before, moviegoers loved the mysterious and beautiful Biograph Girl. Now audiences knew she was a real person, with a name and a hometown and a family. Fans could identify with her; they could project whatever they wanted onto her. The lines between the brave, kindhearted heroines she played and the person she was in real life became blurred. It didn't help that in many films that year, her character was named Flo. By 1912, she was receiving mountains of fan mail every week and appearing on magazine covers. At only five foot three, she quickly became larger than life.

Executives and owners of other companies quickly realized the shortsightedness of keeping actors anonymous and raced to duplicate the success that Laemmle had with Lawrence. Studios soon began crediting their own actors, and filmmakers even started changing their filmmaking techniques to better feature them. Before Florence Lawrence, most films were created with long shots, with the cameras situated far back to catch the entire scene and actors' entire bodies. Studios believed that the

---

47 It wouldn't be until the 1950s that the psychology industry would start using the term "parasocial" to describe these relationships.

more of the actors the audiences could see, the more value the picture had. Ironically, it was D.W. Griffith, the man who fired Lawrence, who helped popularize the close-up, where the camera was placed close to the actors so that their faces were much larger and more recognizable.

By the next year, studios began to submit the names of prominent cast and crew members of films to trade magazines, including actors, directors, and writers. Movies were making the permanent shift from anonymous productions to screen credits.[48]

Eventually, Florence Lawrence went on to appear in over three hundred different films, and the star system she launched went on to create one of the most exciting eras in Hollywood history. Now that the stars were in the spotlight, it was impossible to stuff them back into obscurity. Fans demanded them.

More than anything, they demanded the female stars.

This was because audiences were largely women themselves. Thanks to the gigantic push from theater owners to attract female audiences, and the directing of fan magazines toward female readers, in the 1910s, film fandom was a girl thing.

Women seated in movie theaters, who were for the first time frequently venturing out in public and thinking about their rights, wanted heroines. They wanted to see women on adventures, women getting romanced, women in charge. They wanted to see a world where women mattered. They wanted to pretend—more so, they wanted to believe—that they too were capable of saving the day. In their heart of hearts, these women also wanted to be larger than life. Even if just for a little while.

Film critic Iris Barry, who would later go on to become the first curator of the film department at the Museum of Modern Art in 1933, remarked that American film during this time existed "for the purpose of pleasing women." The best way to do that? Make a movie about a woman.

---

48 Although the long end crawls with hundreds of credits were years and years away.

Just as female consumers decided which of the era's brands and products succeeded, from soaps to soups, they also decided which actors became stars. Hollywood's first crop of movie stars included, along with Florence Lawrence herself, Mary Pickford, Gloria Swanson, Dorothy Davenport, Marion Leonard, twins Lillian and Dorothy Gish (who wore different colored ribbons so directors could tell them apart), and Tsuru Aoki, who was possibly the first Asian lead actress in American cinema. There were male stars, certainly, including Roscoe "Fatty" Arbuckle, Wallace Reid, and Sessue Hayakawa. But Hollywood, by and large, was a lady's world. In 1914, Beatrice DeMille, screenwriter, theater actress, and one of the founding members of Paramount Studios, told the *New York Daily Mirror* that "this is the women's age."[49]

What did these stars do with all that power?

Well, they made movies.

Would you believe that over a hundred years ago, during the fabled "good old days" that conservative politicians are always trying to wrench the country back to, women were making movies about sexuality, oppression, abortion, and women's rights? You bet your corset they did.

Actress-turned-director Cleo Madison released the feature film (one of two she directed) *Her Bitter Cup* in 1916, a tale of unionized female workers suffering under their oppressive male boss. It was a very early precursor to *9 to 5*, with no catchy songs. Madison also directed *A Soul Enslaved* the same year, about a young woman becoming the mistress of a rich man so she can escape poverty, then later on, suffering the judgment from her boyfriend about it. Madison's films often explored female sexuality and power dynamics, and were firmly rooted in storytelling from a female perspective. She was an innovative director, and her 1916 film *Eleanor's Catch* is one of the first ever films to have a twist ending. (I won't spoil it for you, even though it's been over a hundred years.)

---

49   Yes, she was also the mother of Cecil DeMille.

Madison was quite sure of her ability, telling *Photoplay Magazine* in 1916 when asked if she was scared to start directing, "Why should I be? I had seen men with less brains than I have getting away with it, and so I knew that I could direct if they'd give me the opportunity." She went on to say that "One of these days men are going to get over the fool idea that women have no brains, and quit getting insulted at the thought that a skirt-wearer can do their work quite as well as they can. And I don't believe that day is very far distant, either." Even though Madison knew that she and her female colleagues were good, they were acutely aware that they were defying convention. Director Ida May Park said that there was "no finer calling for a woman" than directing movies.

Seeing such bold assurance was exciting and refreshing for the mid-1910s, and unfortunately, would still be exciting and refreshing today. Women have always been expected to diminish themselves to make space for the egos of others. And, good lord, if you're good at something, at least have the decency to be humble about it so you don't make men around you feel inadequate!

Women who are damn good at what they do and deservedly confident about it still set people back on their heels. This interview Madison did caused many film historians to remark upon her confidence, yet confidence is rarely something pointed out in male film directors. While it's wonderful that Madison was confident, it's frustrating to see it pointed out as a salient part of her creative persona. As she might say, "Why shouldn't I be?"

Arguably the greatest director of the time, female or otherwise, was Lois Weber. Powerhouse does not begin to describe her. She started her career as an actor, and developed into one of film history's most important and prolific directors. You might call Weber one of the original social justice warriors. It's believed that she directed between two and four hundred different films, many focused on women's social issues. Weber leveraged her power as a star director to make controversial films. Birth control and abortion, for example, were subjects she felt passionately about.

Film historian Anthony Slide calls her and D.W. Griffith the first American auteurs. Weber was an innovative director, and is often credited with the first use of the split-screen technique in American cinema. Weber involved herself in all aspects of her productions and used her films to express her ideas about the world and the way it should be. In 1914, she said in an interview, "In moving pictures I have found my life's work. I find at once an outlet for my emotions and my ideals. I can preach to my heart's content, and with the opportunity to write the play, act the leading role, and direct the entire production, if my message fails to reach someone, I can blame only myself."

As cool as it is that Weber and her female colleagues were making movies from the female perspective and spreading their ideas, they were championing a very early and underdeveloped form of feminism. So underdeveloped, in fact, that the word had at the time just begun to be used. Aside from being mainly for white, non-marginalized women, it was often (but not always) the sort of proto-feminism that preached equality with men, and in the same breath, told you that your skirt was too short and that you were wearing too much makeup.

For example, in 1914, Weber directed *The Spider and the Web*, where Weber herself played a femme fatale that reveled in seducing and ruining men, until she adopted an orphaned baby and through the cleansing power of motherhood, learned the error of her wicked ways. You know, *that* kind of feminism.

A couple of years later, in 1916, Weber wrote and directed the wildly popular film *Where Are My Children?*, a film about abortion that fiercely advocates for birth control. While it is thrilling and almost mind-boggling to think about a film about abortion being released before the First World War, let alone one that played to packed theaters, the film is a mixed bag. It's about a male attorney who, while prosecuting a doctor who provides illegal abortion services, discovers that his wife and her high-society friends have all used his services. This would be a radically progressive film even by today's standards. Unfortunately, Weber, while strongly supporting birth control, falsely portrays abortion as a procedure that's mentally and physically harmful. The film is also positive on eugenics, providing examples of "good" desirable children, and "bad" undesirable children. Woof!

While I like to give her the benefit of the doubt, and hope that a few modern feminist thought classes and a stack of books by authors like Lindy West, Ijeoma Oluo, and Roxane Gay could set Weber on the right track, it's important to point out that the ideas behind these films had a long way to go.

We can hold both pieces. Many of these filmmakers helped perpetuate harmful ideas with their movies. Even so, they were certainly trying to make change in their own, misguided way. As Ariana DeBose would say, they did the thing.

The same year Weber released *The Spider and the Web*, in which she directed twenty-seven films, she became the first American woman to direct a feature film with an adaptation of the Shakespearean play *The Merchant of Venice*. The year before, in 1913, she directed *Suspense*, which many historians name as one of the greatest American films. Tom Gunning says that no other work before the First World War exhibits a "stronger command of film style" and insists that she outdoes "even Griffith for emotionally involved filmmaking."

In 1915, Weber made more film history by shooting the first non-pornographic nude scene in her film *Hypocrites*. Also called *The Naked Truth*, the film featured actress Margaret Edwards naked as the embodiment of truth, exposing the hypocrisies of the Christian church.[50] The film was banned in some states, making Weber one of the first directors to come under the fire

---

50 Weber shot the nude scenes on a closed set, which means that no one was allowed aside from Edwards, Weber, and the cameraman.

of film censors (who would become a very big problem in the not too distant future) who did not approve of seeing Ms. Edwards's boobs projected onto the big screen. Tell people about *The Naked Truth* when they say that movies today have too much nudity and "woke politics."

Some of the most successful women in film during this time were not directors, but writers.

As the industry developed, screenwriting became more specialized. Soon, it was common to have a dedicated screenwriter, instead of multiple people putting together the screenplay. This meant the director was able to focus on the overall vision of the film and the whole production was more balanced between the director, the producer, and the screenwriter.

Now that movies were getting longer and longer, audiences cared more about the narrative. Talented screenwriters, those who could tug at heartstrings and send thrills down spines, started to rise to the top. These writers gained influence and were soon able to develop their own projects.

Grace Cunard, who reportedly wrote hundreds of short films, worked with her longtime collaborator Francis Ford, who credited Cunard in interviews as the one who usually came up with the ideas for the films they made. They made wildly popular films of all genres, and were called "the king and queen of melodrama" by *Photoplay Magazine*.

Jeanie MacPherson wrote over thirty films for Cecil B. DeMille over the course of fifteen years, who said that she brought him "many, many ideas." MacPherson went on to help found the Academy of Motion Picture Arts and Sciences. She started her career by acting in almost thirty short films before moving into the, as it was called, scenario department.

Even though women made and enthusiastically watched every type of film available—Westerns, adventures, mysteries, romances, thrillers, you name it—there certainly were "women's films."

By now, cinema had begun to edge out theater and vaudeville

as the preferred entertainment of the masses. As its popularity spread, people started to notice how influential film could be. Different organizations looked into the best ways to use the medium to spread their message, whether it was for politics or social movements. One of the era's biggest campaigns was hugely influenced by the movies: women's suffrage. Suffrage organizations were among the first groups of activists to start using films to push their ideas.

At the start of the 1910s, the United States' two biggest suffrage organizations were the National American Women's Suffrage Association (NAWSA)[51] and the Women's Political Union (WPU). By this time, they were seeing progress from their efforts. Between 1910 and 1912, five states—Washington, California, Arizona, Kansas, and Oregon[52]—had granted voting rights to women. The campaign to make it federal law was building momentum. In 1913, Congress, for the very first time, debated women's enfranchisement[53] and began to give it serious consideration.

NAWSA and WPU knew that this was a critical moment. If they could activate enough public pressure, more and more politicians could be swayed to give women the right to vote. But how could they reach as many women as possible? The one form of entertainment that attracted and considered them more than any other.

Movies were an ideal way to spread the NAWSA/WPU's message because films (good ones, anyway) are machines for em-

---

51   It's important to note that this organization was not promoting voting rights for all women. At this time, NAWSA was criticized, notably by W.E.B. Du-Bois, for not allowing Black members. This was partly because they wanted to raise support for women's voting rights among white southern politicians. This kind of thinking was, and always will be, trash.

52   Wyoming, Colorado, Utah, and Idaho had already done so before 1910.

53   Which sounds like giving women the ability to open franchises of themselves all over the country like a pizza chain, but really means the giving of a right or a privilege, usually to vote.

pathy. Like a novel, a movie can intimately invite an audience into the emotions, the struggles, and the dreams of a character. But in a country where millions couldn't read, films were the more effective medium to reach people. And even though the intended audience for these films was a middle-class white woman, they attracted all types. Young women, old women, immigrant women, single women, mothers, poor women. These suffrage films were able to reach them all...and get them thinking.

Between 1912 and 1914, NAWSA and WPU released four different feature-length films promoting women's suffrage. The organizations were cautious in the creation of these movies; they didn't want to appear too radical and scare anyone off. All directed by men, but mostly written by women, the goal of the films was to show how women's rights would actually improve society, not screw everything up.

In *Your Girl and Mine*, a young, white everywoman marries a cruel alcoholic who forces her to endure destitution and the loss of her children. The film highlights the fact that she must go through these hardships because she is legally unable to get a divorce and lives in a state that does not grant rights to women. Her crappy husband is eventually killed (sadly not by her) and the protagonist moves to a new state, where the governor signs a bill granting women the right to vote. Our everywoman is so turned on by finally having rights that she marries the lieutenant governor and they live happily ever after. The message of the film was as much for male audiences as it was for women. If you let women vote, they won't do anything ridiculous. They'll be so happy, they'll want to marry you! Giving ladies rights is like, so sexy.

This plot sounds heavy-handed and maybe even a little bit silly today, but in 1914, it was a goddamn hit. Some review publications thought that the story was a bit much, and *Variety* said that it was "melodramatic." However, the women in those theater seats loved it. *Motography Magazine* praised the film, and noted

that the story "drove home the suffrage argument" and that female audiences applauded throughout the screening. Chicago
film journalist Kitty Kelly (who I'll tell you more about later)
said that audiences responded with "waves of enthusiasm." The
film ended up running in theaters for two years.

Two other suffrage films, *Votes for Women* and *80 Million
Women Want—?*, although fictional, used actual footage from
women's suffrage events and featured cameos by prominent female suffrage activists. *Votes for Women* also tried to appeal to
male audiences and featured an engaged couple to show that
women would not immediately become man-hating harpies
if they got some rights. Historian Shelley Stamp says of these
films that while they push their message, they "cloak demands
for political equality with reassurances that traditional notions of
womanhood will endure with full citizenship, and that heterosexual relations will not be destabilized."[54] Women, as a survival
mechanism, are highly attuned to male anxiety. NAWSA/WPU
knew that male politicians and voters would not grant them a
single thing if they thought their ability to get some would be
threatened by women's suffrage.

Although these films were shunted into the often dismissed
subgenre of "social problem films," female audiences took them
quite seriously. Many women brought the ideas they saw up on
the big screen back home and began to discuss them with their
friends. The popularity made male critics around the country
nervous. Many said that the films were propaganda. A male
journalist in a Connecticut newspaper said that the message of
Your Girl and Mine was akin to socialism, and Edward Toole of
the *New York Tribune* claimed that the film was filling the heads
of uneducated female viewers with false information and "fake
impressions" about laws and government. How dare these filmmakers trick the poor, naive women into thinking that they de-

---

54 A warning sign at the world's creepiest laboratory: Do not destabilize the
heterosexual relations!

serve equal rights? Even if they weren't sure how they felt about women getting the right to vote, seeing female audiences around the country become politicized, even radicalized, made critics concerned. Male fears about the growing power of women, economically, culturally and politically, were reflected in these panicky reviews.

Some women's groups opposed the films, such as the Massachusetts Association Opposed to the Further Extension of Suffrage to Women. Their official publication, the *Remonstrance Against Women's Suffrage* (which is exactly as much fun as it sounds), called *Your Girl and Mine* melodramatic and lurid.

And not all female filmmakers were interested in making preachy suffrage films. Anti-suffrage films (mostly comedies) were being churned out alongside the pro-suffrage ones. Screenwriting legend Anita Loos, who became the first on-staff screenwriter in Hollywood when D.W. Griffith hired her a couple years earlier in 1914, penned the film *A Cure for Suffragettes*, where a group of suffragettes are so fired up for their cause that they forget to take care of their babies, who fall into the hands of a group of bumbling police officers. There were also anti-anti-suffrage films that mocked those who opposed women's rights. All of this shows how everyone, no matter what they believed in, was at least recognizing the power of motion pictures to reach the public and influence their opinions. Film ended up playing a huge role—on both sides—in the debate for the vote.

Most comedies of the time, however, were not political in nature. Audiences always want to see someone getting hit in the face with a pie.

The first actor, of any gender, to provide theatergoers with that particular thrill was Mabel Normand. Normand was known as the queen of "new humor" which gained popularity in the 1890s. "New humor" replaced Victorian narrative-based humor and involved physical slapstick that was fast-paced and often a little violent. From the start, because it appeared to be less cerebral than narrative-based humor, new humor was considered low-class, lowbrow, and decidedly unfeminine. In new humor scenes, which began in vaudeville and moved to motion pictures, social rules and acceptable behavior were presented and then immediately smashed to bits. Over-the-top chases, silly fights, and exaggerated falls were mainstays of the genre.

There were many talented and influential female comedians of the era, but none more than Normand. She starred in, wrote, and directed over a hundred comedies. Physical comedy was her specialty, and Normand was as comfortable throwing a punch as she was throwing a pie. She was quite happy to be aggressive and excessive on-screen. Many female stars in the 1910s, such as Mary Pickford, were beloved for their sweet and demure ways, but Normand was completely uninterested in that sort of persona.

Normand and her female colleagues were important trailblazers because the prevailing wisdom was that women weren't, and couldn't be, funny.[55] Female audiences were thought to be too refined and sensitive to enjoy humor, especially new humor, let alone create it.

What that really meant was women were not powerful enough to be funny.

Because that's what humor and ridicule is, an assumption of power. Deciding what is funny puts you in control, and dismissing women's humor is to deny them access to that power. Traditionally, women in comedies are the butt of the joke. Putting them in the position of power, making women decide who to laugh at, throws the whole system off.[56] As historian Kristen Anderson Wagner says, "The pervasive denial and suppression of women's humor by both popular culture and academia is essentially a denial and suppression of women's social and cultural power." You are conditioned to identify with whoever is

---

55 A laughable (no pun intended) idea that has unfortunately stuck around.

56 This is part of why (aside from a boatload of transphobia) that it's such a long-standing tradition to laugh at men dressed like women.

in power, so why would you want to laugh along with someone who popular culture tells you is of lower value?

A funny lady was the exact opposite of the kind of women Victorian ideals praised: gentle, refined, subdued. Everything that comedy stood for was the antithesis of what it meant to be a "lady."

All of this makes up the boneheaded idea that women aren't funny. When Normand was making films, it wasn't just an annoying idea, it was massively controversial. Women performing any kind of physical comedy caused a stir. Physical comedy challenged the prevailing gender roles because comedy heroines could reduce men for once, whether that meant their bosses, husbands, policemen—any sort of man in power could be taken down a few pegs and made into a laughingstock. Female comedians offered an alternative way of being a woman.

At the turn of the century, it was even believed that many women didn't *have* a sense of humor. They couldn't have a sense of humor because women were the morally superior ones, and laughing at a person is just a little bit wicked. If directed at someone specific, it could be taken as a criticism, especially if directed at a man. During this time, it wasn't even considered appropriate for ladies to laugh out loud, which was thought to signify a lack of self-control. Women shouldn't be seen *or* heard. This is why many male film executives operated under the assumption that female audiences did not like comedies.

In reality, women loved to get rowdy in the theater and laugh at female comedians. And the one they loved the most was Mabel Normand.

Normand didn't care one bit about being considered lowbrow. She told a reporter in 1920, "I am not a highbrow. If I were, I wouldn't be earning my living by being funny—or trying to be."

She started her career at Keystone Studios, which was founded in east Los Angeles in 1912. Normand quickly began to direct films, many of which featured her own name, such as *Mabel's Adventures*, *Mabel's Stormy Love Affair*, and *Mabel's Awful Mistakes*. These films usually featured Normand getting into some ridiculous situation and having to do even more ridiculous things to get out of it. Many of them featured popular comedian Roscoe "Fatty" Arbuckle, and many more featured a young comedian named Charlie Chaplin, whose career Normand played a key role in developing.

Normand convinced Mack Sennett, the founder of Keystone Studios, to give Chaplin a chance, and then convinced him again when Sennett saw one of Chaplin's films and doubted that he would be a hit. Even so, Normand had a conflicted relationship with Chaplin. The two were often co-stars and Normand often acted as his mentor while he adjusted from working on the stage to working behind the camera. They starred in twelve films together, and his first appearance using his "tramp" character was in *Mabel's Strange Predicament*, directed by Normand. But Chaplin frequently chafed at being helped by Normand, and especially didn't like being told what to do by her. Many of the films they were in together were directed by Normand, and Chaplin often wouldn't listen to her, refusing to follow her direction. He told her that she was just a "pretty girl" and would even try to take directing credit from her.

Despite being plagued by mustachioed jerks, Normand was a hit. Film critics were often disdainful about female comedians, but she won them over. *Photoplay Magazine* described her in 1919 "Whether she is falling down a well, leaping through an upper window in a ball gown...she is startling, vivacious, girlish, and always funny."

So, these were the behemoths of burgeoning Hollywood. Not just the *female* behemoths, but the filmmakers creating the most popular, influential, and groundbreaking motion pictures at this time. Lois Weber, Grace Cunard, and Mabel Normand were especially significant. Weber, with her progressive, uplifting films, Cunard with her popular genre pictures, and Normand with her comedies. Of course, they are joined in the pantheon by male directors like Cecil B. DeMille and D.W. Griffith. But they aren't part of a separate subgenre of important *female* filmmakers.

Many female filmmakers (myself included) have an incredibly

conflicted relationship with the word "female" being placed in front of their profession. This applies to writers and artists, as well. Honestly, it applies to just about any job you can think of.

You see the need, in a society that still has a gender pay gap, to recognize women in your field and give special support to the things they make. You see the benefit of it, in a world where women are still having historic firsts, particularly when it comes to showing young girls all the things that they are capable of.

But it feels just like a bra, like an extra piece of equipment you're expected to use to functionally exist in society. And just like a bra, it can be awkward, uncomfortable, and annoying, even while it is also supportive.

So often, the *female* part becomes the focus, instead of the thing you created. People want to ask you about what it's like to be a woman doing that particular thing, instead of actually asking about that particular thing. As comedian Beth Stelling says in her 2020 HBO stand-up special *Girl Daddy*, "I've been called a female comic so many times, I'll probably only be able to answer to 'girl daddy' when I have children."

Suddenly, you've gotten a new job, an extra job that sits on top of your other job. You are now an official spokesperson for your gender. Unpaid, of course. You are doing this instead of, or alongside if you're lucky, talking about and promoting the thing that you actually do. To go along with the pay gap, there is another gap, where you get a little less time and space to champion yourself and your work. You actually don't mind talking about being a woman, but usually only with other people who get it, unless you are being paid to (which you rarely ever are). You like being a woman, but you don't like having it pointed out, but you recognize that you live in a world where you probably should point it out, especially if you look around in a given situation and realize there are no other women around you (which happens more than you'd like).

So you stand, adjusting the underwire that comes with this prefix to your profession as it digs into your armpit, and wait for a better world.

All of these women were frequently asked about how their gender came into play when they were making movies, and all of them balked at the notion that they would ever be unable to do something just because they were women. Then they continued to do what they did best: make the sort of motion pictures that they wanted to see. Lois Weber said, "One of my chief aims in producing a picture, in writing a story, or supervising the dressing of a set, is to please women."

Well, there was another one about to join their ranks, another titanic female filmmaker who would not only help change the cinematic landscape, but would completely change the course of Helen Gibson's life.

Now that Helen was on the payroll at the Kalem Film Company, it was time for her acting career to truly begin.

Kalem's California office, which they opened specifically to shoot Westerns, was located in what is today known as the Pacific Palisades. It is a secluded neighborhood with a multitude of gigantic, marvelous houses tucked into the steep hills that rise up from the coastline. Today, if you're in the Palisades, you're either rich, a celebrity, or a visiting surfer. But back then, it was just a beautiful neighborhood north of Santa Monica. This was perfect for Helen, since she was still living nearby in Venice Beach.

Even though Kalem's office was new, they were a fairly established company who had been making popular motion pictures for several years. Kalem had already shot films all over the world. Besides their offices in Florida and New York, they had sent crews to Ireland, Egypt, and Palestine.

Kalem put Helen to work right away. Pat Hartigan, the director who test photographed her, found the perfect first role for his new find. *Ranch Girls on a Rampage* was shot in Santa Monica and released in May of 1912. Hartigan directed the film which starred Helen, Phyllis Daniels, Jane Haskins, and Ruth Roland. The rampage in question involved a group of wild ranch girls who arrive in Venice Beach, dressed in their fringe-laden cowgirl finest, to frolic in the amusement park. They ride several rides, including a roller coaster, a merry-go-round, and a miniature train. Hardly *Girls Gone Wild*. But their excessive merriment is simply too much and the local police give chase, until the girls are finally apprehended and the party comes to an end.

STILL FROM *RANCH GIRLS ON A RAMPAGE*, 1912. TAKEN FROM IMDB.

A still from Ranch Girls on a Rampage; *Helen is all the way to the left.*

Other than being rather silly, *Ranch Girls on a Rampage* is not particularly noteworthy, film history wise. However, for Helen it was monumental. She was now convinced: acting was her new career. Kalem offered her more small roles throughout the rest of the year and she took them eagerly.

Now, the film industry is many things, but consistent is not one of them. For Helen, however, this was a major perk. In between films, she was able to compete in nearby rodeos to pick up some cash, keep her skills fresh, and of course, have fun riding horses. At this time, Helen was still acting and appearing in rodeos until her birth name, Rose Wenger.

For many actors and filmmakers, the first year living in Los Angeles is usually brutal. For Helen though, her first year was a happy one. She definitely had to budget the rodeo and film money that came in spurts, but this twenty-year-old was living life exactly as she wanted to. She was free, while most young women in the United States in 1912 were not.

At the start of 1913, Helen decided to enter a local Los Angeles rodeo. While riding in one of the races, she caught the eye of one of the event's investors. J. Barney Sherry, himself a prolific Western actor, was deeply impressed with Helen and saw winning potential in her. He offered to finance a rodeo tour, in which he'd pay her expenses and she'd give him half her earnings. The offer didn't interfere with any films she had planned at Kalem, so she accepted. What really convinced her was that Sherry had a ranch up in Pendleton, Oregon, where she could ride and train for a while before setting out. Helen told an interviewer later that, "I worked his horses every day, and learned new forms of trick riding."

Not long after she arrived on the Pendleton ranch, so did another young rider that had received the same offer as Helen. Hoot[57] Gibson was a talented—Helen called him "fancy"—cowboy, born Edmund Richard Gibson in Nebraska, only a few weeks before Helen on August 6, 1892. Also like Helen, he had a history in rodeos and Wild West shows, and had an interest in being a Western actor. Hoot got his start at the Selig Polyscope Company, and wanted to become a star.

With such similar backgrounds and dreams, Helen and Hoot immediately got along. After a short time training up in Pendleton, the pair were sent out together to hit the rodeo circuit. In June, they appeared at a rodeo in Salt Lake City, and as Helen says, they "won everything: the relay race, the standing woman

---

57   He got the nickname because he was a delivery boy for the Owl Drug Company as a teen.

race, trick riding, and the pony express race." They went to several rodeos around the country and even up to Canada. In between, they headed back to Los Angeles so Helen could appear in more Western shorts for Kalem, such as *A Girl of the Range* and *Old Moddinton's Daughters*.

By September, the pair was nearly finished with the tour. Their final show was back in Pendleton and it was set to be a huge event. The only problem was that by the time they arrived, the town was so overrun with rodeo people that all the possible lodgings were full. Helen and Hoot found riders sleeping in the hallways of hotels and outside on benches. They were unsure of what to do, until a wild idea dawned on them.

Married couples were always given preference when it came to rooms.

Helen and Hoot, after many months of travel, had become close friends. They were both trying to make it in the same two industries, and they loved working together. It made perfect logistical and financial sense to get married. This was a time where many marriages were business arrangements rather than romantic ones, only the arrangements usually benefited the parents of the bride and the groom. So why not enter a marriage that benefited the two of them instead? With a mutual understanding that this wasn't for love, Helen and Hoot went looking for someone to officiate. Helen told a reporter later in life, "It's strange how marriages occur! Hoot and I had become good friends but had not thought of marriage."

The pair found a justice of the peace, a judge named Joe Parkes, and a few witnesses, including the president of the roundup association T.D. Taylor, roundup association directors Mark Moorhouse and S.R. Thompson, and the deputy sheriff George Strand. As soon as the vows were finished, Helen and Hoot were loaded into a car decorated with a "NEWLYWEDS" sign and driven to the rodeo grounds. That night, a landlady gave the newlyweds her own room to stay in.

As two decorated trick riders, Helen and Hoot's rodeo fame warranted an article about the wedding in a local paper, the *East*

Oregonia. The piece was titled "Cupid Ropes Ed 'Hoot' Gibson" and stated that:

> Fewer cowboys are more expert with the lariat than Edmund Richard Gibson, known all over the west as "Hoot" Gibson, but Saturday he became a victim of an expert as great as himself, for Cupid, aided by Judge Joe Parkes, tied him by the holy bonds of wedlock to Miss Rose Wenger, relay rider and cowgirl, with scores of victories to her credit won in wild west shows all over the western half of the United States.

In the end, Hoot got the better end of the deal than Helen did. (More on him later.) Soon, it would be Helen's name in the headlines.

LOS ANGELES TIMES, MAY 1, 1915.

Rose Gibson, rodeo star.

The power couple cleaned up at the Pendleton rodeo, and used their cut of the winnings to travel back to Los Angeles. They were both eager to get back to their burgeoning film careers and the warm California sun.

At the end of 1913, Hollywood had only a few remnants of its previous incarnation as a well-to-do subdivision left. Newly made Model Ts chugged along the wide, newly paved streets past the beautiful newly built homes owned by actors and directors. Cows could still be found grazing in the dusty fields of future subdivisions, but horse-drawn graders were working furiously to level out the land to make space for more construction. Studios (mostly long, low buildings) were peppered among the homes and vacant lots. Hollywood Boulevard was studded with new streetlights and electrical poles, and belted with trolley tracks.[58] There were scores of stores and shops selling glamorous clothes and the latest dazzling inventions, like the power clothes washer and instant coffee.

However, the colossal Hollywood sign and swaying palm trees, the most recognizable symbols of Los Angeles, did not decorate the skyline yet.[59] What mainly lined the streets were shady pepper trees. These sort of look like a weeping willow and are covered in tiny red berries that rain down on the sidewalks when the hot, dry Santa Ana winds whip through the branches in the fall. Which was when Helen, now called Rose Gibson, returned to Los Angeles.

While Hoot and Helen were on their rodeo tour, Kalem had

---

58 There were no telephone poles yet and Hollywood only got its first telegraph office that year, in 1914. Telephones were around, but there were no lines to New York yet, and every night, some very tired person at each studio had to send long reports back to their East Coast offices via telegraph.

59 Palm trees were not planted in huge numbers until the 1930s. There actually is only one species of palm tree that is native to the area, the California fan palm. It does not, however, grow naturally anywhere near Hollywood, for they need a huge amount of water to grow, something Los Angeles has in short supply. Eventually, Mexican fan palms would be planted in mass quantities, but I'll tell you about that later.

opened up a second studio to the east of Los Angeles, in a town called Glendale. They found a beautiful spot in Verdugo Canyon and started shooting Westerns there.

The only work the producers at Kalem continued to give Helen was small or background roles, in which she was sometimes put in makeup to make her look like a Native American. There were two problems with this. One, of course, is yikes. The second is that even after almost two years of working with Kalem, no director or producer really knew quite what to do with her, other than showcase her riding skills. Helen had been featured in several films at this point, and had been in the background of many others. She continued to ride in local rodeos and win big prizes. Helen kept catching people's attention, but hadn't gotten a big break yet.

Turns out, she just needed to wait for a brand new type of film.

5

The Hazards of Helen

1914 was the year that the American film industry got a very big boost in a very unfortunate way.

The First World War, like any war, was an absolutely devastating event that caused uncountable losses. One great loss was that of the European film industry. The violence, the destruction of millions of lives, the disruptions to travel and supplies, and just the overall decimation completely crushed the blossoming motion picture scene in many European countries, no matter which side they were on. But people all over the world still wanted to see movies, to escape into them, maybe then more than ever before. And what cinematic enclave was comparatively untouched by the war? Los Angeles, baby.

After 1914, American film dominated the international film market. While other countries, especially European ones, took years to catch up with the United States in terms of film technology and infrastructure (some never did), America continued to churn out movies.[60] What were American filmmakers churning out? A new type of motion picture that was utterly sweeping the country.

When it comes to action movies, you probably think of Arnold Schwarzenegger in one of his many iconic roles. The Terminator, perhaps, or Commando. Whatever you are picturing, it's likely something from the 1980s, the heyday of the American action film. The 1980s were only the heyday of the American *feature* action film, however. There have always been films with action and adventure elements in United States cinema, and they had a much earlier heyday. These films were not led by sweaty, muscle-bound hunks, shooting things up without a shirt on. These action stars were much smaller, skirted, and had to keep their shirts buttoned up.

Serial melodramas, or serials, were short (ten to twenty minutes usually), episodic thriller motion pictures. They were typically centered around a main character and their wild adventures. There were some serials featuring a male lead, but the biggest stars? They were all women. And while they eventually helped spread female empowerment, serials began as a way to sell something.

In 1912, the Edison Film Company entered an arrangement with McClure's *Ladies' World*, a popular women's magazine. McClure's wanted Edison to create a series of film adaptations of short stories, to be released at the same time as the stories were published in the magazine. The hope was that women would see the film and rush out to get a copy of McClure's to read the story it came from. The film series was meant to be a promotional gimmick for the magazine, not the main attraction.

---

60   This has had far-reaching effects and hugely contributed to the cultural dominance of American music and movies. In their own country, Americans mainly consume American media. I do encourage you to look further afield, however. The sentiment is best summed up by award-winning director Bong Joon-ho, who refers to the Oscars as a "very local" film festival, and tells audiences, "Once you overcome the one inch tall barrier of subtitles, you will be introduced to so many more amazing films."

What Happened to Mary starred Mary Fuller and consisted of twelve episodes that ran from July 1912 to June 1913. It told the story of Mary, a young woman orphaned at birth and now in the care of a shopkeeper who was under instruction to marry her off when she came of age. If he succeeds, there's a thousand dollar reward, held until then by the family lawyer. Only when Mary turns eighteen, she doesn't want to get married yet, and sets off seeking excitement instead. Her exploits included traveling by land and sea, fleeing from dastardly villains, escaping from imprisonment, climbing down tall buildings by a bedsheet, and generally having a wild time.

Audiences ate it up.

What Happened to Mary was such a hit both on screen and on the page, that soon after its release, the Selig Polyscope Company film studio wanted to make their own bigger and better version. They teamed up with the *Chicago Tribune*, a newspaper desperately looking for an edge in the fierce circulation battle they were in at the time.

Just six months after the last episode of *What Happened to Mary* was released, *The Adventures of Kathryn* came out. Kathryn, like Mary, was a young white American girl who set off on adventures to avoid a strange stipulation of inheritance. Unlike Mary, Kathryn had inherited a throne in India, which came with its own string of ridiculous problems, the least of which being that the plot was completely full of holes. However, the photography and Kathryn Williams's acting were very compelling to audiences. The *Chicago Tribune* received a 10 percent bump in circulation from readers eager to check out Kathryn's next adventure. Soon, serials exploded.

Mary and Kathryn were followed by *The Exploits of Elaine, The Perils of Pauline, Lass of the Lumberlands, Ruth of the Rockies,* and other similar "Nouns of the Girl" titles. By 1915, almost every single big film company was producing at least one serial, and some made several. Vitagraph, Kalem, Universal, Edison, and others were all in on the game.

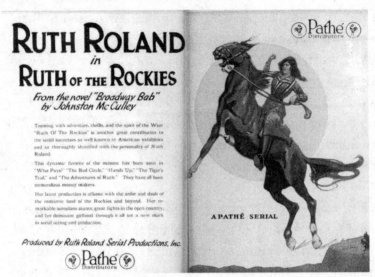

An advertisement for Ruth of the Rockies.

For them, the popularity of serials couldn't have come at a better time. Audiences wanted more feature-length films, but most studios did not have the infrastructure nor the needed money to invest into making them. Features took longer to develop, write, produce, shoot, edit, and all of that cost more money. Serials, on the other hand, were cheap, quick to shoot, and reliable moneymakers. If a company wanted to put a little extra umph into them, with better writing and cinematography, it was likely to yield profitable results. Sinking it all into a feature that might fail was a much bigger risk. In fact, making serials helped some companies eventually get into making features, because the extra profit from the serials could be funneled into feature production.

Serials acted as a critical transitional link between the short films made at the start of the American film industry and the features-only approach that would take over in the coming decades. With their use of stars, particularly female ones, multimedia promotion, and slightly longer run times than the typical five-to ten-minute short film, serials helped studios figure out modern filmmaking and modern film marketing.

When motion pictures were first advertised as public entertainment, it was usually at street level. Theaters put out posters and set up displays in the lobby. The turn of the century was still the age of the curbside barker. Essentially, movies were advertised in places that women were just beginning to go to. You didn't attract *ladies* by yelling things at them, despite what many men on social media still seem to believe. Newspapers and magazines, however, came straight to the home, to the domain of women. Delivering film advertisements cracked open a whole new audience.

Serials even changed the way that films were released. It seems wild in this age of trailers, teaser trailers, teaser posters, all months and months before the film is even released, but before serials, theater owners didn't receive much advance notice from studios and distributors. Plus, short films typically played for only a few days, not the weeks or months that features eventually would. There were no promotional displays, and any publicity a theater had typically focused on the theater itself, and all its comfort and amenities. But knowing that a serial was coming soon and how many episodes it was guaranteed to run for, all with the same star, meant that theater owners could put up posters and banners and advertise tickets well in advance.

Today, most movie watchers stream in the comfort of their own home (and sweatpants), where even the promise of a new, anticipated movie might not be enough to motivate them to go to a theater. In the mid-1910s, however, hordes of people, especially young women, thronged to theaters every week to see their favorite serials. Producers soon realized that if an episode ended on a nail-biting cliffhanger, interest in the next episode could get ramped up even further.[61] This seems obvious, but in a time before television, studios were still figuring out what worked and what didn't.

But why were serials so popular? What drew audiences in?

They offered a glimpse into a whole new world.

Imagine, you're getting off of work for the day. Maybe you're at a cigar factory like Helen was. After twelve hours on your feet in thin-soled shoes, because the eight-hour workday isn't widespread yet and neither are sneakers,[62] you and your friend walk to the movie theater before you have to trudge home and hand over your meager paycheck to your father.

You make your way down the aisle, trying to pick the best seat you can. You've been thinking about this all day, all week really, since last week when you were left perched on the edge of your seat, wondering how it was possible for your hero to get out of the predicament she was in. You sit, adjusting your worn, handmade dress just as the lights dim. A hush falls over the crowd. For the next twenty minutes, you are transported. Away from the cigar factory, away from the crowded streets, away to a place where girls can do anything. Where you can do anything.

There are few pieces of popular culture that showcase the idea of the New Woman better than serials. Serials featured a lot of the same hallmarks that other entertainment directed at women did: romances, female protagonists, and a centering of women's feelings. But in serials, women were dynamic and dynamite. They went out on adventures and they kicked ass. A girl, doing stuff. Who'd've thunk it?

The main element of serials was female heroism. In serials, women got themselves into trouble, and they usually got them-

---

61   In fact, it's believed that the term "cliffhanger" actually originated with serials, owing to the prevalence of episodes that ended with the heroine literally dangling off of a cliff, with no obvious means of escape.

62   Sneakers did not start getting mass produced until 1917.

selves out of it. They exhibited qualities that were typically reserved for male characters. "Serial queens," as they were called, were courageous, strong, independent, and in charge.

Serials toppled almost every traditional gender expectation. It was a way for female audiences to explore a whole new type of womanhood. Most importantly, they featured serial queens *outside of the home.* These women were the absolute opposite of the Victorian ideal of a lady shut up safely in a sock drawer. Serials showcased heroines leaving the home and having fun. Of course, they also showed the perils that came with leaping into the public sphere, but there wouldn't be much of a story if they didn't.

Although serials were also popular with male audiences, they were definitely marketed toward women. They built upon and tapped into the mass readership for "women's fiction," which usually just meant adventure stories that featured a romance element. Female-focused stories had been serialized in monthly magazines and daily newspapers for almost two decades at this point. Thanks to the spread of public kindergartens, more working class women were able to read, and they devoured stories with continuing narratives. Following these stories was a part of working girl culture, a lunch break escape from whatever factory drudgery they did to make a living. These women made up a large portion of dime novel customers. It made perfect sense to translate this fan base to film.

Studios started using women's magazines to hold writing contests, in which viewers submitted their ideas for serial episode endings and the winner won a cash prize. These became an easy way for studios to see what audiences were interested in seeing. And of course, get story ideas for almost free.

Serials coincided with the rise of the New Woman. They reflected both a frustration with the current world and the progress that had been made. These films paralleled the real changes being made in society...just with a few more leaps from moving trains. Ladies were now out doing things in the world and they wanted to see themselves reflected in the stories they read and watched.

We see this phenomenon today. Romance is one of the most popular book genres and women make up the majority of readers. It's not just the steamy sex that is drawing women in. Romance is one the few types of entertainment that centers women's stories, with all their feelings, needs, and wants. Serials became wildly popular for the exact same reason. Historian Shelley Stamp says that serials "marked the industry's first sustained, deliberate attempt to cultivate (and cater to) female patronage on a national scale."

They were like a factory worker's daydream brought to life. Most serial queens were childless and husbandless. Like many Disney protagonists, their mothers and fathers were often absent or dead. Many of these heroines were what so few women in real life were: without obligation to anyone but themselves.

Minus the car chases and gun fights, serials mirrored the experience that many young working class women were going through in the 1910s. Lots of them had moved from farms and rural towns to the city for work, and were away from their families for the very first time in their lives. Instead of feeling small, overwhelmed, and even frightened by their new autonomy, these women could feel like their favorite serial queens: brave, bold, even heroic.

There were some constraints and safety rails in the stories, though. Baked into many of these plots was the assurance that these young women were only on these adventures temporarily, and the safety of a husband, an inheritance, or a family awaited them at the end. In *The Perils of Pauline*, the heroine, played by Pearl White, is an heiress who is under an agreement wherein she gets to embark on a full year of adventures, including hot air balloon rides, car races, horse chases, and submarine excursions…as long as she returns to get married after the year is up. Cue the sad trombone.

Even so, these heroines were armed with skills that women were not traditionally encouraged to have. Serial queens had quick reflexes, muscular strength, and phenomenal coordination. They got in fistfights and shootouts, and leapt from heights and landed unscathed. They rode cars, trains, planes, and horses. They sometimes were even the ones rescuing men, sitting behind the wheel while the men they helped were their passengers. Serials reversed gender expectations *and* gender roles.

PEARL WHITE in 'PLUNDER'

Pearl White in The Perils of Pauline, *doing what many young female factory workers would have loved to do to their bosses.*

Seeing serial queens behind the wheel was a particular delight of female audiences, and controversy for male ones. This was an age where it was popular to joke (and really believe!) that women were much physically weaker than men, and lacked the intellectual capacity and coordination of the opposite sex. A stock joke in many comedies was that female passengers were unable to get on or off trolleys without help.[63] Many *doctors* even thought that women shouldn't ride on trains, in case the momentum would detach their uteruses, which would then bounce around their insides like a popped balloon.

The terrible lady driver was a popular stereotype in the 1910s (just like it still is). In 1904, *Outing* magazine, a publication dedicated to "sport, travel, and adventure" released an article about what terrible drivers women were. It claimed that "Motoring and, indeed, all outdoor pleasures are masters of iron, especially to a woman, who always, in a fashion, has to adopt them, while a man takes to them naturally." That "lack of concentration is the most common failing" of women drivers, and that it is a "feminine fault" more than a masculine one.[64] Serial queens gave a big middle finger to all of these garbage ideas. Female audiences, seeing them skillfully handle cars and big machinery, got a satisfactory thrill over the proof that this bullshit being passed off as scientific fact was just that, bullshit.

Seeing a woman's ability to do all the things men could do, maybe even do them better, was incredibly thrilling. In addition to being wildly entertaining, serials were practically agency porn.

The funny part is that serials were almost a cautionary tale for women leaving home, reinforcement for all those outdated ideas that women didn't belong in public. Serial queens were kidnapped, bound, shot at, tied to railroad tracks, and chased. Look at all the terrible things that can happen if you go out into the world!

The truth is, however, that female viewers loved serials because of, and not in spite of, the over-the-top danger and violence. You could connect the early twentieth-century female

---

63 Maybe if they were encouraged to wear practical clothing, like flat shoes or pants, they'd have an easier time.

64 In modern America, there are more licensed female drivers than male ones, and the male ones make up 70 percent of those receiving traffic violations.

serial fandom to the modern female true crime fandom. Despite the high percentage of true crime media—documentaries, podcasts, or books—being about female victims, the audience is mainly female. Why on earth would women want to consume stories about people like them getting maimed and murdered? Perhaps they're weird, or creepy, or screwed up in some way? Au contraire. These ladies are doing research.

Studies show, including one released in 2010 that was featured in the *Journal of Social Psychological and Personality Science* titled "Captured by True Crime: Why are Women Drawn to Tales of Rape, Murder, and Serial Killers?", women's fascination with true crime is not just strange entertainment, but a way for them to prepare for the very real possibility that they too might have a serial killer take their skin and make it into a hat. It's reassuring to feel like they understand how criminals work and can therefore better avoid them. It's nice to feel like you're a little prepared.

One hundred years ago, serials fans felt the same way. They had been warned for so long that the public sphere was not a place for them and that terrible things could happen if they ventured into it. Well, there they were, watching those terrible things happen to their favorite serial queens. Elaine and Pauline and Kathryn and Ruth got attacked, kidnapped, and generally put in harm's way, over and over and over again. There's something incredibly cathartic about finally seeing the thing you've been anxious about. And then, seeing your heroine face it, battle it, and ultimately defeat it.

In an age where things happened to women, it was thrilling to watch women happen to things.

The very best part of the serials, though? Usually, it was the heroines themselves making them.

It was common in the mid-1910s for the serial queens to star, write, co-produce, and even direct. *Lucille Love, Girl of Mystery* was co-produced by, written by, and starred Grace Cunard. She and her longtime collaborator Francis Ford were tapped by Universal to create a serial and join the craze in 1914. They created fifteen twenty-minute episodes of the show, where Cunard played Lucille Love, a daughter of an army general. Love's father has some top secret documents stolen from him by his longtime nemesis, and Love vows to get them back at any cost and embarks on a wild, hair-raising, extremely ridiculous quest to find them. Posters and newspaper ads for the show promised airplanes, lions, tigers, cannibals, shipwrecks, and explosions.[65] Over fifty newspapers across the country promoted it.

To get a sense of how popular *Lucille Love, Girl of Mystery* was, it cost thirty thousand dollars to shoot the entire fifteen-episode run, which garnered one and a half million dollars at the box office. That's one and half million *1914* dollars. That's almost forty-five million dollars today.

But of all these serials, none of them ran as long and successfully as *The Hazards of Helen*.

No, not that Helen. Not quite yet.

After the release of *The Perils of Pauline* in the spring of 1914, the Kalem Film Company (like all the other studios) wanted a piece of the action. They turned their focus to the athletic young woman they had signed the year before: Helen Holmes would be perfect as a serial queen.

Holmes got her start in Hollywood a few years earlier, thanks to her friend Mabel Normand. She was originally a stage actor, but Normand convinced her to come out west and give the film industry a try. Normand got her a job at Keystone Studios where she was

---

65   Most of these episodes are considered lost films. A few were recovered in the great Dawson Film Find in 1978, when 372 silent-era films were discovered buried under an abandoned hockey rink in Dawson City in Yukon, Canada. The cache was found when a construction crew accidentally dug into it. Luckily, the Canadian permafrost preserved the delicate silver nitrate film. The treasure trove was filled with movies by silent legends like Grace Cunard, Lois Weber, Pearl White, and Lon Chaney.

The films were stuffed under the hockey rink in 1929, when the treasurer of the hockey association took all the old film reels that were used to screen films to the Dawson Amateur Athletic Association a couple decades before and laid them under the rink to help level it out.

making all her comedies, and Holmes acted in a few small roles there. But the executives at Keystone didn't think that Holmes was glamorous or beautiful enough to be a leading woman.

In late 1913, she left Keystone in hopes of finding bigger roles, and good for her. Kalem signed her soon after, disagreeing with Keystone's opinion on her looks. They quickly noticed that she had a natural athletic ability and realized she'd be the perfect fit as the leading lady of a serial they were developing. The story was about a telegraph operator for a train depot in the fictional town of Lone Point who gets into all sorts of hair-raising exploits trying to keep the trains running on time and free of robbers. Born in 1892 (the same year as our Helen), Holmes was the real-life daughter of a railroad clerk. It was the perfect fit.

Even though Keystone didn't believe Holmes could be a silver screen babe, beauty standards were changing. Victorians liked their women delicate, pale, and done up in so many petticoats and ribbons and corsets that they looked pretty but precarious, like a tiered buttercream cake. But when the age of the New Woman dawned, it demanded a new beauty standard. As scholar and author Tressie McMillan Cottom says in her book *Thick*, "beauty is the preferences that reproduce the existing social order." A new social order called for a new body type for women to strive for.

In the 1890s, American artist Charles Dana Gibson created illustrations for major magazines that featured a woman who came to be known as the "Gibson girl." She was white, tall, slim-waisted but a little curvy, and absolutely not delicate. The Gibson girl was athletic and she was usually depicted in the midst of some activity, such as swimming at the beach, striding across a golf course, or bicycling. She certainly didn't stay shut up in the home. The illustrations featured her in the newest fashions, which were more practical—and smaller, more manageable hats. There were sadly no sports bras yet, so the Gibson girl made do with corsets that were a little looser and more forgiving. This girl was not passive. She was active, and she soon became the new feminine ideal. The Gibson girl characterized the New Woman.

By the mid-1910s, girls who looked like they could do stuff were "in" and so was Helen Holmes.

Besides being her first big leading role, Holmes was thrilled to learn that the producers at Kalem wanted her to help write the serial. In fact, the first ever episode, "The Girl at the Switch," was written by Holmes. Over the course of the production, Holmes ended up not just writing, but also stepping in to produce and direct. Since many serials were named after the leading actress to make them seem more real, they decided to call it *The Hazards of Helen*.[66]

The Hazards of Helen was usually shot at the studio in Glendale. For some episodes, however, the crew had to load up their gear and, depending on what the episode called for, travel to the forests or deserts to the north of Los Angeles, or the San Pedro pier to the south.

The first run (they weren't called seasons as in television) of *The Hazards of Helen* was twenty-six episodes long and began to appear in November of 1914. There was a romance subplot that formed some connective tissue between episodes, but it was not a priority for Helen. For this serial queen, her focus was keeping her beloved trains running.

Even among her daring colleagues, Holmes's strength and agility stood out. And Helen the serial queen attracted an immediate fan base for her intellect, independence, and spirit. Except for one episode where she is kidnapped and held captive in an abandoned railroad car (where she uses her smarts to escape), Helen was usually the one doing the rescuing.

From the start, *The Hazards of Helen* differentiated itself from other serials because the stunts were bigger, more dangerous, and much more exciting to watch. Holmes believed that there was no stunt too intense to perform for the show. And she did perform almost all of them herself. She even came up with most of them. Holmes told a film journalist in 1916 that "If an ac-

---

66   Except *The Perils of Pauline* and *The Exploits of Elaine*, both played by Pearl White.

tress wants to achieve real thrills, she must write them into the scenario herself."

During this time, most serial queens did their own stunts. If there was a feat that she couldn't (or didn't want to) attempt, a stuntman would dress up in a wig and duplicate costume. Stunt-women did not exist.

Yet.

Right before *The Hazards of Helen* started shooting in 1914, our Helen was still working with Kalem, but mainly as a background rider. It was a frustrating state of affairs that she hadn't gotten her big break yet, but she kept busy (and paying her bills) with nearby rodeos. She now rode under the name Rose Gibson. Taking Hoot's last name helped sell the illusion that they were a deeply in love married couple who needed discount accommodations.

As a champion rider, Helen was still making headlines. The *Los Angeles Times* mentioned her in multiple articles the next year and printed several features about her. They reported on her many local rodeo wins, including a "cowgirl contest" and winning the title of Pacific Coast Women's Champion. That spring, they ran a feature titled "All Cowgirls Don't Know How to Milk Says Rose Gibson." There was a short interview with Helen next to a gigantic photo of her. The reporter called "handsome Rose Gibson, conqueror of wild horses" a "pretty equestrienne" and said she "looked out frankly from two eyes as big as four." Helen disputed the notion that all cowgirls were farm girls. "No, I'm not Rose of the Rancho. That sentimental line might go all right with some women, but I'm a businesswoman." She might have been the best female rider on the West Coast, but what she really loved was putting on a show. She loved the action, not the ranch life. "My business," she assured the reporter, "is furnishing thrills."

Although Helen was the best at her trade, she did have a lot of competition. The articles always made sure to mention the other women she rode against, fellow champions like Vera Mc-Ginniss and Hazel Hoxie. Even with the rivalry, a lot of these women were Helen's friends. While she had long left her childhood friends behind in Cleveland, Helen's life was not a lonely one. There were always other cowgirls to spend time with.

Her best friend was a rider about five years older than her named Edythe Sterling. Sterling was also working her way into the film industry through Westerns, and the two deeply bonded. They rode against each other that spring in Los Angeles's Cowgirl Classic, competing for a total of five hundred and fifty dollars in prize money. The *Los Angeles Evening Express* covered the event and ran a large photo of the two friends. "Rose Gibson and Edythe Sterling...although best of personal friends, both are keen rivals for the gold belt."

Horse girls forever.

LOS ANGELES EVENING EXPRESS, APRIL 28, 1915.

Thanks to all the successful rodeo work, Helen was able to buy, stable, and ride her own horse in these competitions. The horse's name was Zenobia, after the great ancient warrior queen.

Hoot was working as a background rider with Selig at their studio in Edendale (which today is known as the Echo Park/ Los Feliz neighborhood). Seeing more potential than Selig did, the folks at Kalem, who were only a few miles away in Glendale, snagged him and put him on their payroll. When it became clear that their new serial would need some serious stunt support, they asked Hoot if he wanted the job. So it was that Helen came to find out about *The Hazards of Helen*.

The serial was an immediate hit and Kalem tasked Holmes, the director J.P. McGowan (who Holmes would soon marry), and the rest of the team with creating a new slate of episodes for 1915.

The only problem was that in April, while they were filming, Holmes came down with pneumonia and could not work. In film, time is money, and Kalem did not want to delay the shoot to wait for Holmes to recover. They needed a replacement, not just a stunt double. One of the directors at Kalem, James Wesley Horne, or as Helen called him, Jimmie, had seen Helen riding in a Los Angeles rodeo recently and suggested her as a temporary stand-in.

Once McGowan and the rest of the team saw Helen, they realized that they couldn't have dreamed of a better replacement. Not only were the two women the exact same age, same height (five foot six), but they both had dark hair and athletic builds. They even both had hazel eyes, not that audiences could tell from the black-and-white footage. The two women look so much alike that it can be difficult to tell them apart in photos. But the very best part? Helen could do the stunts, even better than Holmes could.

KALEM KALENDAR, APRIL 1915.

MOVING PICTURE WORLD, JULY 15, 1916.

Helen Holmes on the left, Helen Gibson on the right.

If Helen was such a perfect fit for the role, why didn't Hoot suggest her earlier? Well, that's a great question. One certainly worth keeping in mind.

From the moment Helen stepped foot onto the train depot set in Glendale, it was clear this was the type of work she was meant to do. This was the opportunity that she had been waiting for.

As exciting as it is, being on a movie set is overwhelming. Even though movie crews were much smaller in those days (there was a lot less to do), the hustle and bustle of moving cameras, equipment, lights, props, and set dressing around was constant. Because this was still in the era of the silent film, it didn't matter if the crew made a huge racket while the camera was rolling. The faster that things get set up and taken down the better, so a set is always changing, moving, thrumming with activity. Decisions are made on the fly, there's always someone to find, something to be delivered, some fire to be put out. And that's if you're not in front of the camera.

Being the center of all this work and planning, having so many people focused on you, what your hair looks like, what your clothes look like, what you're saying, how you're moving, it can be dizzying.

But compared to a rodeo? This was a piece of cake.

Helen was used to being the center of thousands of people's attention. She was used to executing a difficult stunt in one try, not in several takes. She was used to a director calling out what she was supposed to do. In these ways, being an actor was easier than riding in a rodeo. Plus, there was a lot less horse manure to worry about.

She took to the work like a duck to water. To some degree, it was what she had been doing most of her life, ever since she first picked up a stick and ran through the mud along Lake Erie.

Initially, Kalem hired Helen to appear in "possibly" two episodes, depending on her performance and Holmes's speed of recovery. Helen's first ever appearance was the forty-fifth *Hazards of Helen* episode, "A Girl's Grit," in which a couple of bank robbers hold up the train station and force Helen to give them train tickets. They then lock her inside the attic and board the train. Helen watches from the window and just as the train is about to speed away, she smashes the glass, climbs out onto the steep roof, and with a perfectly timed leap, lands onto the last train car. She crawls along the roof of the speeding train until she gets to the engine. After jumping inside the engine room, Helen tells the crew that they've got a couple of bank robbers aboard. When Helen and the crew rush to accost the criminals, they find them about to jump out of the window. Helen, however, will not let them escape so easily. She, too, jumps out the window and lands on the ground. Helen proceeds to fist fight *both* men until the train is halted and the crew can come help her.

Standing up on that roof, feeling the rumble of the oncoming train car, Helen might not have realized that she was about to make history. The moment she jumped, the moment her feet left the shingles, white dress billowing, Helen, still as Rose Gibson, became the first ever female stunt double in American film.

STILL FROM THE *HAZARDS OF HELEN,* "A GIRL'S GRIT," 1915. TAKEN FROM IMDB.

And the landing? She nailed it.

Helen did the stunts for the next episode, number forty-six, "A Matter of Seconds," and she nailed those, too. When it was time to shoot episode number forty-seven, "The Runaway Boxcar," something a little unexpected happened.

In the modern world, women are often pitted against each other in the workplace. It is so difficult for women to break into industries like film because of this shitty myth that there is only one spot or role for a woman. A studio might only decide to put one female-directed film on their slate for the year, or only buy a script from one female screenwriter.[67] Popular culture would lead you to believe that women are catty and cutthroat, eager to fit in with the guys and destroy each other for that one spot. Like Highlander, but with a better skincare routine.

---

67   This is a real occurrence and some studio executives pat themselves on the back afterward, knowing they've checked "lady film" off their to-do list for the year.

What really happens, most of the time, is that women, especially in male-dominated industries, meet each other and form instant bonds. Honestly, it's the best part of working in film. Women support each other, suggest each other for jobs, and offer advice. They share information about the best people to work with, and the worst.[68]

Most of all, they hire each other. Just as it was in Helen's time, movies and television shows with women at the helm tend to have more women on the crew. According to the website Women and Hollywood, "On the top 500 films of 2019, movies with at least one female director employed greater percentages of women writers, editors, cinematographers, and composers than films with exclusively male directors." The study concluded that the rise in numbers of female crew members in both television and film was "due to increases in the percentages of women working as executive producers and producers."

The real story is that, when given a chance, women *help* other women. Women in positions of power, as the saying goes, send the elevator back down. Which is part of why all of this matters, and why it has mattered since Helen's time in Hollywood. Getting more women behind the camera contributes to real, systemic change.

This is all to say that Helen and Holmes did not become bitter rivals. They became immediate friends.

It would be reasonable to expect Holmes at least bristled when she learned that during her absence her producers found a woman that could have been her twin, and who was more skilled with stunts. Once Holmes returned, however, she was deeply impressed. One of her first orders of business was to give the job of her stunt double to Helen. Why would they bother putting a dress on Hoot when they had a woman that could do the stunts better?

---

68 If you're a scummy guy working in film, rest assured that every woman you've ever worked with has and will tell all her female friends about you.

Even in female-dominated Hollywood, there were certain jobs that men believed women could not do. Putting Hoot in a wig and a dress was obviously not ideal, but male executives (and some female ones) thought that being a stunt double was too dangerous for women. On modern movie sets, female stunt doubles still say that one of their biggest obstacles is that men feel the need to protect them, while hindering their ability to do their jobs.

With one leap, Helen helped change all of that. Her incredible physical ability and courage proved that women were just as capable.

The top executives at Kalem's New York City office agreed with Holmes. They saw the footage from Helen's episodes and told the folks at the Glendale office that she should stay. Hoot was given the boot.[69] But don't cry for him. He quickly found work in some Western films and another serial called *Stingaree*. Plus, he occasionally acted in background or villain roles on *The Hazards of Helen*.

With Holmes back in place as the lead actress, Helen continued to do some of the riskier stunts for the next few episodes. They were the perfect episodes for her because they involved horse tricks. In episode forty-seven, "The Runaway Boxcar," Helen must chase an errant boxcar on horseback while it speeds down a track toward the path of a moving train. Holmes was quite happy to let an expert rider take over the stunts in those episodes.

She soon had bigger plans in mind, for both herself, and for Helen.

---

69 You truly have no idea how difficult it is to hold back on the Hoot jokes.

6

Women-Made Women

So far, women had come to Hollywood, they had seen Hollywood, and now it was time to conquer Hollywood. They were some of the most popular screenwriters, successful directors, and the highest paid actors. The early studio executives were right. Once they started advertising the names of their stars, those stars wanted more and more and more. What was next?

In the late 1910s, female stars such as Mabel Normand and Mary Pickford earned some of the highest salaries, not just in Hollywood, not just in the United States, but in the entire world. Thanks to Carl Laemmle and Florence Lawrence, the industry was now run on the star system, which was the creation or the management (or both) of publicity around a key performer or creator—a star—to fuel demand for their films.

This really put the studios in a bind because no matter what, they needed the stars. It was their performances that drew audiences in and their fans that guaranteed the financial success of a film.

The problem was that, at this point, studios didn't know how to make a star. Producers and executives assumed that the only way to become one was by audience decision. They couldn't just grab a star from the theater scene, since popularity on the stage didn't always translate to the screen. While some film actors did come from the stage, many theater actors struggled with the transition to film. This is why the stars had so much power.

And it was time to put it to good use.

The stars used their power not just to get themselves paid more, but also to change how the film industry worked to suit them better. For example, one thing that big-name actors hated was block booking. Block booking was a system where studios and distributors forced theaters to buy films in a unit, usually with one high-quality film with stars, and several lesser quality films with lesser known actors. So, in order to get a good movie that was guaranteed to make money, theaters had to buy the whole unit. But actors didn't want their films associated with inferior films. They wanted their films sold separately, and so did the theater owners. Mary Pickford demanded that Lasky, the studio she was working with, if not sell her films on their own, at least sell them in a better unit with other top-quality films called a "star series." Unable to stand up to the star power of America's sweetheart, Lasky relented.[70]

Once these popular actors, directors, and screenwriters realized how badly the studios needed them, they also realized that maybe they didn't need the studios at all.

What was next for them?

How about owning the whole damn production?

With their own production companies, these women would be in charge. They'd be paid more money, or at least a higher percentage of the overall budget. They'd have more creative control over their projects. They could develop their own films,

70   Eventually the entire practice of block booking was outlawed all together in 1948.

either directing them themselves or choosing which director they wanted to work with. Most importantly, they wouldn't be forced to deal with anyone else's bullshit. It was a no-brainer.

Of course, there was a lot more responsibility in owning and running a production company, and a lot more financial (and possibly career) damage if a movie didn't do well. But if you could be in charge, why not?

Now is probably a good time to tell you the difference between a production company and a studio. A film studio is a movie company that has its own facility to make movies and can do all parts of the film process, from shooting to post-production to distribution and marketing, in-house. Usually, they also have financing for their movies. A production company is a company that makes movies, but doesn't have a facility to make them in, and doesn't distribute their movies. They might already have financing, they might not. For example, Elizabeth Banks's Brownstone Productions is a production company that made movies like *Pitch Perfect 2* and the reboot of *Charlie's Angels*, but they signed a deal with Universal Studios to help them make and distribute. If a studio is a big well-appointed hair salon, a production company is the stylist that rents out space inside.

A production company can be headed up by a legal team or a creative team, or both. In the late 1910s, popular pairings were director and actor, or a director and writer, or both with a businessperson (usually, but not always, a businessman[71]). Unlike production companies that were created and helmed by businessmen, however, production companies created by female stars already had a proven asset: themselves.

Female Hollywood powerhouses were inspirational in their

---

71   The Liberty Feature Film Company, founded by Eleanor Gates and run by businesswoman Sadie Lindblom, was the only production company of the time to be owned and managed entirely by women. Their first film was *The Poor Little Rich Girl* starring Mary Pickford, which decades later would be remade starring Shirley Temple.

real lives, too. Almost every star—such as Mary Pickford, Grace Cunard, Tsuru Aoki, and Mabel Normand—kept her maiden name, outearned her husband, and called the shots on her films.

As you can imagine, most of the male-owned studios were not thrilled by this. Historically, men in power do not respond well to women wanting to be independent. Especially since there was a good chance that if a star working at a studio became ultrapopular, she'd go off and start her own company. These female-owned indies made studios even more upset because the established studios were having a difficult time adjusting to feature films. Many of them already had a fixed system for making short films, and had to spend a lot of money to change it. Independent companies, however, had a lot more flexibility to get into the feature game.

The first film star (of any gender) to get into independent production specifically to make features was Helen Gardner. In fact, she was the first actor to form her own production company. Known for portraying strong characters, the first film she produced (and starred in) was a feature-length movie about Cleopatra.

Another early star to capitalize on her own stardom was Marion Leonard. In 1911, she and her husband, director and screenwriter Stanner E.V. Taylor, created the Gem Motion Picture Company. They made mostly short comedies, and eventually made a deal to have Universal distribute their films.

Mary Pickford jumped at the chance to become independent. It meant she was no longer forced to deal with directors who insulted her, then tried to ask her out (like D.W. Griffith). It meant she could do things the way that she wanted to do them.

The idea caught on, and soon, other female directors started to create their own production companies, including Lois Weber, Cleo Madison, Mabel Normand, Alla Nazimova, and Lule Warrenton. In fact, Weber would go on to open up her own studio in 1917, the very first woman to do so. She could make all the movies with tits and abortions that she wanted, and no one could stop her.[72]

Warrenton was an actor who appeared in over eighty films, but she became more well-known for her directing. She is notable both for having a production company with an all-woman crew, and for focusing on motion pictures made especially for children. This was an unprecedented move at the time. Family-friendly movies are colossal moneymakers today (hello, Disney!), but in the late 1910s, few filmmakers thought to appeal to children. Warrenton was particularly skilled at working with child actors and loved to make, as she called them, "films for little ones."

Nazimova made her film debut as an actor in 1916 at thirty-seven years old, and went on to become a director, screenwriter, and producer. She was a notable filmmaker, and her personal life was equally notable. Nazimova was bisexual, although closeted for the safety of herself and her career. She was part of a close community of queer women in Los Angeles, and is believed to be the one to coin the term "sewing circle" to describe this community. As in, "Oh, Marlene Dietrich? She's part of the sewing circle."[73]

Looking back on photographs from this time, it is tempting to think of these women, with their ankle-length dresses and demure curls, as being innocent and virtuous. But these ladies could get *wild*. These women were up to their corsets with power and money. Of course they were going to party. Nazimova was well-known for throwing outrageous parties full of debauch-

---

72 Let's take a moment to give a little shout out to Carl Laemmle. Laemmle founded Universal Studios and was, of all the early film heads, the one who most supported female film directors like Lois Weber and Cleo Madison. He made a huge difference in the development of their careers and therefore, made a huge difference in the amount of successful female film directors I get to write about. Just like in today's world, supporting and giving a chance to women in the film industry had a systemic effect. Thanks, Carl!

73 Which she was, along with many legendary filmmakers and actors of the time, like Talullah Bankhead, Greta Garbo, and Joan Crawford.

ery at her Hollywood mansion, right off of Sunset Boulevard. She dubbed the gorgeous, gigantic house the Garden of Alla.

These female-owned production companies weren't always independent. Some worked inside the greater framework of a male-owned studio. The women had less control this way, but more access to studio resources, such as camera gear and film marketing, than they would have on their own.

Whether independent or not, however, in the late 1910s there were more production companies with women's names on them than there were men's. Female stars of the film industry were shaping Hollywood to their will, including the types of stories being told on screen. They wanted to make movies where women triumphed.

Or at least had some fun.

It didn't matter if the characters were heroes or villains, wives or mothers, sexy vamps or pure angels. These filmmakers got to make movies where women had jobs, had sex, had opinions and feelings that took center stage. And moviegoers ate it up. Audiences clamored for female characters who were bold, seductive, funny, even dangerous. Every trait that could get you marked as a noncompliant demon woman in the late 1800s gave you the makings of a big star in the late 1910s.

In *Mabel's Lovers*, Mabel Normand has so many male admirers that she puts them to a test to help her choose the best one. In *A Soul Enslaved*, Cleo Madison explores workplace double standards as a woman fighting for better conditions at her factory. In *Unmasked*, Grace Cunard plays a jewel thief who meets her romantic match when they both try to steal the same necklace. These characters were kicking the Victorian feminine ideal directly in the face with their heeled, lace-up boots.

Films in which women booted cheating husbands to the curb, took lovers, and had kids out of wedlock mirrored the lives of real women. Conservative America's myth of "the good old days" when women were *ladies* is just that, a story. For all the women born between 1890 and 1900, one of four lost her virginity before marriage. This was bumped up to seven out of ten for those born between 1910 and 1920.[74] And with the First World War raging between 1914 and 1918, many were seeing first-hand just how short life could be. Why wait for marriage when your crush could be sent off to war, and maybe never return?[75]

Between the control, power, money, and freedom, female stars had every reason to start their own production companies. It started with directors, but soon, the idea began to spread like wildfire.

In early 1915, Helen Holmes, like her fellow female stars, wanted to aim higher. At the start of the year, her now husband J.P. McGowan became ill and was hospitalized for a short period of time. Just as McGowan had when she was sick with pneumonia, Holmes kept *The Hazards of Helen* shoots running. She took over directing duties, wrote episodes, helped produce the show, and managed the shoots. But when these episodes aired, she was not credited for any of her work, nor paid extra.

It got her thinking. If she could do the work of running a production company, why shouldn't she create her own? Why not do the same amount of work for more pay, more credit, and more control?

After forty-eight episodes of *The Hazards of Helen*, at the very height of its popularity, Helen Holmes decided to bow out.

She and McGowan left Kalem to create their own production company, Signal Film Corp. They continued to make popular action films with Holmes as the star. The following years, they made a serial called *The Girl and the Game* that reportedly grossed $2,253,000 (about sixty-one million dollars today).

---

74   In 2019, condom brand SKYN did a sex and intimacy study that found that for Gen Z respondents, the number of women who lost their virginity before marriage was…seven out of ten.

75   You might be surprised to learn how much the advent of cars had an effect on this. Cars, and a little bit of that newfangled feminism, kicked the concept of chaperoned courting right to the curb. It's tough to keep an eye on couples riding around in cars. Even if they're parked. Just look at what happened in *Titanic*.

Now, Holmes knew that Kalem wanted to keep *The Hazards of Helen* going, so she made a plan before leaving.

She would hand the torch to Helen.

Kalem agreed to the plan, on one condition: their new star would have to change her name to keep with the established title and credits.

So it was that Rose Wenger finally became Helen Gibson.

Helen accepted the terms. Just like that, she had, without any formal education, family money, or industry connections, finally got her break. With a little luck and a lot of grit, a working-class girl from Cleveland became a Hollywood star at twenty-three years old. She had gone from the cigar factory floor to the big screen in seven years.

And Helen Holmes? The two women would remain friends for the rest of their lives.

With their new Helen, Kalem immediately went into production on a fresh crop of episodes. Instead of trying to hide the swap, Kalem made a big announcement, and many film industry and fan magazines picked up the story. That summer, *Motion Picture News* ran an article that said:

> With "The Hazards of Helen" railroad series approaching the end of the first year of its existence, and with motion picture exhibitors and patrons urging that it be continued, Kalem has taken steps which indicate that this remarkably successful series is to run on indefinitely.
>
> Of paramount importance is the announcement that Helen Gibson has been engaged to succeed Helen Holmes as the heroine of the series.

The article promised that the new run of *The Hazards of Helen* would be "better and more sensational than ever." Now it was up to Helen to deliver.

Even though she had been making a living off tricks and stunts for years, this new gig carried just as much risk as it did reward. Stunt performers have a 100 percent injury rate. It's not a matter of if, but when. Helen wasn't a stunt double anymore, taking over on the occasions when Holmes couldn't do a scene. She was the star and had to do it all: every stunt, every scene, every episode.

WorkSafe British Columbia[76] did a study from 2002 to 2006 that concluded stunt performers routinely partake in activities with a high risk of neurotrauma, with female performers being especially susceptible to injuries like concussions.[77] Because the costumes they wear are typically less protective than their male colleagues, female stunt performers must use less padding and safety gear, not to mention having to do stunts in heels. Elizabeth Davidovich, who has doubled for Gal Gadot, told *The Guardian* in 2017 that sometimes "all it takes is one little pin to not be screwed in all the way and that can cause death."

The Center for Safety in the Arts recorded forty deaths in American film productions from 1980 to 1989. Advances in performer protections have helped those statistics dip in recent decades, but incidents still happen. Just in 2017, professional racer Joi Harris was killed in a motorcycle accident on the set of *Deadpool 2*.

And that's in *today's* film industry, with all the latest safety precautions and equipment. Modern stunt performers use air bags and thick cushions for their landings, special gel padding under their costumes, harnesses attached to rigs and wiring systems to catch them if they fall, and a whole crew of riggers, supervisors, and coordinators to oversee, check, and recheck everything.

What did Helen have in 1915?

Helen had Helen. There was no cushion for her to land on, no pads to hide under her dress, no safety harness to wear. No

---

76 Notable because so many shows and movies are shot in Vancouver.

77 These numbers are probably much higher considering that stunt injuries go incredibly underreported. Stunt performers regularly hide injuries if they are able to so they don't miss out on work.

one on the set of *The Hazards of Helen* was in charge of supervising the stunts or the safety of the star. No one but Helen herself.

The script for her first official episode (the forty-ninth overall) included a fire, a gun, a physical fight, and *two* leaps onto speeding trains. The intrepid telegraph operator of Lone Point station gets accosted by criminals inside the station and locked inside of a closet. After the thieves rob the place, one of the men accidentally knocks over a lantern, setting the station on fire with Helen inside. In the nick of time, she picks the closet lock with a hairpin. Just as Helen escapes the burning building, she sees the criminals have jumped aboard a passing train. She spots another train on a parallel track, runs, and swings onto the last car. Next, Helen alerts the crew of the train and they catch up to the criminals.

Another hair-raising leap later, Helen lands aboard the train manned by the thieves. She flings a wrench to knock out one of the thieves and whips out her pistol to hold up the others. Before they can put up a fight, the train reaches a spot where men are waiting to arrest them. The title? The aptly named "A Test of Courage."

Actors had been injured or even died doing similar stunts before. That same year, 1915, a background actor fell off a roof and broke some of his ribs on the set of *The Birth of a Nation* (karma?), and in *The Girl of the Golden West*, a prop pistol exploded and severely burned the actor holding it. In *The Captive*, one background actor, unaware there was a live round in his pistol, fatally shot another background actor. Soon, actor Wallace Reid would suffer such heavy injuries in a train crash while making *The Valley of the Giants* in 1919 that the studio, Famous Players–Lasky, gave him morphine to finish the shoot.[78]

So, you know, no pressure.

Today, train stunts are typically created using computer generated imagery (CGI), or miniatures, such as the train scene in the film *RRR*. Even the king of practical train stunts, Tom

---

78   He became addicted to the drug and eventually died in 1923.

Cruise himself, had a train specially built for the scenes in *Mission Impossible: Dead Reckoning*. All the train-top fights in that movie were shot with multiple cameras, and all the performers wore harnesses attached to safety wires.

On the day of the "Test of Courage" shoot in Glendale, it was just a single camera and Helen. A thin layer of dark pantyhose protected her legs from the rocks and gravel she would land on if she missed her jump.

But Helen didn't miss.

A TEST OF COURAGE
An Episode of the
HAZARDS OF HELEN RAILROAD SERIES

MOVING PICTURE WORLD, OCTOBER 1915.

The jumps, the run on top of a moving train, the fight. She nailed every scene. Helen passed the test of courage. And with one under her belt, it was time to shoot the other nine episodes in the run.

Over the course of that summer, Helen won fistfights with men, rescued children, got into car chases, and jumped on and off speeding trains so many times that it's hard to keep track. In one episode, called "Danger Ahead," Helen jumps from a speeding car *to* a speeding train. Both were going thirty-five miles an hour. Each and every threat the Lone Point station faced, Helen was there to thwart it. The day was saved, the villains apprehended. All in a day's work.

Helen did each and every stunt, each and every shoot Kalem set up. What's really impressive is that she made it through ten episodes of this with only some bruises and a couple of sprained ankles.

Whenever she got her script for the next episode, Helen looked it over and thought about how she could make it better, more thrilling. In episode fifty-seven, "Crossed Wires," the script called for her to jump to the handrail of the train from a speeding car and hold up a criminal at gunpoint. However, Helen, as she told a reporter, thought that a "plain leap to the handrail was nothing out of the ordinary." So, she told the crew that she wanted to up the tension with a physical struggle between Helen and the man, while she is halfway on the train, halfway in the car. Writing about the episode, a reporter for the *Miami Herald* said, "Had either the auto or the train varied its speed the slightest during her struggle with the convict the result is easy to imagine."

KALEM KALENDAR, DECEMBER 1915.

Helen loved this work, and she was damn good at it. She had a flair for knowing what would excite audiences, what would look great on camera, and most importantly, what kind of stunts she could push herself to do. Kalem was thrilled with the final product. Now it was time to launch the new run and see what fans thought about their new Helen.

"A Test of Courage" was set to premiere on October 16, and Kalem began a publicity push to prepare. The Kalem Kalendar, a monthly release advertising the studio's offerings for that month, had Helen's face on the cover. They sent publicity stills from the episodes and photographs of Helen to various trade papers and fan magazines.

KALEM KALENDAR, OCTOBER 1915.

Kalem and the whole *Hazards* crew believed they had a hit on their hands. However, it's impossible to predict exactly how audiences are going to feel. *The Hazards of Helen* already had an audience, but they might not like the change. This was Helen's big shot. If it failed, she might never get another. Would fans miss Helen Holmes? Would the new star win everyone over?

7

Unusual Feminine Daring

["A Test of Courage"] will convince even the most skeptical exhibitors and photoplay fans that 'Kalem's new Helen' is beyond all question the bravest girl in motion pictures to-day.

...the new Helen has already completely filled the daredevil shoes left by her predecessor.

...Miss Gibson is admirably suited for the role. It is because of her absolute lack of fear—the positive delight she seems to take in performing the most hazardous feats—together with her protean ability, which have caused her to be added to Kalem's galaxy of stars.

The moment "A Test of Courage" was released, America fell in love with Helen Gibson.

Critics loved the new star of *The Hazards of Helen* and had effusive praise for her performance. *Motion Picture News* reported that "Miss Gibson, by exhibition of unusual feminine daring...

gives foretaste of excitement," and that Kalem kept their promise that "there will be no let-up in thrills."

Most importantly, however, was the praise of the fans. The extra care Helen took to raise the stakes of each stunt, to push herself to the limit, to make each episode as thrilling as possible, was immediately noticed by audiences. Helen had single-handedly taken the show to the next level, and *Hazards of Helen* fans new and old were enthralled. They adored Helen, and every Saturday for the next few months, flocked to movie theaters to see the brave telegraph operator's next adventure. An exhibitor in Indiana reported that "We find the Hazards of Helen railroad series constantly increasing in popularity."

A month later, Kalem had a big announcement to make. With the overwhelmingly positive response to their "new Helen," it was clear that Kalem must continue the series. If fans had rejected Helen, Kalem might have never released the rest of the run. Now the studio would not only release all the episodes, they wanted to make more. This was obviously wonderful for Helen and the whole crew, but it also made history. With the November release of the fifty-third episode, titled "The Girl and the Special," *The Hazards of Helen* officially became the longest-running serial, more than *The Perils of Pauline*, *The Exploits of Elaine*, or any other serial headed by hero or heroine. Helen was now a queen among serial queens.

The benchmark was a huge deal in the trade magazines and many of them featured articles about the series. *Moving Picture World* noted that thanks to "requests by many exhibitors," the series would continue "indefinitely." *Motion Picture News* wrote that *The Hazards of Helen* "is an example of what quality will do for a series" and that it "seems likely to run on forever...it is actually increasing its hold upon the public." The same article included feedback from theater owners around the country, including one theater owner in Kentucky, "There has never been anything like [*The Hazards of Helen*] for genuine thrills and hairbreadth escapes. My patrons wait with keenest anticipation for the next episodes....For the past fifteen years, I have exhibited almost every class of picture that has been filmed, but [*The Hazards of Helen*] possesses a fascination for me that is simply indescribable." Another owner in Brooklyn said that he believed the series had any other serial "beaten by a mile" and that it made "the patrons come back for more."

To capitalize on this wave of adoration from fans, Kalem raced to create *The Hazards of Helen* merchandise. Serial queens were major stars and almost every studio that was putting out serials (which was practically all of them by now) developed a wide array of items to sell to fans, including posters, postcards, pennants, and other products that didn't start with *P*. Serials helped launch a new film business model that included extensive marketing and multimedia tie-ins. This was the next development in the star system; not just using names to sell movies, but goods, as well.

An advertisement for felt pennants featuring the name of your favorite serial queens.

The short tie-in stories for the serials were wildly popular. Sixty major newspapers published them, with a combined readership of eighty million. In 1915, the United States had one hundred million people living in it. That means that *most* of the country was exposed to these stories, even if they didn't read them (and many did). They were also helpful for theatergoers during the silent film age, because even with title cards, it could be difficult to pick up on finer plot details.

Of course, it wouldn't be an American film if its viewers weren't being sold something. While serials were being advertised in women's magazines and sewing pattern monthlies, so were the clothes the heroines were wearing in them. In many serials, the camera lingers on whatever the main character is wearing. Serial queens often sported luxurious outfits and were covered in feathers, furs, and silks. These clothes helped sell the fantasy that serial queens had it all: power, freedom, and glamor.

Seeing as her show was about a telegraph operator, not an adventuring heiress, Helen was a bit less glamorous than some of her colleagues. However, quite a few episodes of *The Hazards of Helen* featured her in smart (but practical) outfits.

KALEM STUDIOS PUBLICITY STILL, 1915.

Helen proves that you can look stylish while you beat up bad guys.

KALEM KALENDAR, DECEMBER 1915.

Helen models the latest in stomping-on-men-with-your-boots fashion.

Out of all the film genres, serials were most suited for fan culture. Not only did most of them use the actor's real name, which blurred the line between fiction and reality, but they encouraged their audiences to identify with and become enamored by their heroines. Quickly, serials developed a devoted, fanatic following.

These fans were hungry for more information about their favorite serial queens, and magazines were happy to deliver. Two of the most popular magazines were *Ladies' Home Journal* and *Photoplay*, both of which developed the concept of Hollywood gossip as real news. Actors got interviewed for personal profiles that contained information about their backgrounds, their hometowns, their beauty routines, and their romances. It turns out that stars have been hounded to drop their skincare routines for over a hundred years. Readers clamored for the hot gossip and beauty tips, but deep down, what they really wanted was to compare their own lives to that of their heroes. If their favorite serial queens came from humble origins, maybe they had a shot at greatness, too.

Instead of just being a mysterious screen presence, actors' personas now had to include parts of their real lives. Fans wanted to see publicity photos, wanted to meet them at personal appearances, read in-depth interviews, and see them do promotional stunts as if they were really the characters they played on screen. Today, this is a given part of the job for actors. In the late 1910s, however, it was a new trend, and serial fandom helped develop this type of journalism. Celebrity culture rose in popularity alongside serials.

One thing that hadn't been invented yet, however, was fact-checking. Instead of offering their real biographies, studio publicists concocted backstories for serial queens that tied into their characters. For Helen, this meant fudging her childhood details to be more like Helen Holmes's. She suddenly had a father who was a train clerk that raised her among giant engines, and grew up in California as a "real" Westerner. *Motion Picture News* reported that "she actually ran her father's locomotive when but twelve years old." That's publicity, baby!

One thing fans loved to read about was the athletic abilities of their heroines. Knowing that their favorite stars could actually do all the feats they saw up on screen made their theater experience all the more thrilling. Helen Holmes, for example, told reporters that she could bust her seams by "doubling up her biceps" and that being strong was "essential for the modern woman."

As a whole, journalists struggled to write about serial queens. They wanted to highlight the (what seemed to be) novel strength and ability of these women, but also wanted to assure readers that the actors were ladylike. Don't worry folks, these ladies aren't losing their femininity just because they can punch a robber's lights out. After a paragraph about a heroine's big muscles, the writer would immediately praise her beauty or remark on her charm, maybe even tell readers about some domestic hobby the serial queen loved, such as sewing. Whether or not these hobbies were real, it's hard to say. Helen was said to "love trimming hats" which seems…a little tame for her. Writing about strong ladies was a tough job in the late 1910s, when brawn and beauty were considered mutually exclusive.

Magazine and newspaper editors soon realized that female readers could best be reached by female writers. In the Midwest, Audrie Alspaugh, or as she was known to the *Chicago Tribune*, Kitty Kelly, was a massively influential film writer. Historian Jan Olsson says that she could "make or break a film" with Midwest audiences. Her column, titled "Flickerings from Filmland," was read by over a hundred thousand people. The Women Film Pioneers Project says that Alspaugh's "own sense of judgment and taste was always so perceptive that her criticism often served to 'train' fans in what to look for while watching movies." She encouraged her readers, many of them women, to assess the narrative construction of a motion picture, to pay attention to its atmosphere and editing.

The queen of film writing, though, was Louella Parsons. Regular columns devoted to film reviews began to pop up in newspapers in the mid-1910s, and in 1914, Parsons wrote America's first Hollywood gossip column for the *Chicago Record Herald*. If you wanted to know which stars and filmmakers mattered—and why—you went to her. She eventually formed a strong business relationship with newspaper mogul William Randolph Hearst, who syndicated her Hollywood column for the *Los Angeles Examiner*. At the height of her influence, Parsons was read by twenty million people in hundreds of newspapers all over the world.

As much as her creation came to harm many women in the industry over the next few decades, Parsons originally conceived her column as a space to champion them. She gave the majority of her coverage to the struggles and achievements of actresses, directors, and screenwriters, much more than she wrote about men in the business. Parsons explored the topic that was on many women's minds in the late 1910s: What did femininity mean in the era of the New Woman? Which actresses and filmmakers were presenting femininity successfully and how to emulate them?

Parsons also enthusiastically encouraged her female readers to try their luck in Hollywood. She herself moved to Los Angeles, found career success there, and stayed for the rest of her life. As a journalist writing about all the incredible women conquering motion pictures, she saw what an opportunity this new city and this new industry was.

She believed this was an age for "women-made women."

Parsons and her colleagues were pioneers in a business that was, and still is, dominated by men. According to the Center for the Study of Women in Television and Film, even though women today make up half of film audiences, male reviewers outnumber female reviewers by more than two to one. First conducted in 2007, Thumbs Down[79] is a study that considers the representation of individuals working for print, radio, television, and online outlets in the US and whose reviews appear on one of the country's most popular sources for film reviews, the website Rotten Tomatoes. In the opening months of 2022, men comprised 69 percent of reviewers, while women made up 31 percent, and nonbinary reviewers less than 1 percent. The real bummer is that for female reviewers, this is actually a decline from the 35 percent they made up in 2020. Further, male critics outnumber female critics in every job category, type of media outlet, and film genre considered.

The study also found that male reviewers award slightly higher average quantitative ratings to films with male protagonists than women reviewers, that films directed by women comprise a smaller proportion of reviews by men than women, and that when reviewing films directed by someone of their own gender,

---

79 Since 2007, Thumbs Down has analyzed almost thirty thousand reviews written by almost two thousand reviewers. It is the most comprehensive and the longest-running study of women's representation and impact as film reviewers available.

male and female critics are more likely to mention the name of the director in their review.

What does this mean? People care about people who are like them. Consequently, people care about art that is made by people who are like them, whether they are conscious of it or not. This is why it's important to have representation from all types of film reviewers. It seems like a crap idea to have the people publishing film reviews be unrepresentative of the film's audience. Author Mary Robinette Kowal put it best when she tweeted in December 2014, "It's not about adding diversity for the sake of diversity, it's about subtracting homogeneity for the sake of realism."

Film writing was quite different in the days before Rotten Tomatoes. The internet has both greatly improved and degraded the world of movie reviews. On one hand, it has opened up the field to marginalized writers who have a harder time breaking into the world of film journalism. On the other, it feels strange to be able to assign an algorithmic grade to something as subjective as art.

While female filmmakers in the 1910s did not have to worry about their projects being "Certified Fresh," they did have to worry about bad press. Not every journalist was as excited about women-owned production companies as Louella Parsons was. *Photoplay* called it a "her-own-company epidemic," as if these women's companies were simply cutesy little projects, to be shelved next to their dollhouse and Easy-Bake Oven.[80]

To the dismay of these party-pooping sexists, this epidemic continued its spread. As film historian Karen Ward Mahar says, "Women in the American film industry had thus far enjoyed more latitude and leverage than women in any other industry..."

With the success of *The Hazards of Helen*, Helen could now officially call Los Angeles her home.

During her years as a background rider, Helen continued to travel all over the United States and Canada for rodeos. But now

---

80   These didn't come out until 1963, but you get the idea.

that she was the star of the most successful serial in film history, it was time for her to settle down.

It was a good time to do so, as Los Angeles was rapidly racking up modern conveniences. The city now had a railroad and a cheap electric trolley system. Cars began to multiply on the avenues, following all the wealth pouring into the city.[81] Private cars and chauffeurs slowly replaced horse-drawn carriages and wagons. There were now one hundred businesses dotting Hollywood Boulevard, selling everything you can imagine, from fashionable clothes to appliances. Many of the stores catered to those in the motion picture industry, actors specifically.

Drugstores and beauty parlors sprang up like wildflowers to service the hordes of performers. In the mid-1910s, the film industry was still practicing a tradition from theater where actors did their own makeup and hair. Without a dedicated person to apply it, the makeup and hair usually looked slightly different (at the very least) from scene to scene, sometimes from shot to shot. The first makeup department would not be set up until 1917, when a hair stylist named George Westmore[82] started one at Selig. The idea didn't fully catch on until the 1920s, when other studios started setting up their own hair and makeup departments and relieved actors of the responsibility. Until then, if you went to get your hair done on Hollywood Boulevard, there was a chance you'd be seated next to your favorite serial queen.

Studio facilities were also changing. Most films were still shot outdoors, until an art director (the first, in fact) named Wilfred Buckland helped bring the industry inside. He started using carbon arc lamps—intensely bright lights—to light film sets. They were, and still are, called klieg lights, after their in-

81 And if you currently live in Los Angeles, it feels like they haven't stopped.

82 If you've read my first book, you know all about George and his…interesting family.

ventors, the Kliegl brothers.[83] Soon, enclosed stages popped up all over the city.

With the ability to shoot at all hours of the day and night, studios went into overtime. Universal Studios filmed with multiple units all day, six days a week. When you could build an indoor set that looked like anywhere, from the South Seas to the streets of New York City, why bother shooting somewhere else? Filmmaking finally became *the* industry of Southern California, the largest and most profitable, ahead of even real estate (although that was booming, too).

The complete takeover by the film industry turned the city into the weird place people love today. Los Angeles absolutely changed the film industry, but the film industry also deeply changed Los Angeles.

Non-Angelenos love to mock Los Angeles by calling it a place of plastic surgery and avocados. You know, Tinseltown. The thing is, they're not incorrect. The avocado part is certainly true. But this reputation hides the very best part about living in the city.

No one cares about you.

This is a good thing, a great thing. You can be so goddamn strange in Los Angeles and no one cares. Sure, many people, especially budding actors and internet stars, intensely focus on how they look, how much they weigh, or how balanced their chakras are. But if they're so focused on themselves, they don't care about *you*. And frankly, it's wonderful. No one gives a shit in Los Angeles. It's not that they don't like you (they wouldn't tell you either way), they just don't care what you're wearing or what you're doing.[84]

For a lot of people, Los Angeles lets them be themselves. Almost everyone is from somewhere else, so almost everyone is in the process of reinvention, or showing off who they've always

---

83 The lights were so intense that the ultraviolet rays they gave off caused some actors to develop an inflammation that was called "klieg eye," which sounds like the name of a crusty old pirate.

84 Unless you can get them a job.

been deep down. It's very easy to be cynical about the city, especially when you haven't had a big break. It's an expensive place to live with too many cars and not enough public transportation. But there's something really special about a city full of people who traveled hundreds, maybe thousands of miles to make their dreams happen. And get to eat avocado toast outside in January.

While it was nice to *feel* at home in Los Angeles, Helen could now *buy* a home in Los Angeles. The success of *The Hazards of Helen* made the executives at Kalem want to secure their new star, so they gave her a salary increase. With the money, she bought a beautiful, sprawling two-hundred acre ranch in Glendale, near the studio. Helen immediately filled the ranch with cows, mules, and other livestock.

And of course, she bought horses. Helen finally had her own barns and stables, and filled them with her own horses. This cowgirl no longer had to pay to stable Zenobia.

Helen Gibson, the "Hazards of Helen" girl, owns and manages a 200-acre ranch in California and is on very good terms with the stock.

FILM FUN, NOVEMBER 1916.

Helen with several of her large and furry family members.

Even better than a house and a barn, Helen finally had *more*. She was living a big life, bringing thrills to the entire country instead of a rodeo audience. She was living in a city where it was impossible to be too much. She was living her dream.

The final episode in Helen's inaugural *Hazards of Helen* run was released on Christmas Day, 1915. This meant that, just like they do today, fans could head to their local movie theater and watch a new, anticipated film after opening their presents. Thousands and thousands of women across the country, wrapped in their warmest jackets and shawls, sat down to watch Helen prevent a head-on train collision and rescue a child in "The Boy at the Throttle."

KALEM KALENDAR, DECEMBER 1915.

Helen swinging in to save the day, and a small child.

For Helen, she had all the makings of a phenomenal holiday. She was pulling in more money than ever before and had a big, glorious house to set up a Christmas tree in. When the clock chimed midnight on New Year's Eve, 1916 looked like it would be her best year yet. That night, lying in bed, Helen could practically hear the city around her buzzing with possibility. After years of toiling in background roles, her big break had finally hit.

It's easy to say that the young women stampeding into Hollywood just wanted to see their faces on the big screen, and maybe that was part of it. But seeing stars like Mabel Normand and Mary Pickford control their own lives, buy gigantic, dreamy mansions and cars, or in Helen's case, a ranch full of beautiful horses, while they were stuck sharing rooms and sometimes beds (not in a sexy way) (okay, maybe sometimes in a sexy way) with other young women as they hustled at multiple service jobs? That was another part.

Most waitresses made a mere four to five dollars a week (besides their tips), some working in cafes and restaurants for ten to fourteen hours a day. By 1917, the cost of living in Southern California was fourteen dollars a week. As the star of *The Hazards of Helen*, Helen was making many times that.

And now that Kalem was ready to shoot more episodes, it was time for her to earn that salary.

A journalist at *Motion Picture News* wrote in December of 1915 that it would take more than fan fervor to keep the series going. Whether or not *The Hazards of Helen* would be a continued success was "up to Helen Gibson, however, for it is that petite player who must bear the brunt of the perils and dangers."

She was up for the task. Her reaction to the news of *Hazards* being the longest-running serial of all time was a "mere" smile. She told a reporter that she "promised to contribute her share toward the celebration by doing any feat that scenario would call for." Helen didn't care about the accolades. She cared about the stunts.

One of the best parts of *Hazards* was that, like Holmes did before her, she got to write and work on the show behind the scenes. Unlike Holmes, Helen never used a stunt double. This serial queen did everything herself. After her work as a trick rider, planning and executing her own hair-raising stunts was easy for Helen. It was also safer. No one knew better than Helen just what she was capable of, and on *Hazards*, she did not hold back. Helen devised all sorts of stunts, many of which she knew none of her colleagues could do.

One episode, "Danger Ahead," featured Helen perched on the back of a car speeding toward a moving locomotive. As soon as it pulls up alongside the train, Helen leaps from the back onto a flat car. Her jump has so much momentum that she nearly flies off the other side of the train. But she manages to hang on, get up, and save the day. Take that, Vin Diesel.

KALEM STUDIOS, 1916. TAKEN FROM IMDB.

Helen was so confident in her abilities that she issued a challenge to the other serial queens. Kalem publicized her as "the most daring actress in pictures" and Helen declared that she would ask the studio to remove this title if anyone could do the same stunt.

No one even tried.

There was only one downside to being "the most daring actress in pictures." After her first run of *The Hazards of Helen* episodes, Helen did what every actor who lands a secure job does: she tried to get insurance. But all she received in reply to her application was a letter informing her that she was "engaged in an extra hazardous pursuit" and therefore she was an "unsound risk" for the insurance company. *Moving Picture World* reported the story, and concluded that the insurance company must have sent an agent to the *Hazards* set to observe her in action.

There were two episodes shot during the period between Helen applying for the insurance and receiving the rejection. In one, "The Haunted Station," Helen fights off a determined villain while they are both dangling from the same rope over train tracks.

In the other, "When Seconds Count," Helen, as *Moving Picture World* explains:

...is lashed to a handcar, is sent speeding down grade... while a train is tearing along another stretch of track that diagonally crosses the one on which the handcar is running. Through perfect timing, the handcar passes between the rear and front wheels of the train, though it may be readily seen that had the handcar arrived at the intersection a second too soon or too late a frightful accident might have happened. The scene was rehearsed for a full morning with a handcar loaded with sandbags before Helen was allowed to attempt the feat.

The magazine surmises that after witnessing these stunts, it "must have sent the insurance investigator back to his office with a few gray hairs as a memento of the occasion."

The story made for great publicity for our serial queen... but Helen really did need that insurance! She was intrepid, but she wasn't invincible. Over the course of the next episode arc, Helen sustained several injuries, some minor and some serious. Her desire to push every stunt to its limit occasionally backfired.

That spring, when the *Hazards of Helen* crew were shooting up in Utah at the Salt Lake City railyards, another stunt went awry. In the scene, Helen was supposed to be leaping from a boxcar to the train's engine. Only the engineer hired to run the train had it going thirty miles an hour, instead of the requested fifteen. The doubled speed caused Helen to fall and injure her leg so severely that production had to be delayed.[85]

Moving Picture World reported another accident in the summer, one Helen was lucky to survive.

The fearless Helen of the "Hazards of Helen" series met with a rather painful accident this week...making a jump from a motorcycle off the end of the Long Beach drawbridge. Instead of landing in the ocean, the young lady miscalculated the distance and fell on a pile of rocks. While bruised and battered, she escaped serious injury...

It's tempting to say that Helen was the luckiest woman in the world, or that she was experiencing a series of miracles, but remember that years in the rodeo taught her to make split second decisions about how and where to fall. There was some skill involved in cheating death. Okay, maybe a little luck, too.

Helen loved making *Hazards* so much that she enjoyed even the ill-fated shoots. The same magazine reported on the shoot for "The Record Run" (the seventy-fourth episode) "...that while speeding along a road, Helen lost control and the car flew off the track. She crashed right into the camera, 'destroying it, and barely missing the director and cameraman who were stand-

---

85 The episode was apparently supposed to be titled "Trap of Death" but I believe it was scrapped because of Helen's injury and the subsequent delay, and never released.

ing beside it.'" The article started that Helen "came up smiling in the midst of the wreckage and was not hurt" but the camera was "reduced to splinters."

Accident at Kalem Studio.

MOVING PICTURE WORLD, MARCH 18, 1916, PAGE 1807.

Kalem was fairly lenient when it came to approving Helen's stunt ideas, but sometimes other authorities had to step in. In May, the producers leased a train for a *Hazards* shoot, but once the railroad officials found out what Helen wanted to do with it, they put a stop to the stunt. She wanted to attach a rod between two train cars on parallel tracks, and crawl across it while both trains were in motion. *Motion Picture News* reported that the officials found the stunt "too hazardous" and "prohibited" the train engineers "from carrying out the orders of the producing organization."

Even a lack of health insurance did not deter Helen from attempting the most spectacular feats she could think of.

Now, where was Hoot in all of this?

Despite many magazines and newspapers calling her "Miss"

Gibson (probably to blur the lines between her and the *Hazards* character) Helen and Hoot were still legally bound.

The biggest question, of course, is whether any romance developed between the two rodeo stars. By now, they had been married for three years. The pair never had any children, (although that's not proof of anything). The marriage suited them while they were traveling on the rodeo circuit. It certainly saved them money, as two young people trying to make it in Hollywood. With Helen's ascent, now Hoot got to live at her beautiful ranch in Glendale.

But did they ever get curious, a la Joey and Rachel on *Friends*?

Frankly, it's hard to imagine that they didn't. Even though this was a time when it was not uncommon for married couples to sleep in separate twin beds,[86] I'm sure there were many situations, including their wedding night, where the room they were staying in had only one bed. If you've ever read a romance novel, you know where that goes.

The truth is that we'll probably never know.

Overall, it seems like the relationship between Helen and Hoot stayed platonic and businesslike. They were both quite focused on their careers and benefitting professionally from the marriage. At least at the start, it was a publicity boost for each to be hitched to a fellow rodeo star.

Although he had gotten work as a stuntman and a background rider for several years, and had landed small roles in many Westerns, Hoot still hadn't broken out. He certainly was not a star like Helen was. In fact, newspapers and magazines began to refer

---

86   For about a hundred years in the United States, from 1850 to 1950, it was considered both modern and healthy to sleep in a separate bed from your spouse. Many Victorian doctors believed that the stronger, healthier person would get their vitality drained by the weaker, less healthy person while the pair slept. How this sleep vampirism was accomplished is anyone's guess. It didn't seem like a wild idea at the time however, and by the 1920s, it was fashionable to have two twin beds in your bedroom.

to him as "Helen Gibson's husband." Hoot was, shall we say...
not quite thrilled to receive the title.

Remember how Hoot wasn't the one who recommended
Helen for Holmes's stunt double, despite the fact that Helen was
quite literally the most perfect person on the planet for the role?
As far as cinema history knows, Hoot had never gotten Helen
a job, even though for years before *Hazards*, he had worked in
the same genres—action and Westerns—that she was trying to
break into. Hoot had never done anything to hamper Helen's
career, but he certainly seemed uninterested in helping it, either.

Now, you can imagine how a guy like that reacted to being
referred to as "Helen Gibson's husband." It was probably extra
grating, considering that Helen was the one who bought the
giant ranch. Working as a background actor in *her* show, Hoot
made five dollars a week. She was making many times that. In
later years, Helen would tell a reporter that Hoot had an in-
flated ego. As Helen's star rose and rose, that ego began to rear
its ugly head.

Hoot's irritation echoed the way that many men in Hollywood were beginning to feel about female filmmakers as they
pushed for more money and more control. After harnessing their
power as star filmmakers and actors, women were now knocking
on the gates of the last male-dominated bastion of the industry:
finance. This was a step too far for many executives. Remember, the wave of female-owned productions was being called a
her-own-company *epidemic*. It was about to be treated as such.

8

Strong Female Protagonist

Financing was one of the few parts of the filmmaking world that women did not help develop. They never had a chance. Even at the dawn of American cinema, when women were flourishing in all other areas of the industry, it was difficult to find a woman working on the financial side of things. There were a few, but on the whole, that was still a man's world.

It always had been, really.

During the late 1800s, middle-class or white-collar work was largely the domain of men, and various clubs and lodges were established for these guys to gather in. They were newer and less exclusive than some of the older orders, like the Masons, meaning that less connected, newly middle class guys could join and have access to the facilities (usually some sort of meeting hall) and a network of potential friends and business partners. You could probably guess that these were mostly white-only spaces.

Some of these clubs got sort of weird and cultlike, enacting secret rituals and assigning specific rankings or tiers to their members. Others were just a bunch of dudes who worked in the same trade and wanted a cool clubhouse. A few of these orders are still around, including the Loyal Order of Moose, the Benevolent Protective Order of Elks, and the Knights of Pythias. In fact, this period of time in America is known as the "golden age of fraternalism."[87]

Then, women entered the workforce in the early 1900s, and made these lodges, orders, and clubs even more popular. Since women had now so rudely intruded upon offices and factories, these male-only spaces became a sort of refuge. In these exclusive halls, men could do manly things, like spitting and smoking and drinking and cursing, away from the delicate eyes of women.

Now, getting into a big meeting hall where a bunch of guys are spitting may not seem all that appealing. But access to these spaces included huge financial advantages. Lots and lots of business deals went down underneath the plumes of pipe smoke.

When the filmmaking industry sprang up in the early 1900s, many of its trade organizations and associations were modeled on these men-only clubs and societies. The Motion Picture Directors Association was founded in 1915 as a "fraternal order," two words that struck fear in the heart of any woman trying to get support for her film career.

Despite the prevalence of successful female directors in Hollywood, the MPDA was not particularly welcoming to them. It took them a whole year to admit Lois Weber, and even then, she was only made an honorary member and the leaders of the association told her that the rules had been "set aside" for her. Weber, remember, was arguably one of the most successful and influential directors of the time.

Then, the MPDA announced that they had quite enough women now, thank you very much, and that no more "members of the gentler sex" would be included in the organization. One was plenty. They didn't add another female director until 1923.

Exclusion from these associations meant that female filmmakers were denied access to networking with their colleagues, and

---

87   A phrase that my brain immediately interprets as a threat.

potential collaborators like screenwriters, actors, and producers. Worst of all, they were denied access to potential investors. With filmmaking costs skyrocketing, and more and more female directors, actors, and screenwriters becoming independent, being barred from these spaces was a massive disadvantage.

Many businessmen did their dealings in male-only spaces outside of these lodges, as well. This was a time in America when women were largely unwelcome in bars, a longtime favorite location for meetings and deals.[88]

What this all boils down to is that often women were literally not allowed to enter the spaces where many film or distribution deals were being made.

Even if these women *were* able to schmooze with potential investors, those investors were often uncomfortable with giving money to women. That is part of the reason why it was rare to see female executives on the financial side of production companies and studios, and why there were so many husband and wife teams in the independent production space. In 1916, the prevalent belief in American culture was that men and women were fundamentally different. Women weren't trusted to make sound financial plans and decisions because of their weak, tiny lady brains. These investors and businessmen were happy to make money off of the creative talents of these women, but preferred to have a man in charge of the numbers. As female filmmakers in Hollywood continued to aim higher and push further, this was becoming more and more of a problem for them.

But, in Helen's case at least, maybe it wasn't a bad thing that she wasn't in charge of *The Hazards of Helen*'s finances. She would have spent it all on horses. Kalem, pleased by the success of *The Hazards of Helen*, was ready to beef up its budget. There was one thing Helen really wanted to spend it on: horse-

---

88 If you would like to read a history of women in bars, check out my second book, *Girly Drinks*.

back stunts. They were her specialty, and would make the show stand out even more from other serials, especially since none of the other major serial queens could ride like Helen. Although she had everyone else beat in stunts, "the most daring actress in pictures" always wanted to go one step further to give her fans a thrill.

The studio happily granted her request, and she was even allowed to choose her own equine co-stars. It was no easy task to find a horse that felt comfortable in the chaotic atmosphere of the set, with loud cameras, speeding vehicles, and people rushing around. Trains in particular were known to spook horses.

Luckily for Helen, in her search for a suitable mount, she got word that a horse she had ridden in the Miller Brothers 101 Ranch Show was wintering with another rodeo in California. The horse's name was the rather unoriginal Black Beauty, and it had the necessary calm temperament for galloping alongside a speeding train. Most importantly, it was a horse that Helen trusted and had experience with. Kalem bought the horse off the rodeo for, as *Moving Picture World* reported, "what would make a satisfactory one-year contract for many a famous screen star." With all the work Black Beauty needed to do, it was money well spent.

Kalem purchased additional horses for Helen to train herself. Even among veterans of the rodeo circuit, it was difficult to find animals suited for her needs. One horse that Helen trained was a tough bronco who was so ornery that few people besides Helen could get on his back. She named him Hazard.

To add to this bill, Kalem started construction on new sets. Spur lines, secondary train lines that branched off a main route (also known as branch lines), were built for the series in eastern Los Angeles. This serial queen got her own train tracks. They also hired a crew to build a massive water tank and new trick stages. *Moving Picture World* reported the start of construction in September 1916: "A large tank is now being built for water scenes and additional traps are being built into the stage, one with a hydraulic hoist with sufficient power to raise an entire set."

The budget was further expanded for what is now an action movie staple: the destruction of cars.

The sixty-fourth episode of the show, "Tapped Wires," involved Helen fighting criminals in a speeding car, then jumping from the vehicle before it careens off a cliff. Shooting the scene involved sending an actual car flying off of an actual forty-foot cliff. The whole affair lasted for fewer than sixty seconds on-screen, but Kalem spent fifteen hundred dollars to make it happen. Cars had been rising in popularity for about a decade now and the time was clearly nigh to start driving them off cliffs.

MOVING PICTURE WORLD, JANUARY 8, 1916, PAGE 214.

Helen being quite sick of jokes about women drivers.

After horses, trains, cars, and motorcycles, Helen set her sights…a little higher. She wanted to jump out of a plane.

During the mid-1910s, aviation was still being developed. Over in Europe, airplanes were being used en masse for the first time in a military capacity. The first Atlantic crossing and first airline were still over a year away. Planes were still very new, and very risky. But to Helen, they were a new type of vehicle to conquer.

Airplane stunts have always been dangerous. During a night shoot for *The Skywayman* in 1920, two pilots were killed when their plane crashed, including the film's star Ormer Locklear, a famous aerial stuntman. Even the shoot for one of the most famous aviation films of all time, 1986's *Top Gun*, was deadly. Legendary stunt pilot Art Scholl died shooting the climactic scene when Maverick's plane enters a downward spin. The only things recovered from the crash were a few pieces of debris from Scholl's plane.

Helen wanted to do an aerial stunt in 1916, when aviation technology was still being developed.

Other serial queens had taken to the air before. *The Perils of Pauline* featured Pearl White in a hot air balloon. Ruth Roland had jumped from the top of a moving train to a rope ladder hanging from a passing airplane. But no one had jumped *from* a plane yet. And Helen being Helen, she wanted to push the stunt even further. Episode eighty-four of *The Hazards of Helen*, "A Race Through the Air, " called for her to jump from an airplane *onto a moving train.*

Kalem hired a pilot for the shoot, and once the man discovered what Helen wanted to do, he refused to fly. He would only agree to take her over the train if she promised not to jump out of it. The producer, James Davis, would have to find a way to creatively edit the footage to make it look like Helen had actually jumped. She was unhappy, but Helen finally relented so the shoot could continue.

However, once the cameras were rolling and the plane took off, Helen started silently wriggling her way out of the safety straps. With her hair whipping around in the wind, she had to shout to be heard over the whirling propellers and the rumbling train below them. Helen told the pilot that no matter what, she was going to jump out of that plane. "Now, you had better go through with the drop as I first planned or I'll jump out right here. The camera's grinding...we're going to have a thrill of some kind. It's up to you to say what it will be." What could he do? Drop one of the most famous serial queens in the country to her death, or position the plane so that she landed in her intended spot on the roof of the train? He acquiesced. Satisfied, Helen got into position. With absolutely no safety gear, she leapt.

Helen flew twenty feet down to the train, and completed the stunt as planned. Well, mostly as planned.

She sprained her ankle on the landing, but the crew got the shot. Helen did it in one take. The pilot told a reporter later that he came "close to heart failure."

Helen's only consequence was needing to spend several boring days in the hospital so her ankle could heal. The victorious serial queen told reporters that she was "now stumped" on how she would top this stunt, but that she'd "think of something" while she was laid up in the hospital.

Jumping from the plane was so much fun that Helen did it again six episodes later in "A Plunge from the Sky." This time, she jumped from a plane into a river. *Motion Picture News* announced that the camera "caught every electrifying thrill" but did not say whether or not it was the same pilot. Hopefully Helen didn't send the first guy into retirement.

MOTION PICTURE NEWS, AUGUST 5, 1916, VOLUME 14, NO. 5, PAGE 762.

All things considered, it was truly a miracle that Helen was still alive. She didn't have a manual to work from. She didn't take any classes. There was no governing body that oversaw stunt work in films. Helen simply decided that it was time for her to *jump out of an airplane* and she just...did it, without any practice or training. When she got back home from a day of shooting, Helen lay in bed at night dreaming up new episodes of *Train Station Impossible,* and all it took for those wild ideas to become a reality was the executives at Kalem saying, "Yeah, sounds good." Everyone was just making it up as they went along and hoping for the best. Or at least, the coolest shot.

This sort of fly-by-the-seat-of-your-ankle-length-skirt stunt work was risky for Helen. With horses and airplanes and bigger stunts, she was certainly pushing the envelope for serials. But an increase of thrills came with an increase in injuries.

In the seventy-first episode, "The Girl Who Dared," written

by Helen herself, the brave telegraph operator stands on a pair of horses galloping toward a moving train. She catches a rope dangling from a bridge, and swings from the horses onto the train. Helen told reporters that she wrote the entire episode around this particular "risky stunt." Only when it came time to shoot the scene, her skirt got tangled in the rope. Instead of landing on top of the train's engine, she got clipped by the top of one of the train cars and landed further down the train. The cameraman got the shot, but Helen had to spend a full week in the hospital afterward.

MOVING PICTURE WORLD, JANUARY 1916.

Writing and pulling off this stunt, despite the accident, caused Kalem to raise Helen's salary by fifty dollars a week. It was the least they could do for her after she literally *got hit by a train*.

As long as Helen survived, the studio loved to publicize her injuries. Hearing about them made fans eager to see the newest episode of *Hazards*, knowing that all the stunts were real and that there was a chance they could see the serial queen get hurt. *Moving Picture World* reported that audiences felt "tense" watching these scenes because they were "able to see clearly the girl's danger."

People get injured all the time in very ordinary ways and Helen figured that she might as well get injured doing something that she loved. On a day off from shooting, after spraining her ankle getting off of a trolley car, Helen told reporters, "That's what I get for trying to be careful like other people."

Even with all the danger, Helen was having *fun*. There was nowhere in the world she'd rather be than on top of a speeding locomotive. This was her dream career. In a 2017 article about stunt work, stuntwoman Lisa Hoyle told the *New York Times*[89] that "there's nothing else I'd rather do. It's the best job in the world....I did a ninety three foot fall for the Charlie's Angels movie...leading up to it, it was the first thing I thought about when I woke up, and the last thing I thought about before I went to sleep. My palms would get a little sweaty. But that day, it was euphoric. On the first take, the director said, 'That's great, I got it.' And I thought, 'You mean I don't get to do it again?'"

Fans loved to watch Helen risk life and limb, but they also worried about her. Kalem received lots of fan mail for their serial queen, and some of these writers urged her to be a little more cautious. One fan took the time to add up all the feet of film she had appeared in during *The Hazards of Helen*, and was concerned because Helen was soon to reach a total of thirteen miles of film. This person was afraid that something terrible would happen to Helen when she hit this unlucky number, and urged the star to consider her safety. It's too bad this person died before Twitter was invented.

The letter, while flattering, made Helen laugh. She told re-

---

89 Writers Amisha Padnani and Daniel E. Slotnik interviewed her for a piece titled "It's Not for Wimps': 8 Stuntwomen Reflect on Their Careers".

porters that she aimed to make her thirteenth mile of film her most dangerous yet. Her name in the *Hazards* credits was "Fearless Helen," after all.

When the series celebrated its two-year anniversary at the end of 1916, "Fearless Helen" renewed her vows to thrills. Kalem and Helen saw a bright future to the series, and its star promised to keep providing hair-raising stunts. A reporter once asked her if there was any stunt she would not do. Helen laughed and said, "I haven't met it yet."[90]

This was always Helen's promise when interviewed about her work, that whatever she did next would be bigger, wilder, and more exciting. Thus far in Helen's life, she was right. From rodeo star to Hollywood background rider to the star of the world's most thrilling serial, Helen continued to go up, and up, and up.

In between *The Hazards of Helen* shoots, Kalem cast her in short Western films where she could show off her riding ability. On top of that, when Helen wasn't filming something, she continued to defend her various rodeo titles, such as the Pacific Coast Women's Champion. Her vacation time was spent traveling around the United States to different rodeos, both with and without Hoot. She showed audiences that becoming a Hollywood star hadn't caused her to go soft; she could still win races and bust broncos.

Kalem wasn't thrilled that Helen was risking her well-being with her extracurricular rodeo performances—defending the Pacific Coast title, for example, cost her another ankle injury—but she always recovered quickly and returned to work. Plus, it was good publicity for the show.

This serial queen lived her life just like she performed her stunts, looking straight ahead, focused only on the task directly in front of her. Helen Gibson never looked down.

At twenty-four years old, the star of the longest running se-

---

90   Around this time, Helen asked Kalem if she could jump a horse over a moving train. They turned her down.

rial wasn't thinking too much about her future. This was, after all, the woman who got married for a hotel room. She had no long-term plans for either her life or her career. So far, Helen simply pursued what was exciting to her, and took advantage of any opportunities that were offered.

Unbeknownst to her, as a new year dawned, another big one was coming her way.

9

A Daughter of Daring

In 1917, the United States got involved with a little thing which came to be known as the First World War.

It had been raging for almost three years by that point, but the United States had just entered the fray, like a teen arriving late to class with an iced coffee. President Woodrow Wilson and Congress decided it was time to join the Allies in April of that year, and the rest of the country was immediately swept up in a frantic scramble to support the war effort.

With so many men heading to the front lines, millions of women were hired to take their places as postal workers, bus drivers, railway guards, firefighters, and tram operators.[91] As previously closed doors opened up, some decided to look toward something a little more glamorous.

Arriving mainly by train, the steady stream of women into Hollywood became a flood. In 1918, a shopkeeper remarked to a journalist, "There are more women in Los Angeles than any

---

91 Some positions were opened to Black women as well, for the first time ever.

other city in the world and it's the movies that bring them."[92] Luckily, with productions becoming bigger than ever before, there were lots of job opportunities for these newcomers. Although women were being shut out of the financial side of the film industry, they continued to shape and innovate and influence it.

Before Frances Marion became the most successful screenwriter (of any gender) of the age, she worked as an assistant at Lois Weber's production company. She was a very beautiful woman, and Weber encouraged her to try her hand at acting. But Marion was never comfortable in front of the camera, and preferred behind the scenes work. What she was really eager to do was write.

Producer William Fox, founder of the Fox Film Corporation, discouraged Marion from this, and told her she should really be an actor instead of trying to be a screenwriter. His advice was that she should "gamble on herself" and that it was "easy, like tossing a coin." Marion responded by saying, "A coin, Mr. Fox, can only fall heads or tails, and I'll gamble on heads. They last longer."

Weber noticed Marion's screenwriting talent and began to assign her tasks as a writing assistant. When Weber moved to Universal however, Marion decided not to join her. She had become close friends with Mary Pickford, and Pickford wanted Marion to come write at *her* company. A beautiful partnership was born and the two became best friends. Marion would end up penning some of Mary Pickford's most iconic films, such as *The Poor Little Rich Girl.*

In 1917, working as Pickford's official screenwriter, Marion was making fifty thousand dollars a year (about $1,185,000 in 2023). Known for her flair for both comedy and drama, she was one of the highest paid screenwriters of the time. She knew what female audiences wanted to see. Her screenplay for *The*

---

92   From *Go West, Young Women!* by Hilary A. Hallett.

Flapper was the first ever to depict women as flapper girls, who flirted and danced and smoked and did whatever they pleased. Her film *The Restless Sex* depicted a beautiful Marion Davies as a young woman in love with multiple men.

Marion always said, "I owe my greatest success to women."

Screenwriters were especially inspirational for women of all classes because writing is the one part of the filmmaking process that you don't need anyone else for. You can write alone, in your home, without any special equipment or training, or most importantly, a Los Angeles address. With a fountain pen, some paper, and a few cents for postage, women all over the country could write a story and send it to a studio or enter it into a screenwriting contest.

Writers usually worked closely with the director and the producer, which often gave them some creative control and authority. As films improved, with higher production values and better stories, the scripts became much more important. This helped elevate female screenwriters into positions of power, and helped some become directors. It was common to find women who were the heads of writing departments. Before Mary Pickford signed her to a massive, exclusive contract, Frances Marion worked as the head of the writing department at a company called World Films, where she worked on fifty films.

Besides her legendary career, Frances Marion's story highlights something that made this period of Hollywood incredibly special: women's freedom in relationships.

Finding close friends in the film industry like Mary Pickford and fellow screenwriter Adela Rogers St. Johns gave Marion the courage to leave the husband she was very unhappily married to. Because of her screenwriting, and the support of the women around her, Marion could do what many women in America could not: get out.

By 1917, one in seven marriages in the United States ended in divorce, the highest rate in the entire world. That's not the sad part. The sad part is that a much larger percentage of marriages were unhappy and would have ended in divorce if the women weren't entirely dependent on their husbands. Even though millions of wives were making their own money, many of them had to hand off their paychecks to their husbands. Rising freedoms, the suffrage movement, and millions of women now working outside the home were "blamed" for these statistics. But if giving your wife freedom makes her want to leave you, who is really to blame?

Successful women in Hollywood didn't just have control over their careers. They could also control their personal lives. Marion had the money to leave a marriage and set herself up on her own. She had friends who had their own money to help her if she needed it, their own houses where she could stay temporarily, their own cars to pick her up with.

Of course, all the glamor was enviable. The gorgeous wardrobes, the over-the-top parties, the mansions. But underneath the gilding, the real appeal of all this wealth was independence and choice. With mountains of hard-earned money in her bank account and a community of similarly wealthy and powerful women, Frances Marion never had to worry about being stuck with an asshole because she was dependent on him.

This was why it was extra galling that women were still unwelcome in business spaces.

In her memoirs, Alice Guy-Blaché wrote that she was told not to attend meetings with her distributor. She said that she "would have embarrassed the men who wanted to smoke their cigars and spit at their ease while discussing business."

With less access to information and connections, these misogynistic restrictions denied women control. If their male partners had to be the ones to handle all the finances and business, at least on the face of things, these women could never fully be in control, even of their own companies, built on their own talent and savvy. It meant that many female stars, even in the midst of their biggest successes, could be manipulated.

So, despite the fact that female directors, screenwriters, and actors were reigning in Hollywood on the surface, underneath it all, trouble was brewing.

The Hazards of Helen continued to run through the beginning of 1917 in its usual fashion. Speeding motorcycles, galloping horses, thundering trains, and Helen leaping off each one to stop the bad guys, rescue the innocent, and make sure the Lone Point train depot survived another day. Having passed the one hundred–episode mark in autumn of the previous year, it seemed like the serial could go on indefinitely. Helen had told a reporter for *Motion Picture Magazine* the year before, in a piece titled "The Girl with Nine Lives," that as long "as the fans want railroad pictures, I'll keep on taking risks playing in them."

The 119th episode of the show should not have been an unusual one. The content of the episode certainly wasn't. Helen stops a massive train collision, then jumps from the hood of her car onto the ladder of the locomotive and runs along its roof. Ordinary day in the life for her.

No, the 119th episode, titled "The Side-Tracked Sleeper," is notable because it was the last one.

Helen never spoke or wrote publicly about the abrupt conclusion of the series, and Kalem never issued an official reason. *The Hazards of Helen* was still incredibly popular and made lots of money for the studio. Maybe Kalem never announced the ending because it wasn't truly the ending.

Our serial queen was about to get a brand-new show.

There are a few possible explanations why Kalem would want to put an end to *The Hazards of Helen* and start fresh with a new serial, and the real reason behind the change is probably a combination of all of them.

The Hazards of Helen had been running for a historic length of time. One hundred and nineteen episodes is substantial even by modern standards. Even though the show was still hugely popular, it's possible that Kalem wanted to get ahead of the game and start a fresh series before audiences could get bored. A new show meant a new marketing push, potentially pulling in loads of new fans. And it meant that Helen and her crew could have more freedom without being tied to the established world of *Hazards*.

After a mighty *seventy*-episode run, Helen Gibson was no longer the star of *The Hazards of Helen*. At this point, she had been one of Kalem's top moneymakers for about a year and a half, ever since her first full episode of *The Hazards of Helen* aired on October 15, 1915. She had been Helen for so long it was easy to forget that she had ever been Rose.

Now it was time for her to become *A Daughter of Daring*.

A Daughter of Daring was a one-reel show (about fifteen minutes long) just like *The Hazards of Helen*. It starred a...get ready for this...telegraph operator named Helen who worked at the Lone Point station and did wild, dangerous stunts to keep the trains running without delay. Sound familiar? The new serial was basically just *The Hazards of Helen*, but wearing a mustache. It even shared some of the same supporting actors.

Really, the person who *A Daughter of Daring* felt most different to was Helen.

She had inherited *The Hazards of Helen* from Holmes, who developed and shaped it. *A Daughter of Daring* was *Helen's* show. Sure, it was the same story and the same location and the same characters. But it was also a series that was all hers from the very start. And she had more control over the thing that mattered the most to her and to the audience: the stunts. If you could ride it, Helen wanted to do something dangerous and thrilling with it. In *A Daughter of Daring*, this serial queen was set to perform the most impressive stunts of her entire career.

MOVING PICTURE WEEKLY, AUGUST 11, 1917.
VOLUME 4, NO. 26, PAGE 24.

Helen checking the framing of a shot.

Kalem started production right away. The last *Hazards of Helen* episode was released on February 17, 1917, and the first *A Daughter of Daring* episode was set to debut exactly a month later. Just like *Hazards*, *Daring* was shot in Glendale at the "Lone Point" outdoor train station set. Many of the same crew members returned, including director Walter Morton, who had directed the last fifteen episodes of *Hazards*, meaning that Helen was already comfortable with the group behind the camera. Which was fortunate, considering that the first episode of the new serial would feature one of the most dangerous stunts Helen would ever do. The script for "In the Path of Peril" called for Helen to drive a motorcycle onto a speeding train.

Motorcycle stunts are notorious, even today, for being particularly dangerous to shoot. In the 1992 film *Supercop*, Academy Award–winning actor Michelle Yeoh did her own stunts, including the one Helen was about to do. Even with all the training and guidance, she still looks back on the scene and tells reporters, "What was I thinking?!"

One of the most infamous stunt horror stories is from the set of the 2015 film *Resident Evil: The Final Chapter*, where stunt double Olivia Jackson was injured so severely in a high-speed motorcycle chase that she was in a coma for seventeen days and her left arm had to be amputated. Jackson eventually won her suit against the production company shooting the film. Her attorney issued a statement: "Action movies that require people to carry out dangerous stunts should always be very carefully planned and performed. They should also be backed by insurance that can meet the very significant lifelong losses that could be incurred by any member of the cast and crew who is seriously injured."

Well, Helen was about to do this stunt without any of that.

The script featured Helen attempting to prevent a train crash. As she speeds alongside the tracks on a motorcycle, she sees a flat car dragging behind the train. Helen then revs her motorcycle and drives onto the train using the flat car as a ramp.

MOTION PICTURE NEWS, MARCH 1917.

In heeled boots and a long white dress, an outfit almost identical to the one she was wearing in her very first *Hazards* episode, Helen got on the motorcycle. The year before, she had told a reporter that before every stunt, she whispered, "Do or die" under her breath. With the rumbling of the train and the purring of the motorcycle's engine, she probably couldn't even hear her own words. But they worked. Helen drove that bike right onto the train.

And so, *A Daughter of Daring* had begun.

Helen in "A Race to the Drawbridge."

MOVING PICTURE WORLD, NOVEMBER 1917, PAGE 877.

Kalem ordered eleven episodes of the new serial, and everyone got right to work. For the first three episodes, the shoots went smoothly. Helen planned wild stunts, and her trusty crew captured them all on camera. But shortly before the episodes began airing, problems began.

In the first week of March, Walter Morton left the series.

Kalem announced that, starting with episode four, director Scott Sidney would step in. The studio hoped that Sidney would "inject an atmosphere of freshness and spontaneity" in the new episodes. It wasn't uncommon for serials to change directors, but three episodes in a new series was a bit soon. Did Walter Morton leave, or was he fired? Unaware that trouble was brewing, Helen just wanted to continue the shoot. She was focused on making *A Daughter of Daring* into the most thrilling serial of the era.

On March 17, "In the Path of Peril" hit theaters across the country, and fans turned out for the release. *Moving Picture World* announced:

A Daughter of Daring—A Money Maker If There Ever Was One

It is our pleasure to announce the starring of Miss Helen Gibson in a series of one-part railroad dramas, unique in their conception and execution.

Miss Gibson, whose heroic exploits are not approached by any other player of her sex in motion pictures today, needs no lengthy introduction.

Advertisements for the new show started to roll out in magazines and newspapers. Kalem hailed *A Daughter of Daring*'s "seat selling" power to potential exhibitors, and its "rousing action" to fans. Promotional photos and stills for the first episode showed Helen on a motorcycle, poised on the edge of a ramp leading up to a speeding train.

Over the next few weeks, three more episodes were shot, after which Scott Sidney left. Just like Walter Morton, it is unclear why exactly he left. One thing is certain, his departure had nothing to do with Helen. With all the directors she worked with over the course of her serial career, no one ever complained or found her difficult to work with. Even when she accidentally crashed a car into their camera rigs.

James Davis, another *Hazards of Helen* director alumni, returned to Helen's crew to take over from Sidney. His first episode with the series was "The Railroad Smugglers," which featured another one of Helen's biggest stunts. Even though the show was on its third director a mere seven episodes in, Helen was giving *A Daughter of Daring* her all.

In this episode, to prevent some new railyard calamity, Helen hops on her motorcycle and rides it up the freight ramp onto the loading platform at the station. She continues through the open doors of an empty freight car and proceeds to *jump her motorcycle onto a passing train*. Once she lands, Helen jumps off the motorcycle and scrambles onto the roof of the train.

successfully tamed those on her father's ranch. to the unbounded amazement

stopped on her way to the studio to help a stranded motorist fix his car. When she "got out from under," after five minutes' tinkering, the amazed owner discovered that his engine ran as smoothly as if an experienced mechanic had done the job. He didn't realize that the

TYPICAL MADCAP HELEN STUFF—A FLYING LEAP ACROSS THE WIDENING CHASM OF UNCOUPLED CARS

of the regular cowboys. Gradually she drifted into the rodeo game, those exhi-

MOTION PICTURE MAGAZINE, JUNE 1917.

The queen of the rails.

By now, the first four episodes were receiving critical and audience acclaim. Fans loved *A Daughter of Daring*, and critics praised Helen, saying that she "surpassed herself" with her stunts. When the fifth episode, "The Mystery of the Burning Freight" was released, a journalist from the *Louisiana Times* said,

> There may be a few skeptics left who do not believe that motion picture players take any chances and that most of the feats which astound picture patrons are film tricks, performed in laboratories. If so, any of those doubting Thomas's could have been turned into believers had they witnessed the making of "The Mysteries [*sic*] of the Burning Freight," a coming episode of "A Daughter of Daring."

Seeing actors perform their own stunts was becoming more and more important to moviegoers. That year, *Photoplay* magazine reported that fans hated stunt doubles. One complained, "I pay money to see the star and not their double." This was bad news for some actors, but not Helen Gibson.[93] She flaunted her abilities, and Kalem often invited reporters to the sets to see her in action. They didn't call her the "Queen of the Rails" for nothing.

The show continued to draw fans, which meant drawing sponsorships. Helen started to receive offers from various motor companies for marketing stunts. Later that summer, she appeared in several ads for King Motor, a Detroit-based car company. They wanted to push their new eight-cylinder Roadsters onto female drivers, dubbing the car "Essentially a Woman's Car."

For the stunt, Helen drove one of their new Roadsters up Lookout Mountain, a peak to the northeast of Los Angeles, in high gear. The ads featured an illustration of Helen in a black car with the canvas roof down, speeding up a mountainside. The text declared that, "When Helen Gibson at the wheel of

---

93   At least, it wasn't bad news for her yet. Eventually, this type of fan sentiment would come back to bite her, and her colleagues, in the ass.

her KING Roadster successfully negotiated Lookout Mountain, in California, on the high gear, she not only added another record to KING achievements, but she strengthened the KING's claims of being essentially a Woman's Car. Ease of control, so complete that in absolutely no detail of the car's operation was she ever embarrassed in the least by lack of manly strength."

These were the dark days before power steering, and turning the wheel of a car was notoriously difficult. (That's why cars in the 1910s had such large steering wheels, because they were easier to turn.) Now, it's safe to say that Helen Gibson was rarely, if ever, "embarrassed" by her "lack of manly strength," so it seems silly that King Motor Company would choose her for the stunt. If anything, they should have chosen an average woman off the street and had her drive the car up the mountain. But Helen was massively influential. Women all over the country wanted to be like her. Plus, if a car could withstand the stunt driving of Helen Gibson, it could withstand almost anything.

Besides getting a free car, Helen was paid for these sorts of ads and appearances. Extra money was always welcome, especially because Helen was a little bit...spendy. Now, she still had different tastes than many other female Hollywood stars. She didn't drape herself in furs and diamonds. This serial queen didn't buy a fleet of cars, or expensive silk dresses.

Helen bought farm animals.

Ask your nearest horse girl and she'll tell you that horses aren't cheap. After buying her two-hundred-acre ranch, Helen filled it with livestock. Unlike diamonds and silk dresses, an entire ranch of very large and very hungry animals needs to be constantly maintained. A farm needs a steady stream of hay, feed, cleaning, and animal care. Fortunately, for the past year and a half, Helen had a steady stream of healthy income to pay for it all.

She certainly wasn't filling up a savings account, however. Rich twenty-five-year-olds living thousands of miles away from their parents are not necessarily known for their financial prowess. Money came in, and money went straight back out. This isn't an issue when money is constantly coming in. But it can become an issue when it isn't.

Honestly, it's tough to say if Helen knew she was living a little beyond her means, mostly because it must have been difficult, even for her, to tell exactly what her means were. For most people in the film industry, money comes in irregularly sized amounts and unpredictably timed spurts. Helen had occasional payment from companies like King Motor and her salary from Kalem. Although, as she'd soon find out, Kalem's days at that point were numbered.

With films getting bigger and more expensive, and the industry making more money, cinema started to attract attention on the federal level. America was still in its Progressive Era, which began roughly around 1890 and consisted of white Protestants trying to make sure that anyone unsavory, namely immigrants and Catholics, was not in control of popular culture. Their goals were sort of a mixed bag, and they waged political and legal campaigns to prevent everything from sex work (boo) to child labor (yay). And as film grew exponentially in popularity, the motion picture industry became a huge target for Progressives.

Progressive organizations and religious groups started to notice that objectionable sights were being included in motion pictures without any sort of official oversight. No one was stopping sex and violence from being shown on the silver screen. Lois Weber was out there showing boobs, for godssake! Yet just like the boobs do, these films started to attract unwanted attention.

The first American censorship law was enacted in 1907 in Chicago. The law authorized the Chicago police chief to screen any and all films that were to be exhibited in the city and make sure they were fit for public consumption. Detroit followed suit that same year. While those police chiefs probably would have loved to hang out all day and watch movies, it wasn't sustainable for them to integrate that responsibility into their daily law enforcement duties. So cities and soon states began to establish censorship boards with dedicated censors to screen and assess films. In order for a film to be screened in these cities or states, it needed to get approval from the censorship board, for a fee, of course.

Now, film censorship wasn't all bad. It was just mostly bad. Remember, at this time, there was no film rating system to prevent small children from seeing movies. It's not necessarily a bad thing for a five-year-old to be prevented from watching a violent film. But these censorship board positions were usually political, because being on them meant having control over which stories were told up on screen. And most of the people appointed were white and Christian.

Film censorship was often used to further white supremacy. A board could censor or ban films that showed Black characters in positive or empowering roles, while granting approval to films that only showed Black characters in negative or demeaning roles.

When a film was submitted to a censorship board, it faced one of three possible outcomes. The first was that it would be banned outright and therefore could not be legally shown in the city or state. This was long before movies could be rated R. When a film was banned, that meant *no one* could see it, even adults.

The second outcome was that to get approval, the film required edits for any elements that the censors decided would corrupt people or make them commit crimes. The third outcome was that it would be granted approval and could be screened with no changes.

The goal of the boards was to reduce or remove scenes that contained nudity, sexuality, vice, "vulgarity," and in some states like Kansas and Maryland, "racially inflammatory" content. How did these censors know when something crossed the line? In Virginia, they were told to look for content that was "obscene, indecent, immoral, inhuman, or is of such character that its exhibition would tend to corrupt morals or incite crime." Does this sound quite subjective? You bet your film canisters it is. Historian J. Douglas Smith has written about the early days of Virginia's film censorship board, saying that the board members "clearly understood that their mandate demanded the prohibition of films which portrayed Blacks in ways that did not comport with prevailing standards of acceptance."

We can all agree that there are certain acts that are unquestionably unwelcome in films, especially acts that have to do with children and animals. But in most cases, what counts as obscene or immoral in a film is rarely black-and-white.[94] Often, it prevented marginalized filmmakers from telling their own stories about the suffering they faced. This also meant that any films that stepped outside of the heteronormative were doomed.

In 1909, the New York Board of Motion Picture Censorship was established, and it quickly became quite influential not just in the state, but countrywide. New York has long been a cultural hub that other states looked to, sort of how a book can hit a bestseller list in Seattle or Boston, but the list that really matters is the *New York Times* list. The board took advantage of that cultural power and renamed itself the National Board of Censorship, which in 1915 became the National Board of Review.

At first, movie studios played along with the censorship boards. They agreed to submit their films in the hopes that censorship would stay at the local and state level instead of escalating to federal regulation. Unfortunately, this cooperation did not hold off the government for long.

In 1915, a landmark case hit the Supreme Court: *Mutual Film Corporation vs. Industrial Commission of Ohio*. The Mutual Film Corporation was a big conglomerate that owned several studios and production companies. Their Detroit branch claimed that

---

94 Well, everything was in black-and-white during this time period, but you get
    it.

the fees from the censorship board restricted interstate commerce and, most importantly, violated free speech.

This was an enormously influential legal battle. It was essentially deciding whether or not making and releasing a film was protected by free speech. The case went all the way up, from Ohio to the Supreme Court.

In the end, the Supreme Court awarded the case to the Industrial Commission of Ohio. They ruled that movies were "a business, pure and simple, organized and conducted for profit." This ruling marked film's official transition from an art to a business, and once something was legally ruled a business, it could be regulated by state and federal governments.[95] Censorship of cinema was officially constitutional.

In the wake of the case, more and more states established boards that decided what movies could and could not be shown. Several congressional bills had already been introduced to create a Federal Motion Picture Censorship Commission, seeking to establish that "no copyright shall be issued for any film which has not previously received the certificate and seal of the commission."

This was big trouble for female filmmakers.

Lois Weber was one of the first filmmakers that caused trouble with the censorship boards, but it wasn't simply a matter of not being able to go topless on screen. For women trying to push the boundaries of gender roles, and show female sexuality in a positive light, the growing power and influence of censorship boards was a nightmare. Now everything from dramas that depicted abortion to comedies that depicted over-the-top female violence was in jeopardy. If a censorship board was likely to ban it, why would an investor want to fund it? The only way for a film to make money was for it to be seen in theaters.

Now, which type of film challenged gender roles most often? Serials.

---

95   This actually would be changed in a future Supreme Court case, but not for another thirty-seven years.

10

The Hair-Raising Business

The next six episodes of *A Daughter of Daring* continued as expected. Helen provided her signature thrills while she apprehended robbers and stopped runaway rains.

Toward the end of the shoot for the eleventh episode, "The Deserted Train," Helen had to go to the hospital, presumably for an injury sustained on set. She required an operation at nearby Thornycroft Hospital in Glendale, the staff of which was likely on a first-name basis with her at this point. While she recuperated at home, James Davis and the rest of the crew finished the shoot.

Due to her injury, Helen's last stunt in the episode needed to be faked. The editors made a cut that showed her jumping from a barrel on a railroad trestle toward a speeding train, and the next shot showed her landing on the platform. It's safe to assume that between these two shots, when she was flying through the air toward the train, is when the injury occurred. It was the only "faked" stunt during her entire reign as serial queen.

Turns out, it was bad luck.

Helen was injured at the end of May, and after a week or so was finally able to return to work. *A Daughter of Daring* was planned, it's believed, to be twenty or twenty-five episodes long. Helen was ready to shoot the second half of that run.

When she arrived at the Glendale studio, however, she was told that, after eleven episodes, *A Daughter of Daring* would not finish shooting. Her beloved show, which had just barely started, was over. Only five episodes had been released at that point.

That wasn't all the bad news. Helen's contract was also canceled. In fact, Kalem itself was nearly canceled.

From the outside, it seemed like everything was fine at Kalem, great even. A brand-new studio building in Glendale was nearly finished being constructed. It was a spacious place to shoot that included both indoor and outdoor stages. Its completion should have heralded a new and exciting era for Kalem Studios. Instead, it was the beginning of the end.

With several successful projects, *A Daughter of Daring* included, how could Kalem cancel production?

Despite outward appearances, Kalem was steadily losing money. For example, the year before, they produced a fifteen-episode serial drama called *The Social Pirates*.[96] The series was expensive to produce, and it ended up losing the studio a significant amount of money. In February, trade magazines reported that Kalem's Florida studio was being taken over by the United States Film Corporation.

Down a studio branch, with expensive projects losing money, and a costly studio construction to fund, Kalem started the spring of 1917 in dire straits. Even with major successes like *The Hazards of Helen* under their belt, many film studios and production

---

96   It's a real shame this series was unsuccessful because its plot, described as "two women who finally tire of being taken advantage of by men, and vow that they will stop these cads from preying on helpless young girls" sounds incredible.

companies were usually only a few big failures away from collapsing (even today). By June, everything fell apart.

Photoplay Magazine reported at the end of the summer that business at the Glendale location of Kalem Studios "was almost completely suspended." Every single production, with the exception of the "Ham comedies"[97] made by male comedy duo Ham and Bud, was canceled and all the talent were let go. After making close to fifteen hundred films, Kalem finally shut down for good at the end of that year and was purchased by Vitagraph.

So far in her film career, Helen's time with Kalem was the steadiest, most reliable work she had ever gotten. Suddenly, it was over. What was she to do?

Helen did what she was best at. She took a deep breath and jumped.

By mid-June 1917, film magazines were running announcements that Helen Gibson was no longer a "Kalem player." But that was only part of the news. Almost as soon as Kalem collapsed, a bigger studio scooped her right up.

Within days of getting the shock that her contract was up and *A Daughter of Daring* was over, Helen was contacted by Henry McRae, the studio manager at Universal Studios. He offered her a contract and a salary that was nearly *triple* what Kalem had paid her. As Helen later told the *Los Angeles Herald Examiner*, "That was good money in those days." For the grand total of one hundred and twenty-five dollars a week (thirty-two hundred in 2023), McRae wanted Helen to come to Universal[98] and return to her acting roots. He wanted her to make Westerns.

This was a mutually beneficial arrangement. Helen went barely a week without stable employment and got a gigantic

---

97 Completely unrelated to the free hams given out at theaters.

98 I keep saying Universal, but just a reminder that technically, at this time it was still called the Universal Film Manufacturing Company, a much less snappy name.

salary raise. Universal got a guaranteed star who was also rodeo royalty. Thanks to the war, demand for Westerns was rising rapidly. WWI's effect on the country was colossal and Hollywood was no exception.

The American film industry started cranking out pro-war propaganda films, stars helped fundraise for the war effort, and some notable names even headed to the front lines.[99] That year, Mary Pickford starred in *The Little American* (written by Jeanie MacPherson), a romantic war drama about a plucky lady who survives a U-boat attack. Frances Marion became an overseas combat correspondent, officially appointed by the US government to write about women in the service.

Jennie Louise Touissant Welcome created the Touissant Motion Picture Exchange with her husband Ernest, and made films that recognized Black contributions to the war. The two shot a twelve-part documentary series about Black soldiers called *Doing Their Bit*. Some historians believe that Welcome was the first Black female filmmaker in the United States.

The war directly affected Helen's life when, that summer, Hoot decided to enlist. He still hadn't gotten his big break, and was mostly doing stunt and background work for films. With not much to lose, he joined the army and headed to Europe.

Helen, really on her own for the first time in Los Angeles, stayed behind to keep America's mind off of their wartime anxieties.

Just as in the early 1900s, when citizens were nervous about what women's rights reform movements would do to the country, America once again turned to Westerns, this time to soothe its nerves about the war. Westerns were the perfect remedy. You could make them for cheap, they glorified American traditional values, and offered a fantastical escape into a world where the bad guys always lost and the good guys always won. As Rich-

---

99 Some male actors who stayed behind, notably Charlie Chaplin, received a lot of public vitriol.

ard Aquila, author of *The Sagebrush Trail* says, these movies offered "nostalgic visions of a glorious past." It didn't matter that
this past never existed. White Americans wanted a break from
reality. They wanted to watch themselves be the heroes.[100]

Americans were clamoring to spend their money on Westerns, and Hollywood was more than happy to oblige.

Studios threw their production of Westerns into high gear,
including Universal. Kalem's collapse could not have come at a
more apt time. The perfect Western actor had landed directly
into their laps. In fact, Helen Gibson already had experience with
one of the crews making horse operas for Universal: the Bison
Film Company, also known as the 101 Bison Film Company.
Her old friends at the Miller Brothers 101 Ranch.

The 101 Bison Film Company had continued to shoot Westerns, and now they had partnered with Universal. Bison made
the movies, and Universal distributed them. In August that summer, *Moving Picture World* reported that the "widespread revival
of interest in good Western subjects" pushed Universal to up
the delivery schedule for Bison's films. Now Universal wanted a
new feature Western film every other week. The article declared
that "So many requests for full-length Bison pictures have been
forwarded from the various Universal exchanges during the past
two months that it was deemed advisable to devote more attention to the manufacture of this brand."

It was time for Helen Gibson to make her return to the Bison
Film Company. Only this time, she was the star, not a background rider.

By July, Helen was back on set in the Los Angeles summer
heat and shooting exciting action scenes. Her first motion pic-

---

100 This is a long-standing American pattern, and is part of why shows like *Ted
Lasso* and stars like Dolly Parton got so wildly popular right after the Trump
administration ended. The United States turns to media like this when it
wants to feel good about itself.

ture with Bison was similar to *A Daughter of Daring* in that it was a "railroad thriller" called *Mettle and Metal*.

"Mettle and Metal" Is the Present Title of a Forthcoming Universal Production, Featuring Helen Gibson the Popular Stunt Actress

MOTION PICTURE NEWS, JULY 7, 1917, PAGE 93.

Film writers remarked that she performed her dangerous stunts "nonchalantly," in which she had to ride a galloping horse to a hanging derrick, jump out of the stirrups and catch a huge iron hook, and swing herself over the track to catch a runaway train engine. For a serial queen, this was a regular working day. One reporter spoke to Helen afterward, and she grinned while telling them, "I know that as long as I'm doing railroad thrillers for Universal, I'll never get bald. I'll be in the hair raising business!"

That summer, several magazines published profiles on Helen. *Moving Picture Weekly* called her the "girl that tames trains" and declared that "her pictures are some of the most popular on the market." *Motion Picture Magazine* wrote a glowing piece about her that began, "What? You never heard of Helen Gibson? The girl who laughs in the face of the most perilous feats that can be devised for her?"

The next stage of Helen's career was off to the races. Over the course of the rest of the year, Helen starred in four films for Universal, *The Perilous Leap, The Dynamite Special, The End of the Run*, which were all railroad thrillers, and *Fighting Mad*, a Western drama in which Helen got to flex her acting skills instead of just her stunt work.

Shooting for Universal meant a slightly different work pace than Helen was used to. Both *The Hazards of Helen* and *A Daughter of Daring* were one-reelers, meaning each episode came out to ten or fifteen minutes. Most of the thrillers and Westerns Helen made for Universal, however, were two- or even five-reelers, meaning either about twenty or fifty minutes long.

Even though each shoot lasted longer, Helen's daily schedule was familiar, just with a longer commute to the Bison Film Company sets north of Los Angeles, instead of down the street to Kalem. Helen loved to drive, so she didn't mind the change. In fact, Helen loved it so much that in an interview with *Moving Picture World* in September, Helen said that she liked to spend her off-set hours cruising around and outside of the city.

To beat the Southern California heat, she also loved to ice skate. A rink called the Ice Palace had just recently opened up in Los Angeles, and Helen was among a group of movie stars who could be spotted there. You might see Charlie Chaplin or Mabel Normand flying across the rink, only the second one ever built in California. According to ice skating historian Ryan Stevens in a 2018 article "The Lost Years: Skating and The Great War" for the blog *Skate Guard*, it "had a midnight blue lighting system and was decorated with stars to give the illusion of moonlight in the Arctic." Skating was a fantastic way for Helen to exercise, stay out of the sun, and maybe even hang out with her fellow stars.

Because that's what Helen was, a star. Even though *Hazards* was over, she wasn't a flash in the pan. Her cushy contract with Universal proved that. Helen, for all intents and purposes, had made it.

What exactly did it mean, for Helen, to make it? Financial stability, or maybe excess? A mansion? A luxury car? Fame and recognition? Everyone has their own subjective definition. Did Helen know, in that moment, the leather of her car seat squeaking under her skirt, her short, trim nails tapping on the steering wheel, the hustle and bustle of Los Angeles flying past her window?

Publicity shot of Helen looking glamorous.

She owned her own dream home. She was making good money. She saw her name up in lights on theater marquees and in enormous type on movie posters. Most importantly, she had the independence and freedom that the teenaged girl working at a dusty cigar factory in Cleveland always dreamed of. In 1917, even though the world was at war, Helen Gibson was happy.

But she wasn't satisfied.

So far, she still hadn't made a movie that she was *totally* in control of. All her films had been made by studios, so Helen was never completely in charge. Other female stars had made their own production companies, including her friend and *Hazards* predecessor Helen Holmes. The possibility of being completely independent sparkled on the horizon.

Also, Helen was legally bound to someone that she was beginning not to like very much. She told reporters later in life that Hoot's ego was really starting to drive a wedge between them. In fact, Hoot joining the army and traveling thousands of miles away was probably the best thing he could have done for their marriage. While Helen's star was rising at Universal, he was overseas in the Tank Corps.

As 1917 came to a close, the war began to take a toll on the film industry. With so many overseas, supplies being rationed, a new wartime tax on theater admissions, many studios decided to tighten their belts until the conflict was over. In November, *Moving Picture World* reported that Universal was laying off several feature production companies for a month "until we know exactly how seriously the war tax is going to affect us." He said that Universal had a massive backlog of films, "the largest reserve stock of negatives in our career" and instead of spending money to make excess films in an uncertain time, Laemmle decided to pare back the studio, at least temporarily.

It didn't help that November and December often usher in the rare periods of cloud and rain that Los Angeles experiences every year. Laemmle declared that they didn't have enough electric indoor stages for everyone. It's possible that Laemmle was one of the early adopters of the film industry's current practice of shutting down almost completely from Thanksgiving to mid-January.

Helen, however, was not part of the break. Her films were too reliable, and her Western drama, *Fighting Mad*, hit theaters the first week of December. At Universal, Helen's films were usually shown in theaters two weeks after they were finished shooting, a speed absolutely unheard of today.

At this same time, the dregs of Kalem Studios released the last *A Daughter of Daring* episodes. Her serials were some of the final motion pictures Kalem ever released. During the last week of the year, syndicated film news columns reported that "for an indefinite period, Kalem has decided to cease producing pictures." That indefinite period ended up being forever. Helen spent New Year's Eve, 1917, pouring one out for the studio that put her on the map, and toasting to the studio that was paving the way for her future.

By now, it was clear that motion pictures were here to stay. Like plays, books, and newspapers, film had become a permanent part of the American media landscape. The cultural legitimacy of the movies was proven. With the United States at war, the federal government wanted to harness that cultural power and use movies and their stars to support the military effort. They declared that motion pictures were an essential industry, a cultural force so important to keeping American morale up and patriotism high that it had to keep running.

As soon as the United States entered the war, an organization for war propaganda was created. The Committee of Public Information created a film division that made numerous newsreels and short films. Seeing war propaganda films inspired scores of young Americans to either join up, or offer their support to the United States military. Many soldiers began their military careers in theater seats.

What pro-war American films also accomplished was spreading the message of American might and superiority. Remember, the war had absolutely annihilated the film industry in Europe, and American films were being exported everywhere. While soldiers were fighting on the battlefields, Hollywood had been drafted into a cultural war taking place on theater screens the world over.

That year, director D.W. Griffith made *Hearts of the World*, a dramatic love story about a boy and a girl whose love is torn apart by the war. The British government was so eager to stimulate support among the American public that they encouraged the project and gave Griffith access to filmmaking locations that were otherwise forbidden to the public. The narrative casts Germans in an almost laughably evil light and features gruesome battlefield scenes. Despite the intense subject matter, the film was very successful, and star Lillian Gish said it "inflamed audiences."

It wasn't just young men who were being inspired by newsreels and war films. The National League for Women's Service was established before the United States even entered the conflict. In January of 1917, in conjunction with the Red Cross, the NLWS was created by the Woman's Department of the National Civic Federation to provide war services, such as transporting and caring for soldiers, stateside. These women were prepped and ready to help.

NLWS volunteers did everything from cooking meals for soldiers to working as wireless operators. There was a subdivision of female drivers, the Motor Corps, who transported troops and even drove ambulances on the battlefield. In a time where female drivers were often the subject of satirical cartoons, these women were proud to be official members of the Motor Corps. Some of them, no doubt, were inspired by Helen's motor exploits.

Besides making films to inspire these soldiers, workers, and volunteers, many in Hollywood rallied to raise money and materials for the war effort. Filmmaker and actor Douglas Fairbanks wanted to throw a charity rodeo to raise money for the Red Cross. Held in Exposition Park in South Los Angeles, a fairground that is now the LA Memorial Coliseum, the rodeo was called the Douglas Fairbanks Wild West Show. Fairbanks himself signed up to be one of the riders, alongside other Hollywood stars and rodeo champions. But one of the biggest attractions was Helen Gibson.

Helen was such a draw for the show that the *Los Angeles Times* published a feature on her to drum up attendance.

"DAREDEVIL :: HELEN" :: AT :: THE :: RODEO.

Trick Riding for the Red Cross on Saturday.

LOS ANGELES TIMES, JANUARY 10, 1918.

The article informed readers that the audience would "have the pleasure of witnessing Helen Gibson, famous stunt actress of the Universal company, perform a number of her hazardous riding tricks. 'Daredevil Helen,' as she is called, thinks nothing of riding full tilt down a steep mountainside or leaping from cliff to cliff on the back of one of her string of wonder horses; and her railroad feats as shown in pictures on the screen have made many a fan gasp with amazement at the absolute fearlessness displayed by this Universal actress."

Twenty thousand people attended and the show ended up raising fifteen thousand dollars for the Red Cross. Helen's performance lived up to the hype. She galloped around the arena in a red shirt with silver fringe, a satin skirt, and light blue satin hair ribbons. As both a movie and a rodeo star, Helen was an audience favorite. After the rodeo, the *Los Angeles Times* published a follow-up article, declaring that Helen and the other "crack lady riders" were "easily the sensation of the day." The piece declared that "These daredevil sportswomen clung to their mounts at every conceivable angle, rode standing and tandem, whisked bandanas from the ground, and made flying mounts, their gaily colored costumes and sheer intrepidity sending many a thrill through the enthusiastic bleachers." *Motion Picture Magazine* claimed that it was Helen alone who "took the crowd."

Another article about the rodeo declared that Helen was "afraid of nothing outside of indigestion, that's why she didn't take all the peanuts and pop the sailor-lads offered her." One of Helen's tricks was described, in which "with her left foot in the saddle, she throws herself over the pony's side. Her hands and her right foot wave at the onlookers. With her pony racing the limit, she picks a peanut from the ground. Yep, does it with her rosebud lips!"

When the rodeo was over, it was midway through January and time to shake off the holidays and get back to work.

11

Universal City

Helen's first project in the new year was a guest role on a serial that Universal was shooting called *The Lion's Claws*. It starred Marie Walcamp, another successful serial queen. The pair worked well together, because Walcamp, like Helen, took pride in doing all her own stunts.[101] Helen's episode was called "Through the Flames" and involved her sliding down a rope through a gout of flame.

Afterward, Helen began a demanding shooting schedule that had her making fifteen more films before the end of the year. Luckily, Universal was an absolutely phenomenal place to be shooting movies in 1918.

Four years earlier, Carl Laemmle made a big decision. After years of moving locations, trying to find a suitable ranch for his ever-growing film production facilities, Laemmle bought

---

101 Walcamp was called "the daredevil girl of the movies" but never quite gained the popularity that serial queens like Helen and Pearl White did.

a two hundred and thirty-acre chicken farm just over the hills from Hollywood.

None of the other locations had worked out so far. They were too small, or too far away, or too haphazardly put together. His most recent, a ranch in the San Fernando Valley, was called "Laemmle's Folly" by the heads of other studios because it was such a big distance from Los Angeles. They joked that he could film all the free locations that he wanted, since he was out in the middle of nowhere.

After a couple of years, however, Universal outgrew the location. That's when Laemmle ended up on that chicken farm. He spent one hundred and sixty-five thousand dollars for the land in March of 1914, and that's all he got, land. There wasn't much that existed on the farm that he could use. In fact, on one of his early visits, Laemmle's car got stuck in the mud. Fortunately, there was a movie shooting nearby starring an elephant named Jumbo, and Jumbo was persuaded to pull the car out.

Soon, Laemmle hired hundreds of workers to build what he called his "new Universal City." He didn't simply want a full production facility, with sets, indoor and outdoor stages, and dressing rooms. Laemmle wanted a real city, where his film crews and actors could live and have all their needs taken care of.

So, he ordered the construction of a post office, a school, a police station, a fire station, offices, a library, two hospitals, a horse corral, and a bank. After spending a million dollars on its creation, Carl Laemmle had the largest production facility in the world.

Universal City was a surreal place because it was both a real city and a fake city at once. All the sets were designed so that their facades could be easily changed, becoming saloons in a Western one day, and a temple in a fantastical drama the next. But most of them were operational. There were real shops, offices, a mill, a greenhouse, even a forge. *Moving Picture World* reported in October of 1914,

> There is rapidly rising a city capable of accommodating 15,000 souls, built for the express purpose of making motion pictures, the first city of its kind ever constructed by the hand of man....This city has one peculiarity which marks it out from every other municipality. It is a chameleon, or a changeable city...every building which has been put up or which is planned is designed to have a four or five fold usefulness....Every bridge is so constructed that it can take on the aspect of a Japanese arch bridge, a Roman stone paved bridge or a steel cantilever bridge, or in fact any other kind of a bridge for which a director has need in the production of a scenario....The roadways of the city are peculiar in that they are made in different widths and the styles of top dressing so that there will be as great a variety in this respect for the director to choose from as possible.

All of that work and planning paid off. The first year, two hundred and fifty films were made in Universal City. The hustle and bustle were constant. Films were always being shot, with actors in costumes running around, cameras being wheeled from stage to stage, and set pieces being carried all over the place. It was hectic, but it was extremely practical. There were eighty dressing rooms, so lots of actors could be changing into or out of costumes at the same time. There were two outdoor stages that were covered with muslin to soften the powerful California sun. One stage even had water tanks so that it could appear as a pond or lake if the film called for it.[102]

Now, Universal City was not the sleek thoroughfare of neon lights and escalators you can see today. The roads were still

---

102 This stage still exists and can be seen on the Universal studio tour.

mostly dirt, and only some of the buildings had electricity and running water. And there were definitely no rides or gift shops. But one thing was the same. There were tons of tourists.

Laemmle's next stroke of genius was opening the studio facilities to the public. He knew people were curious about motion pictures and would pay a few cents to watch them being made. The entire city was designed not just for shooting movies, but for spectators to see those movies being shot. He had bleachers installed around the sets, and a zoo built and filled with elephants, monkeys, leopards, and lions. The zoo served a dual purpose as both an attraction to the public and boarding facilities for animal actors.

A year after Laemmle first bought the property, he hosted a grand opening of Universal City. For twenty-five cents, you could watch live filmmaking and see your favorite stars. Since motion pictures were still silent, it didn't matter if there was a gigantic crowd of tourists sitting on bleachers next to the scene. The public could wander around Universal City and even approach actors for autographs. The two restaurants were also open to the public, and for an additional five cents, a chicken lunch would be included with admission.[103]

Besides the cheap lunch, there was something else wonderful about Universal City: it was filled with women.

This would become the peak year for female-directed movies at Universal Studios, not just for this time period, but of all time. Including women like Cleo Madison and Ida May Park, there were eight female directors staying booked and busy on the Universal lot.

In 2013, over a hundred years later, Universal Studios combined with their division Focus Features[104] only put out films by

---

103 Maybe that's what happened to all the residents of the chicken farm?

104 According to their own website, Universal Studios itself is only putting out two films directed by women in 2023, out of thirteen films total.

seven female directors. That's after they became the first major film studio to sign up for the #4PercentChallenge, an initiative to boost female directors in the industry. The challenge involved committing to a whopping *one* female director within the next eighteen months. It's wonderful that Universal was the first studio to sign up, but it hardly seems like cause for a parade. The fact that working with a single female director would be considered a "challenge" tells you everything you need to know about the current state of the American film industry.

Carl Laemmle was, even in this era, notable for his encouragement of female filmmakers. Universal City had "official" (but mostly symbolic) town positions and eight of the twenty-eight were held by women. Actress Laura Oakley was named the police chief and Lois Weber was named the mayor.

Even though she was technically the mayor, Weber was really the queen. Laemmle had lured her to Universal by promising that she could make features and the year after the new Universal City opened, Weber directed sixteen of them. Eventually, working with her own personally chosen production team, she became the top director at the studio. Weber was also the highest paid, pulling in five thousand dollars a week. She was worth every penny for Laemmle because her films made him millions. Eventually, Weber had convinced Laemmle to pay for a private studio building for her on Sunset Boulevard, where she could control every aspect of her movies.

At this point, Helen had been working in films for years. She had her own set at Kalem in Glendale with a depot and train lines specifically built for her show. But she had never seen anything like Universal City. Helen not only got to make movies in the largest, most innovative production facility in the world at the time, but she did it while hundreds or even thousands of people looked on. For the next year and fifteen films, Helen Gibson worked in wonderland.

That spring, Helen made a movie almost every week. It was a grueling schedule. Actor Gertrude Astor described her days of shooting at Universal, "You worked hard. You worked Sundays. Lots of times we did two pictures a day. We never had holidays. I think the only holiday we would get the whole year was Christmas Day....At Universal, they had a big stage and 36 companies all shooting at once. It was wild, it was ridiculous, with everyone screaming and yelling, and one doing a Western and one doing a romance."

For the most part, Helen played the lead in Westerns and railroad thrillers, such as *The Midnight Flyer* and *The Branded Man*. These movies were pretty typical fare, with stagecoaches and horses, shootouts and sheriffs. But Universal also encouraged Helen to spread her acting wings and try out genres that were new to her.

Helen was cast in a supporting role in *Bawled Out*, a comedy starring Alice Howell, a huge fan favorite.[105] She also starred in a drama called *The Silent Sentinel*, about a love triangle in a small Western ranch town. She played the part of a gun-toting ranch woman whose love two men fight for, in a big saloon scene, literally. *Under False Pretenses* was a railroad drama whose plot mostly centered around a romance, which was rare for Helen. She got to leap from a horse onto a speeding train, *and* kiss the handsome hero, actor Millard K. Wilson.

But the bulk of Helen's shooting schedule was taken up by her favorite: thrilling stories with horses, trains, or both. That summer, before she turned twenty-seven, she starred in *A Shooting Party*, *The Payroll Express*, *Beating the Limited*, and *Danger Ahead*. Many of these were made with a regular film crew, so even if Helen was dangling from a rope over a set of train tracks, she felt some comfort and stability. It was similar to her days at Kalem, only she was pulling in more money and working in a production facility that was about a hundred times better.

---

105 Some historians call her the "female Charlie Chaplin," but now you know that you can call Charlie Chaplin "the male Mabel Normand."

Most of her co-stars and colleagues were people that were easy for her to get along with. Neal Hart played opposite Helen several times, and he, like her, came into the entertainment industry through rodeos and Wild West shows. Eileen Sedgwick, another hard-working ex-serial queen, appeared in some Westerns with her. Helen had a community of peers, especially of women, to spend time with. Not that she had much chance to stay out late and party when she had to drive the six or so miles over the Hollywood hills every night, back home to her ranch full of hungry animals. In fact, Helen seemed to hardly party at all. Really the only time she was reported to be out on the town was when she was skating at the Ice Palace. It seems like Helen followed the creed of many teenage girls with long braids: fuck boys, get horses.

Unfortunately, as focused as Helen was on her career, when autumn arrived, two events—one global and one quite personal—would stymie her ascent.

★ ★ ★

In the late spring of 1918, people all over the United States started to get a strange sickness that involved an intense fever. Most people who caught the disease recovered, however, and the American public moved into summer without thinking too much about it.

But when summer ended, the sickness emerged again. This time it was much, much more severe: a flu that stampeded over your immune system straight to your lungs. Your throat became sore, then maybe you'd feel a chill, or a fever, or both. Soon, your lungs began to fill with fluid. Breathing became more and more difficult. And then, within days, sometimes within hours, you went into complete respiratory failure.

So began the Great Flu Epidemic.[106]

The disease spread quickly, affecting rural and urban areas alike. It was an international epidemic that soon claimed millions of lives. By the time the flu had run its course around the world, it claimed an estimated twenty to *fifty* million. Headlines read, "U.S. at War. Mystery Virus Leaps around the Globe Killing Scores in Its Path. Scientists Race to Find a Cure."

In America, it affected about 25 percent of the population. Unlike most other flus, this mostly hit strong, healthy adults, instead of the elderly and the immunocompromised. Scientists were baffled, and everyone was afraid.

The United States medical system was almost immediately overwhelmed. The situation was very similar to 2020, except there were no N95 masks, tiny bottles of hand sanitizer, or delivery

---

106 Many called it the "Spanish flu" for the same type of ignorant reasons that some called COVID-19 "the China virus." Because Spain was neutral in WWI, they had more media bandwidth to talk about things other than the war. So, in the early days, Spain reported the progress of the epidemic more heavily than other countries in Europe. This made many Americans, Brits, and other Europeans believe that the disease started there. Meanwhile, people in Spain called it "the French flu" because *they* believed it started in France. The origin country of the flu was never fully determined, although scientists now believe it actually originated in the United States. Go figure. It is quite sad to see how far we haven't come in over one hundred years.

apps to order groceries from. Many poor families died from star-vation because the breadwinner had become gravely ill, or died.

By the start of November, government officials tried to con-tain the sickness by shutting various industries down and en-acting quarantines. Almost everything in the country came to a standstill. Author Alfred Crosby wrote in his book, *America's Forgotten Pandemic: The Influenza of 1918*, that public schools and church services were canceled all over the United States. Busi-nesses like restaurants and saloons were ordered to close. In Chi-cago, "police officers were ordered to arrest anyone sneezing or coughing in public." And entertainment was shut down, from pool parlors and dance halls to movie theaters.

By mid–October, film distribution across the country was suspended, with the exceptions of serials and newsreels. Many producers and studio heads panicked. The suspension only lasted for about a month, but if you lived through 2020, you can imag-ine the uncertainty and fear. No one knew when the epidemic would end and the film industry would be allowed to resume. With film shoots canceled and theaters closed, anxiety was as rampant as the flu.

Some theater owners tried to see the bright side of the situ-ation. *Motion Picture News* reported that "a good many of the theatres are taking advantage of this Spanish Flu season to paint up" their facilities. But not everyone found the quarantine use-ful. *Moving Picture World* reported that many theater owners were upset that they had to close when "department stores are crowded, the sale of soft drinks has not been interfered with, and the public transportation systems are permitted to crowd their patrons into far closer and less sanitary contact than ever existed in the motion picture houses."

Most Hollywood stars made it through relatively unscathed. They had the money and means, even with a work suspension, to keep buying food and to stay away from the general public. Helen did not catch the flu, and spent the month at her ranch, tending to her animals and waiting for Universal to reopen.

All told, the epidemic lasted for about four months. In fact, it burned quicker than scientists could study it, and the medical world never found a cure. By the end of the year, stores and theaters and schools and churches reopened, and the American film industry was back in business. During that period, it's estimated that six hundred and seventy-five thousand people died in the United States.

The epidemic had a lasting effect on American filmmaking. This was the first time in its decade or so of existence that the industry experienced a major financial crisis. Before the epidemic began, studios and production companies were already struggling with the rising cost of production and audience demand for longer, better quality films. With ticket sales hugely (and understandably) down, filmmaking schedules set back a month or two because of the quarantine, *and* a war tax on movie admissions, smaller motion picture studios were in trouble. Some of them even shut down.

As the 1918 holiday season approached, America got a double reprieve. The flu had finally run its course and on November 11, the end of the war was declared. After a devastating war and a devastating epidemic, with Christmas approaching and businesses back open, the country was feeling cheerier than it had in a long time.

But Helen didn't have time to celebrate. She starred in three more films before the year ended. All three were Western dramas: *Captured Alive*, *The Robber*, and *Wolves of the Range*. Guns, horses, the open range. You know the deal. None of them were particularly notable except for the fact that Helen was relying more and more on her acting chops instead of her stunt work. Universal was trusting her more and more to lead a film, even if she wasn't on horseback or leaping from a speeding train.

Which made everything that was about to happen even more infuriating.

As the new year approached, all the soldiers, nurses, doctors, drivers, and volunteers who had been sent overseas started to return home. That meant that instead of a present, Santa Claus put a lump of coal in Helen's stocking. Hoot arrived from Europe right before Christmas.

Hoot had become a sergeant while he was in the Tank Corps and was honorably discharged, along with the rest of his unit. Upon his return, Universal was happy to take back an honored veteran and immediately offered him work. They gave him a contract to appear in two reel Westerns, just like Helen was doing. Maybe they thought she'd be thrilled to work with her husband now that he was back.

Helen, however, was less than pleased and Hoot felt the same. Absence, it turned out, did not make the heart grow fonder. Maybe the distance made Hoot realize he wasn't happy in his marriage of convenience; maybe Helen realized she was happier alone. Maybe it was both. Whatever the reason, Hoot's attitude toward Helen, as she diplomatically said in an interview later in life, "was quite different."

At first, they tried to make it work. Helen and her regular film crew went right back to work after the holidays, and so did Hoot. They were both so busy shooting that there was hardly time to see each other, let alone fight. In January 1919 alone, Helen shot *The Secret Peril*, *The Girl Sheriff*, and *The Canyon Mystery*, the last of which in particular was well reviewed for its "action and remarkable stunts" and "amazing thrills."

Things slowed down a little bit in February owing to a brief flu resurgence. There was another quarantine, although this one was less strict, and only about half of theaters and businesses closed down.

By the time March rolled around, Helen and Hoot couldn't stand each other anymore. The country reopened, but Helen and Hoot decided to close their marriage. It was clear that what began as a business deal no longer suited either of them, and had ceased to be beneficial for Helen for a long time. Now it was only bringing her unhappiness.

Unfortunately, they were now both under contract for the same studio, making the same kinds of movies. Sometimes, making the exact same movie. It's bad enough to have to see your ex, let alone star in a movie with them.

That month, Helen shot another Western called *Riding Wild*, sans Hoot. However, her next film, another Western called *The Black Horse Bandit*, featured Hoot in a supporting role. He wasn't the lead, that was taken by Pete Morrison, another rodeo alumnus turned Western actor.[107] But Hoot was moving up in the film world from stunt man and background rider to supporting roles.

Helen and Hoot in The Black Horse Bandit.

The Black Horse Bandit, more typical Western fare, would be the first of six movies Helen and Hoot starred in together. Helen told a journalist later in life that Hoot mostly worked as "an extra and a stuntman until 1919, when he starred in a two-reeler at Universal. From then on, he was on his way up."

Jack Ford, the director of *The Black Horse Bandit*, took a liking

---

107 The character he played in this film was named "Hugh Manville" which is ridiculously funny.

to Hoot and for the rest of the spring, cast him in supporting roles with Helen: *The Rustlers, Even Money, Gun Law, The Gun Packer,* and *Ace High*. It became clear that Ford and the upper echelon of Universal were grooming Hoot to be a star. With the increase in significant roles, Hoot finally caught the eye of Carl Laemmle himself. Laemmle was impressed by Hoot, and his status as a veteran and history as a rodeo star made him publicity gold.

For the still legally bound co-stars, none of the tension of their marriage is evident in their performances, and not just because they were silent films. Things were beginning to boil over, though.

Luckily, Helen soon got a little break and starred in a film without Hoot. *Down But Not Out* was the eighth film in the *Cyclone Smith* series, Western movies that starred Austrian actor and former circus performer Eddie Polo. She also picked up extra cash doing more product endorsements. She appeared as the spokeswoman for the Racine Auto Tire Company in numerous ads. They had a new brand of "horseshoe tires" with high performing rubber and a horseshoe pattern. What better person to sell them than the daredevil girl on horseback?

That summer however, things dried up for Helen at Universal. Even though her contract continued throughout the year, she wasn't offered any movies until September when she was given a supporting role in the drama *Loot*. It was the last film Universal ever offered her.

Now, if she had been reliably making money for Universal, what changed? Helen was still an incredibly popular star and a guaranteed draw at the box office, not to mention a hard worker with a lot of special skills that other Western performers did not possess. According to Helen, it was Hoot's attitude toward her.

After years of being the uncredited background actor while Helen's name was glittering up in lights, and being called "Helen Gibson's husband," Hoot was more than thrilled to get his turn. Helen claimed his new contract at Universal threw his ego over the top and any fondness Hoot felt toward her evaporated. *He* was the star now.

Helen said in an interview that year that "It was jealousy that turned the trick for us. Hoot was jealous of the salary I was making and the publicity I was getting and we quarreled all the time."

Soon, their arguments cropped up at work. Hoot's and Helen's dressing rooms were directly across the hall from each other. You can bet whoever set that up thought they were doing the couple an adorable favor. Ted French, another Western actor who shared a dressing room with Hoot described the fights the pair got into: "Every time Hoot came out that door he had to duck, 'cause she was sitting there just waiting for him. She'd throw anything she had handy....That old squatty Hooter, he'd just sit back and laugh at us, then he'd come out when she had nothing left to throw."

It was easy for Hoot to laugh because he was in a great position. Word around the lot was that Harry Carey, one of Universal's big Western stars, was not long for the studio. Laemmle was very happy with Hoot's work and saw a lot of potential in him, especially since Hoot was about fifteen years younger than Carey. That summer, Carey's contract was up and Laemmle decided not to renew it. Instead, he offered a cushy contract to Hoot. It was official: Hoot Gibson was Universal's new cowboy star. He starred in ten more films for the studio that year.

And Helen? Laemmle did not renew her contract, either. Why would he renew her contract when she was at odds with his new star? Hoot certainly didn't want her around.

Helen Gibson was no dummy, though. She could see the writing on the wall. Before *Loot* even came out, she accepted a contract with another studio, the Capital Film Company. Now it was clear to her that the studio was not in good shape. Helen knew they were losing money even as she signed her name. But that didn't matter. She just needed something to hold her over while she planned something bigger, and better.

It was time for Helen Gibson to get what she really wanted.

12

No Man's Woman

In the United States, at the start of 1919, things were...off.

Sure, the war was over. But that meant all the women who stepped up and took on traditionally male jobs were in an awkward position. They were expected to happily cede their space and go back home, preferably with a veteran in tow to make babies with. Of course, some women were content to do just that. Many didn't want to, however. They liked their jobs and wanted to keep them. They liked being out in the world. All the same, most women were fired from their wartime jobs.[108] When the boys came home, the girls were booted out.

To top it all off, on January 16, 1919, the Volstead Act was approved by Congress. One year hence, American Prohibition would go into effect, making all "intoxicating beverages" illegal.

---

108 The only exception being secretaries and other clerical workers. Those positions were now seen as pink-collar jobs that returning soldiers didn't want. Despite the fact that before the war, secretarial work was seen as a man's role, now it had icky girl cooties all over it.

1919 would be the last year for over a decade when people in the United States could legally drink.

Woof. No jobs and soon, no booze? This was not the way many American women envisioned the end of the war. At least they were granted the right to vote later that year, when Congress passed the 19th Amendment on June 4.[109] It was ratified a year later, in August 1920.

At this time, things *should* have been looking rosy for women in Hollywood. By now, about 90 percent of all the movies being shown in Europe and South America were American made. Within a year of the war ending, forty million Americans were going to the movie theater every week, more than making up for the wartime (and epidemic) box office slump. Motion pictures, especially feature films, were the dominant form of entertainment in the United States, more popular than stage plays, vaudeville, and concerts. Thousands of people worked in the filmmaking industry, mostly in Southern California, where there were around twenty studios in Hollywood. Eighty percent of all the movies made *in the entire world* were being shot in the Los Angeles area. The industry, on paper, was booming.

People had continued to steadily pour into Los Angeles. Hollywood, once a charming little place dotted with orchards of fruit trees, now was home to thirty-six thousand people, a *720* percent jump from 1910. Like anything when it becomes too popular, the city began to change.

The hordes of aspiring actors and filmmakers no longer looked hopeful and excited: now they looked desperate. The corner of Sunset and Gower[110] was packed with sunburnt background actors waiting for a casting call and a chance to appear in whatever Western was being churned out that day.

---

109 Of course, it wasn't until 1965 when the Voting Rights Act was passed that *all* women in the United States could be guaranteed the right to vote.

110 The masses of cowboys earned the area the name "Gower Gulch." Even today, many buildings and signs on that corner sport Western-themed decor.

Hollywood's newly formed chamber of commerce started to actively discourage film hopefuls. They released fliers and advertisements in national publications telling people not to come to Hollywood. One read,

Don't Try To Break into the Movies in Hollywood.... It May Save Disappointments. Out of 100,000 Persons Who Started at the Bottom of the Screen's Ladder of Fame ONLY FIVE REACHED THE TOP.

Under a photo of a crowd, the caption read, "Thousands buck the line on every call issued for a few movie picture extras. This is a sample of the customary massed assault on the employment bureaus resulting from an ad for a very few men and women to work in an insignificant scene. The wage is meagre for a day or night of hard work." It sounds harsh, but the chamber of commerce wasn't totally wrong. The competition was fierce and the grind to break into film was grueling.

The bigger problem was that Los Angeles simply didn't have enough jobs for all the people moving to the city. By 1920, nearly every waitress was either an actor waiting for her big break or a screenwriter exhausted from submitting her stories to studios. There were only so many restaurants and diners in the city, so the employment overflow fell to the brothels, of which there were many.

It was a tough line to walk because the chamber of commerce *did* want tourists. Well, they wanted their money. Their first order of business was convincing all the businesses on Hollywood Boulevard to keep their lights on past nine to attract customers.[111] What few orchards left were destroyed to make room

---

111 A light salesman named Otto K. Olsen came to Hollywood in 1920 to sell his wares to movie studios. To advertise, he mounted a klieg light on a swivel stand and lit up the Security Bank on the corner of Hollywood and Cahuenga. Ever since, huge lights shooting up into the sky has been a trademark of the movie industry.

for new shopping districts. Instead of serving filmmakers, stars, and studios, Hollywood needed theaters and stores to serve all the tourists coming to see the filmmakers, stars, and studios.

This is also when Los Angeles's infamous traffic problem truly began. As it continued to annex small towns, the city bloated into an enormous mass of roads. Because of the sprawl, train and trolley routes could rarely get you directly where you wanted to go. And if you did hop on, they were crowded and outdated.

More and more residents were buying cars, even though many of the roads were still unpaved. The Cahuenga Pass, which connects Hollywood to the San Fernando Valley, where Universal City and North Hollywood are, was merely a dirt road at this time. It was the third most heavily trafficked road in the whole country, with around seventy-five thousand cars on it every day.

So many nonindustry people wanted to move to Los Angeles to be close to the motion picture glamor that there was a huge post-war construction boom. A Hollywood address no longer felt distinguished, pushing many stars to move out and find houses farther afield, away from the prying eyes of tourists. Even studios began to follow Carl Laemmle's lead and build bigger lots away from the bustle and traffic of Hollywood. Some installed high walls to prevent tourists from getting in.

Just a few years before, you could walk around the city and see movies being shot all over the place. You could wander onto the property of a studio. You could bump into the biggest stars on the sidewalk, or in a diner.

Now, all over town, security was tightening. The boundaries between tourists and industry people became stark. Tabloids were a growing business, and gossip was now currency. Reporters paid telegraph company workers for any juicy bits of information they picked up at work. No one wanted to be seen doing anything scandalous, or talk to anyone they didn't trust. Actors started wearing dark glasses in public to hide their identities. The laissez-faire atmosphere of early Hollywood had come to an end.

The laissez-faire atmosphere of early Hollywood film production was coming to an end, as well. Now that audiences and theater owners alike wanted longer movies[112] with higher production value (better scripts, bigger sets, more elaborate costumes), the cost to make a feature was *quadruple* what it was in 1915. Up until this point, studios funded their features with the profits from the much cheaper to produce short films and serials. But now those weren't enough to cover the cost. ·

So, studios started streamlining and reorganizing productions. The loosey-goosey sets of the early 1910s, where everyone did a little bit of everything and people could easily learn other jobs, began to disappear. Collaborative productions were slowly pushed out in favor of a new way to make movies: the central producer system.

This system took control away from the director and put it in the hands of a producer. Instead of a director having the final say on the script, the production design, the cast, and the shooting locations, those decisions were ultimately up to the producer, whose interests aligned with the studio's.[113] Each department became isolated and stratified, with clear hierarchies and roles. Shooting schedules became strict and rigid. Every element of

---

112 Although, after having sat through enough three-hour-plus films desperately having to go to the bathroom, I think I can speak for all of us when I say that we're all set on longer films. Let's bring back the ninety-minute movie. Please. After this gallon of cherry Coke that I spent approximately thirty dollars on, my teeth are floating.

113 Studio films are still generally made like this today. This is why director's cuts of films, that is, the version of the film where the director has the final say in the edit, are so appealing to fans.

the film and each dollar that was spent needed to be approved of and accounted for.

On the surface, this sounds sensible. However, it's hard to stuff art into a box. Taking total creative control of a creative product away from the creative people making it is rarely a good idea. Every person who has ever made art knows that some things do not go according to plan. The central producer system often meant that experimentation and inspiration got tossed in the name of making the day's schedule.

Now, of course, it's good to have rails on a project. Even a rough deadline and budget can keep things from getting out of hand. There are many stories of films that became too expensive and too ridiculous before they were even shot, one of the most infamous being cult director[114] Alejandro Jodorowsky's planned 1970s adaptation of *Dune*, which spent around two million dollars in preproduction before it ran out of money. But creating strict hierarchies, schedules, and roles on a film set absolutely demolished many of the reasons women were attracted to and welcomed into the film industry in the first place. This meant, for example, that a writer could no longer easily try her hand at directing, and an editor could no longer easily get her foot in the door of screenwriting.

Over at Universal, several writers became directors, such as Ruth Ann Baldwin, Ida May Park, and E. Magnus Ingleton. At Vitagraph, there was Marguerite Bertsch, Lillian Chester, and Lucille McVey Drew. Some actors became directors, such as Paula Blackton, Ruth Stonehouse, Lule Warrenton, Elsie Jane Wilson, and Cleo Madison. Both large and small studios saw women working their way up from assistants to editors, writers, and directors. Now there was no time to learn or teach. Everyone stayed in their lanes.

---

114 In the 1970s, Jodorowsky allegedly said that he raped his lead actress while shooting the film, *El Topo*. The director has since claimed these statements were made for shock value.

The worst part, though? The central producer system meant film studios operated like corporations.[115]

The corporate world, now there was an industry absolutely steeped, drenched, marinated, soaked in thousands of years of sexism. Historian Kathy Peiss says that a "set of gender-coded perceptions and protocols" structured the early twentieth-century corporation. In advertising, newspapers, and magazines, for example, Peiss says that women formed a "small minority" and "rarely controlled these enterprises or held executive positions in them." Publishers and retailers were "predominantly male," and women comprised only about 3 percent of professionals in the big ad firms from 1910 to 1930. Corporations were looking for a staff of "college-educated, white-collar" white men. They were masters at keeping women out.

This stood in stark contrast to the film industry in the 1910s, which had more female-owned production companies than men. Compared to the corporate world, Hollywood was basically Barbieland.

Then, the central producer system came along.

Female directors began to notice that they were only getting assigned low-budget, bottom-rung pictures. They weren't trusted with the financial responsibility of a big-budget film. Most women just made the movie, and then found employment at another studio where they could work on better projects. Soon, however, more and more studios adopted the new system, and options became limited.

At first, the central producer system did more harm to the studios than good. All the top talent hated the new system from the moment it was enacted. Some star actors and directors called it the "factory method" because it was like making a movie on an assembly line. Instead of trying to make art like they were putting together Model Ts, the talent simply began to leave the studios.

---

115 Corporations and corporate law have been around since the late 1700s.

This made the independent market bloom. All those "her-own-companies" were actually ahead of the game. Soon, those adorable little female-led companies were dominating the market thanks to their star power.

This was also when the American film industry saw an effort to make Asian American films and production companies. A woman named E.L. Greer headed up the Fujiyama Feature Film Company, which adapted films from Japanese literature. The legendary Marion Wong had just created her film *The Curse of Quon Gwon*, which is still the only American film made by an all–Chinese American cast and an all–Chinese American production company. Wong wrote, directed and starred in the film, and according to the Women Film Pioneers Project, "always expressed enthusiasm for presenting Chinese culture to Westerners."

Of course, there were still challenges facing these companies. The frustrations of independent production made many stars long for their days at a studio, where work was much steadier and more reliable. Sometimes it's nice when someone else has to make all the decisions and pay for everything. But for most of these stars, it was worth the chaos to be the one in charge.

1919 was the year that Mary Pickford, Charlie Chaplin, D.W. Griffith, and Douglas Fairbanks banded together to form a corporation to control distribution of their independent films. The problem of distribution was (and remains to this day) the most difficult one for indie film companies. Even if they get the financing to make the movie, it's so tough to compete with the gigantic network of resources that big studios have for getting their movies in theaters, let alone marketing and publicity. The four stars called their company the United Artists Corporation, which still exists today.

Forming United Artists was a brilliant move because it meant that the group could make the movies they wanted to make, the way that they wanted to make them, and get them to theaters without having to change anything to meet a studio's demands.

Especially since, having to come back from a wartime slump, those demands were getting worse and worse. The "brass" at studios multiplied while all the creative members of film crews were shackled to the rigid central producer system. Studios were squeezing as much fun and artistry—the uncontrollable or unquantifiable variables—out of the filmmaking process as they could in order to maximize their profits and minimize their schedules. The divide between the studios and the star-run independent companies was now wide and deep.

Helen was thinking deeply about that divide as she signed her contract with the Capital Film Company in the autumn of 1919. Capital was on the downswing, and Helen knew it. But soon it wouldn't matter, because she was getting ready for a new plan.

Capital was quite thrilled to sign "The Railroad Girl" to make two-reel Westerns, dramas, and railroad thrillers like she had been doing at Universal. The executives thought that perhaps signing a star might perk things up a bit for them. By November, Helen was back on set and shooting. She filmed four movies before the end of 1919: *The Opium Runners, The Trail of the Rails, Daring Danger,* and *Flirting with Terror.* These were the kind of movies that Helen could do on autopilot by this point. Which was good, considering that she had big plans stewing.

The 1919 holidays were uncomfortable ones, considering the state of Helen and Hoot's marriage. At some point around this time, he moved out. It was finally time to call it quits. Once the best of friends, the two now hated each other. After seven years, Helen was happy to cut her losses and take her freedom. By the next summer, their divorce was finalized. In an interview she gave to cinema reporters, Helen said, "As long as we

stuck to rodeos and round-ups, as long as we were just plain
show folks, we were happy. Then we got into the picture game
and we struck the domestic snags." In the end, all she got from
Hoot was her last name.

1920 began with four new films to shoot. *The Clutch of the
Law*, *The Broken Trestle*, *The Golden Star Bandits*, *The Border Watch
Dogs*. They were all Westerns, with *The Broken Trestle* advertis-
ing Helen as "Filmdom's Foremost Daredevil."

She originally had signed a contract with Capital Film Company for twenty-four films. By May, only twelve had been shot
and released before they folded. Even Helen's daredevil stunts
couldn't save them. Capital had been steadily losing money,
which meant they had a tough time attracting quality writers,
which meant they had a tough time making quality movies,
which continued the cycle of losing money. It had been months
since they even had a budget for advertising. Her last few films

with Capital were released in May: *Winning the Franchise, Wires Down*, and *Terror of the Rails*.

PROMOTIONAL POSTER FOR *WIRES DOWN*, 1921, CAPITAL FILM COMPANY.

Articles about the end of Capital Film and the end of Hoot and Helen's marriage contained happy news, however. Ms. Gibson, it was announced, now "heads her own company."

Now that she was free from both her marriage and any studio contracts, it was time for Helen to make her own movies. With her company, she would be totally in charge. She could choose the crew, the writer, the director, and her co-stars. She could choose the story, the genre. For the first time in her professional life, after almost a decade, Helen Gibson had to answer to no one.

Over the summer of 1920, Helen took her savings and planned. Just before she turned twenty-eight years old, it was time to launch her production company. Never one for frills, she named it Helen Gibson Productions.

For her first movie, Helen decided to get the rights to a story by screenwriter and author L.V. Jefferson about a dancer who saves a young child who has been kidnapped and then abandoned. The father of the child, a cowboy, first scorns the dancer when he discovers her profession, only to change his tune and fall in love with her once he realizes that she's the one who has been caring for his kidnapped child. It was called *No Man's Woman*.

Helen decided to make it into a Western drama, with her in the lead role as the dancer. After churning out poorly written movies at Capital, *No Man's Woman* was a chance for Helen to make something with substance. Plus, the movie stripped her of her most famous assets: her stunts and her horseback riding skills. It would succeed or fail based solely on her talents as a dramatic actor. Helen was betting on herself.

She tapped Ford Beebe, a friend of members of her old *The Hazards of Helen* crew, to write the screenplay. Leo D. Maloney, a *Hazards* alumni, was hired to play the villain on-screen, and behind the scenes be the production manager and co-direct with Wayne Mack, a relatively inexperienced (and therefore inexpensive) director who only had one film under his belt. The rest of the cast was rounded out with Edward Coxen and Aggie Herring, two actors she had never worked with before. It was a smart move on Helen's part to mix affordable newcomers with experienced filmmakers, especially ones she had already worked alongside.

To shoot the interior scenes, Helen decided to go back to her old stomping grounds. Although Kalem Studios no longer existed, their old Glendale buildings were currently occupied by a small new company called Astra Studios, who agreed to lease her the production space. For the exteriors, Helen wanted shots of wide open scenery. The crew decided to shoot up in the Mojave Desert, a few hours northeast of Los Angeles, above what is now Joshua Tree National Park.

By the autumn of 1920, *No Man's Woman* went into production. Shooting out in the desert during October was perfect timing. The sun was beautiful, warm but not too powerful. And of course, being on set felt totally different for Helen now that she was in charge. She had finally joined the ranks of her friends and colleagues like Helen Holmes and Mabel Normand.

For the shoot, instead of her regular Western costumes, Helen got to slip into sparkling gowns with thin straps, drape a length of pearls around her neck, and have her hair shaped into a curly, stylish bob.

In stills from the movie, Helen looks surprisingly fresh-faced for a woman who just went through a divorce, started her own production company, and was making her own film for the very first time. Most producers, midshoot, look like the only thing keeping them alive is caffeine, spreadsheets, and spite. But Helen looks, frankly, great. More than anything, she looks like she's having fun. Independence always looked good on her.

By the end of the year, *No Man's Woman* was in the can. She had done it. Helen had survived the shoot and made her first Helen Gibson production. Her name, for the first time ever, would be credited on the poster in two places.

PROMOTIONAL POSTER FOR *NO MAN'S WOMAN*, 1921. TAKEN FROM IMDB.

Like many independent production companies, Helen's main problem now was finding distribution for the film. She needed someone to get it printed, put onto reels, and sent out to thousands of theaters all over the country, not to mention craft advertisements and arrange announcements in trade magazines. It's a lot of work to get a film in front of an audience. Making movies is one thing, earning enough money to *keep* making movies is another.

Fortunately, Helen connected with a brand-new, independent distribution company, Associated Photoplays. The man who ran it was named Victor B. Fisher and he had produced the first film that Wayne Mack, co-director of *No Man's Woman*, had directed. Mack knew that Helen needed distribution, and that Fisher, with a new company, was hungry for films to distribute.

There was a risk for both sides. It was the first film made by Helen Gibson Productions, and Associated Photoplays had no track record, no proof that they could sell a film well. Both sides decided to go for it, and the deal was made.

Unfortunately, when *No Man's Woman* was in postproduction, Helen began to run out of money.

As we know, Helen was already not particularly careful with her finances, so she didn't have a huge savings to begin with. She hadn't made any money since that May and so far, had been funding the entire company and production by herself. Her contract with Associated Photoplays was only for a finished film, so she couldn't ask them for help. *No Man's Woman* still needed its intertitles completed. This pushed her toward the worst mistake of her life.

Helen decided to borrow money.

Well, that alone wasn't the big mistake. The mistake was that Helen decided to borrow money from someone who was not involved in the film industry. It makes sense that she wouldn't want to borrow from any friends or filmmakers she knew. Anyone from the motion picture world would likely want some sort of stake in *No Man's Woman*. Helen didn't want anyone else involved. This was *her* movie. Plus, she didn't want the word to get out that her new company hadn't even finished one film yet and had already run into trouble. So, she took a loan from someone outside the industry.

Decades and decades later, no one has been able to figure out exactly who Florence Hoyt Stokes was. The best guess is that Helen did what many first-time filmmakers do, which is to convince some wealthy person they tangentially know (most people usually recommend a dentist) to give them the cash. It's doubtful that Stokes was a dentist, but perhaps the wife of some wealthy person that Helen was acquainted with. Helen's star power helped convince this woman to loan her fifteen hundred dollars to pay for *No Man's Woman*'s intertitles (remember, this was a silent film and those title cards were crucial).

The contract that Helen signed stipulated that she had ninety days to pay Stokes back. Ninety days to ship the film stock from Glendale to where the titles were being done in New York, finish them, and ship the film back. Once Helen had the completed film, she could deliver it to Associated Photoplays, get her payment, and repay the loan to Stokes. Easy, right?

That December, *No Man's Woman* was announced to the press and public excitement for Helen Gibson Production's first film began to build.

Ninety days should have been plenty of time. But like in many productions, there were delays. Helen did not, in fact, get the film back in time. Now she was late on her loan repayment to Stokes, and she had an even bigger problem. She still needed more money.

It's unclear exactly what Helen needed an additional forty-five hundred dollars for, but any filmmaker knows how fast movies can eat funds. Maybe the intertitles cost more than she budgeted for. Why Helen didn't hand the film off to Associated Photoplays is a mystery. All we can guess is that there was some element of the film that needed to be completed, and clearly, it was rather expensive.

To convince Stokes to give her more money, Helen decided to offer her the film itself as collateral. This was another terrible idea. Those reels were the only version of the film that existed. Associated Photoplays had not yet made prints.

As the new year began, Helen was in a bind. She was broke, and could not pay Stokes back the money that she owed, not without delivering the finished reels of *No Man's Woman* to Associated Photoplays. Fisher wouldn't pay for the film until he had it in his hands. Stokes refused to give the reels up until she got her money, and because Helen was late on her payments, wanted an *additional* fifteen hundred dollars.

By March 1922, all of the parties involved went to court because Stokes was starting to threaten that she would destroy the film. On March 18, the film trade magazines began to report the legal drama.

The case dragged on through April. Associated Photoplays claimed that they had spent twenty-five thousand dollars already on publicity and distribution contracts. Strokes said that she was "not interested in the contract between Helen Gibson and Associated Photoplays" and that she was "legally entitled to possession" of the film. Stokes refused to release the negatives directly to Associated Photoplays so they could have prints made and fulfill these contracts, unless they paid her the seventy-five hundred dollars (fifteen for the original loan, forty-five for the second, and fifteen for late fees)[116] that Helen owed her. Stokes claimed that she even sent the film to the Associated Photoplays offices, which "refused to accept them from the express company on their arrival." Why the hell Associated Photoplays wouldn't just take the movie, pay off Stokes, and take it out of Helen's payment is a mystery. As a brand-new company, with no films out, were they, too, out of money?

The judge was also confused, and citing "conflicting allegations" denied the injunction that Associated Photoplays had ap-

---

116 About $127,107 today.

plied for against both Stokes and Helen. By May, it had turned into a "three cornered suit," as *Moving Picture World* called it.

To pay her loans, Helen declared bankruptcy. Stokes got her money, Associated Photoplays got her film, and Helen, as she told a reporter, "ultimately lost everything": all control of, rights to, and any profit from *No Man's Woman*.

She spent the rest of the year selling off her possessions. Her ranch, her car, her beloved horses, and the thing she had worked so hard for—her production company—were gone.

At the end of the year, trade publications announced that Associated Photoplays had sold *No Man's Woman* to Joan Film Sales, probably to get themselves out of the financial hole the debacle had sucked them into. Joan decided to change the name of the movie and design new posters. *No Man's Woman* got an enormous downgrade to *Nine Points of the Law*.

Now you had to squint to see Helen's name. None of the posters or marketing materials mentioned Helen Gibson Productions at all.

Magazines and newspapers announced that *No Man's Woman*[117] was set to be released right after the new year. Before it hit theaters, the film got effusive praise from critics.

…a pulsating western melodrama with splendid suspense…

…well acted, well directed…grips interest…

…general excellence of production…

…a moneymaker…

Acting is praiseworthy…

Helen Gibson makes a heroine that one cannot help but admire.

…has every element of success.

Brand new box office winner…

When a picture can grip you for six full reels, it's got to have something in it and this one has…

Some called *No Man's Woman* Helen's best film.

While her masterpiece was playing to packed theaters around the country, Helen was bereft. Everything she had worked toward her entire career had dissolved. The only possessions she had left were her name and her skills.

---

117 I refuse to call it *Nine Points of the Law.*

★ ★ ★

The most devastating part of what happened to Helen was that she was not alone.

All over Hollywood, female-owned independent film companies were crumbling. A combination of post-war factors began to sap the power that female stars had wielded over Hollywood.

The first problem was with the content of many female-created films.

After the war and a deadly flu epidemic, the United States was pretty burnt-out. The roaring twenties had begun and people wanted to let loose. Skirts were higher, jazz was cranking, and American society generally wanted to have some fun.

This meant that few people were interested in seeing motion pictures steeped in moral lessons. Unless it was sexy and exciting, no one wanted to watch a moving drama about abortion, or marital abuse. This was bad news for filmmakers like Lois Weber, who had built a career on such material. She was the reformer's filmmaker. Right as the roaring twenties started, Weber was at her peak. She had even bought her own studio facilities.

Now her movies began to decline in popularity. As film historian Karen Ward Mahar says, "her morally upright films bored audiences, her crusading unwanted." Weber had a deal with Paramount to distribute her films, but in February 1921, just as Helen was about to go to court, Weber's drama *What Do Men Want?* about a faithful wife and the husband who cheats on her, was dropped. Paramount decided not to distribute it and even canceled the rest of her distribution, period. By April, her studio had collapsed.

Critics began to question the inclusion of any political messaging in films at all.

On the other end of the spectrum, you'll recall that serials were increasingly under attack from censors. At least, the really popular ones, the ones made for and by women. Censors watched society get looser and the separate gender spheres disintegrate, and they pointed the finger at movies. The strange irony of a culture getting more liberal and its media becoming more conservative.

Of course, the boards weren't totally incorrect. Serials had encouraged female independence for years by this point. The boards started to stifle the distribution of serials, asking for edits that were impossible to make. Some refused to clear a film that showed "the laying of a hand on a female character." How could the serial queens fight the bad guys without anyone touching them? Funny how these boards wanted to protect women's sensibilities, but ended up stripping them of agency.

There were outcries from censorship advocates in newspapers and magazines, blaming the recent rise in youth crime on serials. Serials had always been controversial, but now they were low entertainment that featured unnatural women and inspired crime.

Many of these demands came from clubs of rich white women who became extremely vocal after the war. They led the charge to introduce more censorship bills to state legislatures, eventually thirty-two states in all.

In 1921, cities around the United States started to ban serials. In truth, many studio heads were afraid of these clubs and these bills. The National Association of the Motion Picture Industry promised that it would support the wishes of the General Federation of Women's Clubs. The federation wanted to "protect children" by limiting what sort of movies could be shown across the country. In March, the National Association of the Motion Picture Industry adopted a list of limitations. Included on the list of things that could not be shown on screen was gratuitous violence, ridiculing authority, vulgarity, improper gestures, drunkenness, and provocative title cards. Any company or studio trying to distribute a film that did not comply would be expelled from the association.

Helen Holmes's production company, Signal, also fell apart around this time. She and McGowan had gotten divorced and with so much sexist prejudice on the financial side of film, Holmes could not keep the company together by herself. Like Helen Gibson, she was also financially devastated. She ended up taking the Warner brothers to court to get back thousands of dollars that they allegedly owed her. After it was all over, she simply gave up and quit the movie business.

Female-made comedies followed the same story. Censorship boards wanted female filmmakers to tone down the violence and the subversiveness, crucial elements for slapstick comedy. Censorship advocates began to demand the banning of films by the queen of slapstick, Mabel Normand.

Soon, Normand's production company collapsed, as well. She made a movie called *Mickey*, but her distribution deal fell through. Like *No Man's Woman*, it was a major success, some historians estimating that it made around eighteen million dollars. Yet she never did another independent production. Even the stars themselves began to lose their power.

As a way to fire back at the stars, big studios invested in "picture palaces": gorgeous theaters that attracted moviegoers regardless of what they were screening. These theaters featured velvet seats, glimmering chandeliers, marble bathrooms, and smartly uniformed ushers who brought patrons to their seats. Picture palaces, with their luscious, over-the-top glamor, were modeled on opera houses.

When the theaters themselves were the draw, and the studios owned the theaters, it became a way to bring viewers to a movie even without a big star attached. More irony, that attracting female patrons to movie theaters was what gave female stars their power in the first place.

More and more studios practiced vertical integration, where they owned the means to make the movies, distribute the movies, and show the movies. This, of course, made it even more difficult for independent companies to get their projects into theaters. If all the best and most luxurious theaters were picture palaces owned by their competitors, and those were the theaters that audiences wanted to go to, options for indies became slimmer and slimmer. And if they couldn't get their films into good theaters, why would any financers want to give them money?

The final blow came when studios remodeled themselves to attract the attention of Wall Street.

With production costs skyrocketing, and the recent box office slump fresh in their minds, some studios were having a tough time with financing. To pay for features, or big stars, or both, they needed a large reserve of money, or at least a reliable source of outside financing. The big East Coast banks, however, were absolutely not interested in the film industry. Even with all its exponential growth, Wall Street looked at the movie business as too mercurial to invest in. It was just too *weird*. Too West Coast, too loosey-goosey. There were women everywhere, for godssake.

Women in powerful positions may have been the norm in Hollywood for a while, but never on the East Coast, and certainly not in finance. Anything they weren't used to seeing, these bankers did not trust—including a female director or a producer in charge of a film set, whose job was to give orders, command people, correct mistakes—basically all work that these bankers deemed masculine. Seeing a woman director was just too much for these ignorant bankers. Executives realized that if they wanted that Wall Street money, they needed to rethink who they worked with, who they hired, and whose movies they funded.

By 1920, there were no female directors working on the Universal City lot.

Two years before, Carl Laemmle had hired a man named Irving Thalberg to design and enact stricter department separations. Laemmle wanted his studio to run like one of Henry Ford's assembly lines: a well-oiled machine with all the parts working separately. It just so happened that this new businesslike mindset ended up imposing gendered divisions of labor. Soon, all the other big studios were doing the same thing.

You can see how this works, slowly and methodically. It's not as if one day all the studio heads marched in unison out to their front gates and tacked up a sign that read NO GIRLS ALLOWED. But slowly, over the course of several years, little choices here and there, to not renew contracts, to not fund certain movies, to not hire certain people, built up.

Some stars, like Mary Pickford, had made smart business moves and were relatively safe. By creating United Artists with three of the biggest male stars of the era, she insulated herself against a lot of the problems that other female stars were facing. In turn, Pickford's chosen writer and best friend, Frances Marion, was also safe. In fact that year, Marion got to direct Pickford in *The Love Light*, a movie that Marion also wrote.

But most women weren't so lucky.

Marion Wong, creator of the Mandarin Film Company and producer, director, and writer of *The Curse of Quon Gwon*, was never able to land a distribution deal for her film. Despite early rave reviews from critics, distributors didn't think that white American audiences would like or connect to the film, especially since it did not feature any of the racial stereotypes that audiences were familiar with by this point. Essentially, because Wong made a movie that accurately reflected the lives of Chinese Americans, set in the San Francisco Bay Area, in real Chinese American homes and stores, featuring sets decorated in an authentic Chinese style, distributors didn't want it. They wanted the stereotypes.

Wong ended up having to travel around the country, coast to coast, herself to try to sell the film directly to exhibitors. Unsurprisingly, it was not a successful trip. By the time she returned to California, her uncle, who helped her finance the film, declared bankruptcy. When Helen lost Helen Gibson Productions,

Wong had just started work as a touring singer and musician. She never made another film.

In 1921, the production company helmed by Alice Guy-Blaché, the woman who started it all, was in decline. It simply could not compete with vertical integration. The next year, she returned to Paris with her two children. Like Helen, her marriage had also fallen apart. She came back home with no surviving prints of her films, and in her absence, many of them became credited to others. At forty-nine years old, she was a single mother, looking for employment without any tangible evidence of her extraordinary body of work.

All over Hollywood, it was as if women were waking up from a dream. Doors to places they helped build slammed in their faces.

When she launched Helen Gibson Productions, Helen delighted in being no man's woman. No contracts, no studios, no husband. But that freedom also came with risk. Now that her big dream had failed, she had no one to save her. Broke and brokenhearted, Helen needed to figure out her next move.

Act Three

Sincerely
Helen Gibson
12-7-17

13

Scandal and Vice

The only positive for Helen to pick out of the ashes of *No Man's Woman* was that her name was still attached to it. The success of the film showed that Helen still had star power. Not long after it was released, someone came knocking.

Spencer Productions was a brand-new company and flush with brand-new investor money. They wanted to get into the Western game, and bought a screenplay called *The Wolverine* from writer B.M. Bower, an adaptation of her novel, *The Ranch at the Wolverine.*[118] The film was about a female rancher who stands up for an innocent man accused of cattle theft, and the lead role involved lots of horseback riding and stunt work. Of course, our girl was the perfect fit.

The shoot was a new, chilly experience for Helen, as it took

---

118 B.M. Bower was the pseudonym for Bertha Muzzy Sinclair, a wildly successful author of Western stories. She began writing during her first marriage to,
as she put it, "save her sanity." Bower's first marriage was a deeply unhappy
and abusive one, and she decided to start submitting her stories about cowboys and ranch life to gain financial independence from the marriage. They
were a hit, and once she had enough money saved up, Bower was able to
leave her shitty husband. Over the course of her career, she ended up writing
fifty-seven novels, plus numerous short stories and plays. It's believed that her
books sold over two million copies. The best part? Her final marriage was to a
cowboy who was the love of her life, her very own sexy cowboy protagonist.

place in the mountains north of Los Angeles. *The Wolverine* was described by film journalists as "glittering through the great land of snow" and featured gorgeous shots of wintery scenery. Throughout much of the film, Helen is wrapped in thick coats and white fur hats. It was likely the first snow she had seen since she was a kid in Cleveland.

However, thanks to the cold and the distance from the city, the shoot for *The Wolverine* was a grueling one. Long days on set are bad enough when it's warm, let alone when you're freezing your butt off. Snow removal adds time and logistical issues to a production. Plus, snow and ice bring safety concerns, with the need to keep everyone warm and avoid slippery terrain. Film journalists reported that ten horses had died during filming, from both accidents and issues from the cold.

PROMOTIONAL POSTER FOR *THE WOLVERINE*, 1922. SPENCER PRODUCTION COMPANY. TAKEN FROM IMDB.

Overall, the shoot was bittersweet for Helen. Just six months before, Helen was in charge of her own company, her own movie, her own shoot. Now she was back to being a hired gun.

Worst of all? The distributor that Spencer Productions decided to partner with was none other than Associated Photoplays. *No Man's Woman* was making money for them, so it made sense that they'd want another Helen Gibson Western, especially one that had already been paid for and completed. Helen had no say in the decision, and it must have stung to see the words "brought to you by Associated Photoplays" underneath her face on the poster for *The Wolverine*.

When the film was completed, the executives at Spencer Productions were pleased with Helen. They loved the movie and guessed that it would be a hit (it wouldn't be released for another few months). They were so pleased, in fact, that they wanted to get her under contract. Spencer Productions offered Helen four hundred and fifty dollars a week, nearly *quadruple* the one hundred and twenty five she had been making at Universal, about seven hundred and thirty-nine thousand dollars a year today.

This was the most money she had ever been offered in her film career, by quite a large margin. Yet it felt a little hollow. Signing this contract was settling for less than she really wanted. It was a lot of money, sure, money that could restart her life. Even so, it was a step down from the glory of independence. Helen, however, didn't have much choice. She needed to get back on her feet. She signed.

By 1921, Prohibition had been in effect for a year, and the reality of the law had finally sunk in for Americans. "Dry" politicians and activists campaigned on a platform of getting rid of saloons and drunken crime. Many people had voted in favor of Prohibition without really understanding that it meant *all* consumable alcohol was banned, for *everyone*. But now everyone had to live with it.

As soon as Prohibition started, illegal bars sprouted up all over the country. They were all over Los Angeles, an estimated two thousand of them, from grungy dives to glamorous speakeasies. The Hollywood drinking scene thrived during this period.

Cocktail lore says that the classic Brown Derby, a mix of bourbon, honey, and grapefruit juice, was invented at a speakeasy on Sunset Boulevard. Whether it was at a secret club or a party at a luxurious mansion, stars regularly guzzled alcohol. The new law didn't slow the hard partiers down one bit.

Even though there was plenty of bootleg booze to be found in town, Prohibition opened the door for other vices to enter the film industry. Drugs, from morphine to cocaine to opium, had always been a part of the underground Hollywood party scene. But with quality alcohol becoming harder and harder to get as Prohibition continued, many stars looked to other substances to untether from reality.

This became another factor that contributed to their loss of power. The same year Prohibition went into effect, the big Hollywood scandals began. In fact, for the next several years, there was a constant string of shocking incidents that wore the shine off the stars.

At the end of the summer, actor Olive Thomas died of what is believed to be an accidental drug overdose. Just a few months before, she had starred in *The Flapper*, a film written by Frances Marion about a teenage girl living in a small town who yearns for excitement and becomes a flapper. Thomas was the first ever to portray a flapper girl on screen. She and Marion were responsible for popularizing the term for the new wave of young American rebel girls who bucked tradition and turned their backs on social norms for femininity. The actor was in Paris with her husband (actor Jack Pickford, Mary's brother) when, as the story goes, she accidentally drank a medication containing mercury, believing it to be a sleep aid and passed away in a hospital a few days later.

Newspapers quickly saw how coverage of Thomas's tragic death sold heaps of papers. They went wild with the story, churning out unfounded speculation and immediately sensationalizing her death. Soon, it was alleged that Thomas had died not from a terrible accident, but from consequences of alcohol and drug-fueled "orgies," or murder by Jack Pickford, who wanted her money. So it was that Olive Thomas's death became one of the first big Hollywood scandals.

The story added gasoline to the fire that censorship boards had been stoking about the immorality of Hollywood. The American public began to eagerly inhale outrageous tales about the sins of the stars and the newspapers raked in the profits.

The next year, the story of Olive Thomas's death was overshadowed by an even bigger scandal. Allegedly, at a Labor Day party in San Francisco, actor and model Virginia Rappe was assaulted by comedian Roscoe "Fatty" Arbuckle, and died several days later from internal trauma. (Follow this footnote for details.[119] Skip if you find it too upsetting.)

The American press instantly erupted with speculation. Arbuckle went through three separate manslaughter trials and was acquitted in each one. Some witnesses gave compelling evidence in support of or at least exonerating him, such as Rappe allegedly suffering from chronic cystitis or STIs, or both, that would have contributed to her death, and that his primary accuser was a woman who had a police record for blackmail and extortion. Some witnesses gave compelling evidence against him, such as his reputation as an alleged predator. Actor Gloria Swanson went on the record after the trials, saying that "nobody in town ever thought he was all that innocent."

It's likely that the truth of what happened to Virginia Rappe will never be fully known.[120] Though he was acquitted three times, the American public had made up their minds on Arbuckle. Even without the grisly death of Rappe, people read about Arbuckle's partying, illegal drinking, and "lewd conduct" and decided that he was not fit to be a star. The affair annihilated his career, despite the fact that before it began, he had just signed a historically lucrative contract with the Famous Players–Lasky studio.[121]

William Randolph Hearst, one of America's first (maybe first

---

119 It's alleged that Rappe had been violently assaulted, which resulted in a ruptured bladder and internal inflammation.

120 Some historians believe that she actually died from complications from an abortion.

121 After directing films under a pseudonym, a descent into alcoholism, and a brief attempt at an acting comeback, Arbuckle died in 1933.

ever) media moguls, said that the Arbuckle scandal "sold more papers than any event" since the tragic sinking of the *Lusitania*. Newspapers all over the country ran stories of the sordid goings-on in the film industry, from illegal booze to drugs to sex to murder, and readers lapped them up.

Not even six months after the horrible death of Virginia Rappe came the murder of director William Desmond Taylor, a director working, coincidentally, with Famous Players–Lasky. In February of 1922, his valet arrived at his Los Angeles bungalow to find Taylor dead on the ground with a gunshot wound in his back. The night before, Taylor had been visited by his good friend Mabel Normand, and authorities believed that he was shot sometime after he walked her to her car. Although to this day, his murder has never been solved, the American press quickly turned the story into a lurid sex scandal.

Millions of papers were sold that claimed Taylor was embroiled in a bitter love triangle between Normand and young actor Mary Miles Minter.[122] At the scene, the police found scented love letters that Minter had sent Taylor, and allegedly, a slinky piece of lingerie.

Yet, it's widely believed today that Taylor was gay, and trying to redirect Minter's unrequited crush. Normand wasn't involved at all, aside from the fact that she and Taylor were close friends. But the papers turned the murder into a salacious affair, where either Normand or Minter shot Taylor out of jealousy, or hired a man to do the deed. Reporters dug into the lives of both women and revealed secrets, particularly Normand's cocaine addiction. Some papers, like the *Chicago American* (owned by William Randolph Hearst) made even wilder claims, such as Taylor had been murdered by a gay Hollywood sex cult.

Despite the fact that both women were cleared by the police, again, the American public had already made up their minds. Minter, who was famous for playing sweet, innocent protago-

---

122 Say that five times fast.

nists, had her career destroyed. Audiences didn't accept her pure on-screen persona once they knew that she drank and partied.

Normand's career was already in decline, and this scandal was the final nail in the coffin. She made a few more films, each one receiving lots of publicity and support from her colleagues, particularly Mary Pickford. But the damage was done.

After the Taylor murder, beloved actor Wallace Reid's addiction to morphine was made public when his wife checked him into a medical facility to get help. The media turned it into a scandal.

At this point, American readers didn't need any more proof. Hollywood was full of crime, sin, and immorality. Now it was at the center of a culture war.

The stock market was flourishing and many people (white guys) were getting rich quick. There were new technological marvels all over the place and the public was urged to buy them: nicer cars, new radios, and telephones. The war was over, the economy was booming. People were encouraged to spend, spend, spend, and consumer culture was rampant. The migration from rural areas to cities went into overdrive. Millions of Americans were leaving agricultural life and rejecting tradition.

Activists and reform groups blamed the cultural shifts, from feminism to flappers to the spread of jazz, on the influence of the film industry. Censorship advocates were now practically foaming at the mouth to bring Hollywood to heel. For too long, they felt, the American film industry had gone unchecked.

After the jarring discovery that so many of their favorite actors were real people and not actually their pure, heroic on-screen personas, the public felt distrust toward them. With tarnished reputations, many of them, such as Mary Miles Minter, could no longer be counted on to draw crowds at the box office. Guaranteed box office draw had been the driving force behind the power of the stars and star-owned independent companies. Without it, they had no leverage over the big studios. You know, the same studios that were actively in the process of getting rid of their female filmmakers.

Women in Hollywood at the start of the 1920s were caught between a rock and a hard place. They could either go down with the ship of independent companies, or submit to the demands of studios and the central producer system. For many actors, the choice was quite clear. Studios still needed actors to make movies, and were happy to hire them as long as they played by the new set of rules. For directors and screenwriters, they were lucky if they were offered jobs at all.

Some female filmmakers made movies outside of the system, to varying degrees of success. In 1922, Tressie Souders had her film *A Woman's Error* distributed by the Afro-American Film Exhibitor's Company, which was based in Kansas City. There was also Maria P. Williams, who produced and starred in her own film *The Flames of Wrath* the next year. Coincidentally (or maybe not), Williams also lived in Kansas City. Her husband was the manager of a movie theater, and she was the assistant manager. The pair also worked for the Western Film Producing Company and Booking Exchange, for which she was the secretary and treasurer and he was the president. Through the Exchange, Williams was able to get limited distribution for the film. *The Flames of Wrath* is considered a lost film, but historians believe it was written and produced by an entirely Black crew.

Without the structural support of Hollywood, however, most of these independent female filmmakers never made more than one or two films. Souders and Williams each only made one film. And with Hollywood becoming increasingly unwelcome to anyone who wasn't white and male, their work went unnoticed by the industry.

The Wild West era of American film was coming to an end. The time when female filmmakers had the freedom to shoot their own movies and take charge of their own careers was disappearing before their very eyes.

Between censorship boards across the country attacking what was on screen, and newspapers across the country attacking what was behind the scenes, Hollywood needed some public relations help, badly. Once censorship bills started to reach a federal level, several studio heads got together and realized that if they didn't get some sort of internal censorship system in place that the federal government would come in and dictate what they could and could not do.

So, the Motion Picture Producers and Distributors of America was born on March 10, 1922.

The MPPDA began essentially as an industry protection organization. In order to appeal to and placate conservative censorship boards, it appointed Christian Republican and former postmaster Will H. Hays as their first chairman. Hays had a sterling reputation in conservative circles and the studio heads figured that if he was speaking for them, censorship boards might back off a little. Hays's job, to the public, was to "clean up the pictures." It was now his responsibility to fight censorship bills and convince the government that Hollywood could regulate itself.

Cartoon by Cy Hungerford depicting Will Hays poised to rescue the film industry.

For his new Department of Public Relations, Hays went straight to the film industry's biggest critics to recruit. The International Federation of Catholic Alumni doesn't seem like a hot breeding ground for Hollywood PR talent, but Hays figured if he could appoint people from those types of organizations, the censors would trust him.

What Hays didn't account for was that—and now, this might come as a shock—many censors were not in it for the good of the nation. They made a nice salary, about two hundred dollars a month, which is about thirty-six hundred dollars in 2023. It certainly wasn't Hollywood money, but being a censor was a pretty cushy gig: you got to watch movies all day, cut and reedit them as you saw fit, even rewrite their intertitles. Not to mention the power you had. Censors didn't truly *want* to be placated.

Even with Hays in charge, censorship boards continued to trouble the studios. In turn, the studios tried to protect themselves by making "safe" movies and keeping their casts and crews under strict control.

With the stars losing their power, studios no longer needed to cater to their wants and needs. Stars now needed to fully cater to the wants and needs of the studios. Studios cranked out more and more formulaic movies, and stars were now typecast into roles that were difficult to break free from. Actors either became strong heroes or evil villains, innocent maidens or sexy vamps, with little to no say in the matter. They were rarely even shown the screenplays ahead of time. Why bother? It wasn't as if they had the power to change anything.

This period was also the beginning of what became a staple of the studio system: the seven-year contract.

Signing with a studio, whether it was Universal or Paramount or Warner Brothers, meant they controlled your career: what roles you played, what press you had to do, how many days or hours you worked a week. And you were exclusive to that studio; you couldn't do a movie with anyone else. To top it off, it was good for seven years. That really meant seven active years, as in seven years of business days. Holidays and weekends did not count. If you didn't want to do a role the studio assigned to you, they could suspend you without pay. If they got tired of you, they could suspend you without pay. Since you weren't working, the studio could add the length of your suspension—weeks, or months, or years—to your contract. Howard Suber, film history professor at UCLA told *Vanity Fair* in 2020, "It was essentially a form of indentured servitude. These contracts gave all of the advantages to the studio and made it nearly impossible for stars to have a say in their careers."

Even Greta Garbo, who eventually became so famous and successful that she was allowed creative power on her films, originally was shaped by studio heads. Our old pal Irving Thalberg, who moved from Universal to the newly formed Metro-Goldwyn-Meyer (MGM), liked the look of her screen test. With her angular looks, he cast Garbo in sexy, sophisticated roles against her will. She used to complain to Thalberg that she was "just a young girl" (she was only nineteen at the time), but he ignored her protests. By the mid-1920s, female stars and filmmakers, if they were lucky to get work at studios at all, were simply employees.

Even though censorship boards were at war with serials, audiences still loved them. And studios wanted to keep making money from those fans. So, they tried making serials in a conservative way: with squeaky-clean male heroes.

Serials were now the domain of cartoonishly gallant male heroes. *The Adventures of Bill and Bob,* which starred two actual Boy Scouts on their adventures hunting animals in the woods, was about as far from *The Perils of Pauline* as you could get.

Studios tried everything to make serials work. They tried making Westerns that focused on beautiful scenery. They tried "exotic" locations in Europe, Africa, or Asia to interest audiences. They tried adapting popular stories like *Tarzan.*

Despite their best efforts, within a few years, serial profits were drooping. Audiences were just not interested. Serials became popular because of the thrills they provided, the boundaries they pushed. Offering fans a safe, conservative version was like giving your teenager a Kidz Bop CD instead of a Lil Nas X album.

Studios finally began to give up. By 1924, Universal announced that they would be cutting the amount of serials that they made in half.

But what about the old serial queens? Without serials, what were they doing?

Well, they were doing what they did best. Hanging on for dear life.

With her contract signed, Spencer cast Helen in another film right away.

They had purchased the rights to a novelette by author George Rix called *The Girl in Gopher City* and wanted to turn it into a Western. The story was about a woman and her sick father who hide out in an old desert mining town from a group of bootleggers who mistakenly believe that they are federal agents. After *The Wolverine*, what would eventually be called *Ghost City* seemed like the perfect follow-up. The shoot was set to begin in April, 1921.

However, like a cruel joke, on April 1, Helen started to feel ill with a rapidly worsening pain in her abdomen. Before she could get to the hospital, her appendix had burst. Soon, Helen's condition worsened and became peritonitis. It was clear that she was in no condition to work. When someone from Spencer called the hospital to ask about her recovery timeline "the doctors were angered and told them I was lucky to be alive" according to Helen. After all her dangerous stunts, Helen's closest brush with death came from an organ the size of a finger.

Spencer didn't want to delay the shoot, and quickly found a replacement. In a reversal of how Helen started her career, the producers at Spencer Productions cast Helen Holmes in *Ghost City*'s lead role.

For all the same reasons why Helen was perfect to take over *The Hazards of Helen*, Holmes was perfect to take over in *Ghost City*. Even six years later, the two women were the same size, with the same color hair, and faces so similar they could be sisters. While Helen was still fighting for her life in the hospital, *Ghost City* went into production.

She wasn't mad at her friend, though. It seemed like a great solution. Truly no one on earth was a better fit, and Helen assumed that once she was healed, she could start fresh on the next Spencer film.

It took her two full months to recuperate from the burst appendix and the peritonitis. By the first of June, she was feeling good and ready to return to work. Helen went to Spencer Productions, ready to resume her contract.

When she arrived, Helen was told that her contract was canceled.

They no longer wanted her. Just a couple months before, Spencer had offered her a cushy contract, and now, after one medical scare, they were rescinding it. They didn't offer her a different contract, or any more films.

Helen was, understandably, furious. Both parties had signed that contract, after all. She decided to take Spencer Productions to court.

The trial began that August, with Helen suing for breach of contract. She pointed out that there was a clause that ensured she could return to work after sickness or injury. For an actor known for her stunt work, it was common for Helen to ask for these sorts of clauses.

While the case made its way through the system, Helen tried to revive her production company. With, she assumed, ten thousand dollars coming her way soon, she could buy new production facilities and start making a new movie. Helen partnered with another independent production company to get everything off the ground.

It was a bad move. The company ended up folding before the film could be finished, and Helen injured herself during a horseback stunt.[123] In December, she was back in the hospital, waiting for word on what was happening with the lawsuit.

To literally add insult to injury, *The Wolverine* had finally been released to rave reviews. Crowds of Helen Gibson fans lined up outside theaters, stood underneath gigantic signs that featured her name even bigger than the title of the film…all while she was broke and embroiled in another legal battle.

MARGARET HERRICK LIBRARY

Stymied again, Helen had to spend Christmas couch surfing with friends. She was worse off than when she started working in Los Angeles. No other production companies came to offer contracts, and there was no hope of getting back in the serial

---

123 We can assume the film was another Western, but the story and information about what stunt Helen injured herself during is unknown.

game. The roles for which she became known were no longer offered to women.

Helen's case against Spencer Productions was finally settled out of court, for less money than she wanted. Spencer claimed that it was Helen Gibson's old pals at Associated Photoplays that canceled their distribution contract for her films, forcing Spencer to cancel their own contract with her. The same company had screwed her twice. *Ghost City* did not end up being a successful film anyway, and Spencer never made another.

What the judge awarded Helen wasn't enough to cover the debts she had from one final attempt at her own production company. She told a reporter years later that she had to sell what little she had left, her car, her furniture, even her jewelry.

Helen was in a tough spot, along with many of her friends. Hoot's career was still on the rise at Universal, yet he wouldn't help. She said that he "avoided" her. In fact, a month after Helen had settled her case, Hoot was already getting remarried. In a move that would drive historians absolutely bananas decades later, Hoot wedded a vaudeville performer named Helen, who took his last name.[124]

Our Helen Gibson tried to soldier on. She organized some paid appearances across the country in the wake of *No Man's Woman* and *The Wolverine*. These events were usually held at theaters or rodeos, and her fans were always thrilled to see her. But news of her financial situation had begun to spread in Hollywood. All those lovely film gossip columns reported that she was bankrupt, had no assets, and was twenty-four thousand dollars in debt.

Helen continued to tour, introducing screenings of the two films and talking to audiences about her work. She spoke to audiences from California to North Dakota to Wisconsin. After dazzling stories of big stunts, Helen told everyone to remember that when they watched her movies, it was really her up there.

---

124 If you're wondering whether or not this made my research a living hell, you're correct.

"No doubles, and no dummies." She stood in front of the crowd, hiding her broken heart behind a megawatt screen star smile.

When she returned to Los Angeles, finally, an offer came. Roberson-Cole, a studio hanging on the bottom rung of the Hollywood ladder, wanted her to star in a Western called *Thorobred*. She agreed to the role, but it was no career saver. The film was made for a very low budget, and received barely any press. It was released in November of 1922 and it was Helen Gibson's last starring role.

When 1923 began, she was not offered any contracts. By the end of spring, there were no jobs, no offers, no leads. At thirty years old, she was broke, with no career prospects. So, Helen did what many of us do when times are tough.

She made things even worse by getting into a shitty relationship.

Film historians don't know much about William E. Smith, other than that he was good with horses and bad with women. What we do know is that Smith worked at a stable in Los Angeles that provided horses for Westerns, so it's easy to figure out how he met Helen. He was a Texas native, and seven years older than her. We don't know what he looked like. Hopefully he was at least handsome. It's easy to imagine how Helen, at the lowest point of her life, could be charmed by some jerk with the promise of stability.

Helen and William Smith were married in Los Angeles by a justice of the peace on May 22, 1923. Helen was now Helen Gibson Smith.

Unfortunately, Smith showed his true colors quickly. Fortunately, Helen left him almost as quickly. Within two months, the pair separated. By November, the divorce was official. In her only statement to the press about it, Helen said that, "He kept a houseful of bootleg booze. He used to get drunk frequently, and when he did he made life unbearable for me. He called me names, and accused me of misconduct with other men. I couldn't stand it any longer, and we parted." After that, she never spoke about him in public. Sorry, Helen, for bringing it up.

She might have been at rock bottom, but she still knew her worth. Helen shed his last name, and reverted back to Helen Rose Gibson.

That August, she turned thirty-one years old. Twice divorced, career in tatters, she looked out at a changed Hollywood. It had been twelve years since she first started as a background rider in Topanga Canyon. She had seen her name up in glittering lights, illuminating the eager faces of the crowd that had come to see her and get their hair raised by the most daring girl in motion pictures. Now she couldn't even get a callback.

One of the most crushing aspects of losing this magical period of the film industry is that these women didn't have any perspective on what was happening. There was no social media, no Twitter to post on. From a historical distance, we can see the misogynistic connective tissue in all these events. Being shut out of finances, censorship boards, the restructuring of studios to attract Wall Street.

But Helen couldn't see that.

She could only see that the industry had changed greatly, not that there were multiple systems in place working to make sure that she didn't succeed. She just felt that she had failed, individually.

That's how these systems trick you, anyone who is marginalized. They make you think you're not good enough, that you just don't have what it takes, that no one wants you. Looking at the situation from a long lens, you can see all the obstacles put specifically in place to stop you. Up close, however, it seems like the only person to blame is yourself.

For Helen, it was time to take a break. While her colleagues tried to rally a comeback in Hollywood, she decided to return to where it all began.

14

The Sound of Change

Ever since she was a teenage girl, fresh from her factory job and off on adventure across the plains, the only thing Helen Gibson could ever really count on was her own abilities. Her daring and her riding talent caught the attention of the managers of the Miller Brothers 101 Ranch, of Hollywood producers, and eventually, of the movie audiences of America. So, when everything crumbled around her, Helen decided to, quite literally, get back on the horse.

The year before, when she was touring the United States doing appearances for *No Man's Woman* and *The Wolverine*, Helen stopped in to see some old friends at the Miller Brothers 101 Ranch. She really enjoyed being there. It reminded her of a time when life was a little less stressful. Maybe, she thought, it was a good time to step away from Hollywood.

So, when the biggest circus in the world came knocking, Helen answered.

A few years previous, Ringling Brothers and Barnum and

Bailey had merged into one megacircus. When the 1920s began, the "Greatest Show on Earth" was flourishing and decided to add a Wild West exhibition. To do so, they needed trick riders. Even though Helen had been out of that world for a long time, her skills had not atrophied. If anything, she had learned a few new tricks in all her years shooting serials and Westerns. She no longer held any of her rodeo titles, but Helen Gibson could still ride with the best. And the American public still knew her name.

In the spring of 1924, at thirty-one years old, Helen ran away with the circus. She signed a two-and-a-half-year contract, and that April it was time to hit the road.

It was a good time to be getting back in the game, since historians refer to the 1920s as the "golden age" of rodeos. The shows were wildly popular with war-traumatized American audiences and made a ton of money.

Helen traveled all over the country to perform for gigantic, enthusiastic crowds. With all the hustle and bustle of riding and traveling, she didn't have much time to think about and dwell on everything that had happened over the past few years. Life was just her and a horse and the wind in her hair, with Hollywood a mere glittering speck on the horizon. It was therapeutic to quite literally get some distance from the film industry, and reconnect with what made her happy. Most importantly, to reconnect with what she was good at. Helen was reminded that she had talent, something the capriciousness of Hollywood can make you forget. She was in control, even if it was just over her breath and the trick she was about to do.

Helen was often recognized during the tour, and when the season was over in November, instead of bunking in the Ringling Brothers and Barnum and Bailey winter quarters, she continued to make paid appearances. Theaters hired her to introduce screenings of her films and speak to audiences about "the thrills and dangers of picture making."

What she didn't realize was that everything about picture making was about to change.

★ ★ ★

When Helen went off to the circus, Los Angeles was strug-gling to grow up, scrambling to get its infrastructure to the point where it could support the people still pouring in. Although Hollywood was one of the cultural capitals of the world, East Coasters still considered it a backwater town. The lack of big buildings certainly didn't help.

In the mid-1920s, however, it finally started to develop a sky-line. Office buildings, apartment complexes, and grand hotels shot up all over town. The legal height limit was twelve stories, so they certainly weren't skyscrapers, but Los Angeles was begin-ning to look the part of a major metropolis. Some of Hollywood's famous modern landmarks, like the Roosevelt Hotel and Musso and Frank's Grill, were now open to serve the rich and the famous.

This was also a time of frenzied studio expansion. Almost all of them had morphed into huge corporations and moved to loca-tions with bigger, grander offices and huge stages and back lots. A decade before, most studios were a collection of one-story build-ings alongside a dirt road. Now Fox Studios occupied a space that was big enough to shoot twenty movies at the same time.

In 1923, Hollywood's most famous landmark went up: the iconic sign. Despite its association, it had absolutely nothing to do with the film industry and everything to do with sell-ing property. The owners of a subdivision in the Hollywood Hills wanted to attract new buyers. One of the builders, a man named Harry Chandler, figured out a dramatic way to draw attention. He spent twenty-one thousand dollars to buy colos-sal metal letters, fifty feet high and thirty feet wide, get them painted white, and installed them on the side of the hills. Four thousand light bulbs were installed and when the sign was lit up on a clear night, you could see it from miles away. They spelled out HOLLYWOODLAND.[125]

---

125 The LAND was removed a couple decades later when the sign was restored
   and repaired.

Over on Hollywood Boulevard, another landmark was under construction.

Along with his business partners Mary Pickford, Douglas Fairbanks, and Howard Schenck, businessman Sid Grauman wanted to build a grandiose picture palace. The building was designed with Chinese aesthetics, including carved ceilings, murals, giant columns, and the now legendary facade. On November 11, 1925, Grauman brought Chinese American superstar actor Anna May Wong to drive the first rivet into the steel girders that would become the Chinese Theater.

Aside from being the most famous place in the world to premiere a film, the theater is an important part of Hollywood lore because of an accident. While there are a lot of legends, the real story is that one day in 1927, when construction workers were pouring cement, Grauman accidentally walked through a patch. He looked down at the imprints his shoes made, and got an idea. He called Mary Pickford, Douglas Fairbanks, and Norma Talmadge, and when they arrived, he asked them to add their footprints alongside his. Unfortunately, the cement was nearly dry and the impressions were quite faint. So, he asked the trio to come back a few weeks before the grand opening. This time, the three stars pressed their handprints as well as their shoe prints into the cement in the theater's fore court, and a Hollywood tradition was born.

The changes in Los Angeles were not all glamor and glitz, however. By this time, Los Angeles had become a racially segregated city. Certain neighborhoods, particularly the ones filled with rich white people, decided to make themselves off-limits to the growing Black population. Some councils drew up contracts forbidding land or property from being sold or leased to anyone who wasn't white.

All-Black neighborhoods started to form, and so did organizations for Black creatives. The Ink Slingers was created in 1926 for Black writers. One member, Fay N. Jackson, covered the Black entertainment scene in Los Angeles, and ended up founding *Flash*, the first Black West Coast news magazine. The town was full of Black talent, and there was no shortage of actors, writers, dancers, singers, and directors. But the promise and excitement of the early days of film, when all-Black indies like the Lincoln Motion Picture Company launched, were over before they could really start. The problems that plagued white female filmmakers were tenfold for Black filmmakers, particularly the women. Getting financing and distribution was almost impossible.

Many Black actors broke in by getting hired for service or background work. Some, like Ethel Waters and Carolynne Snowden, were able to get through and become stars. Snowden, for example, was hired to teach jazz dancing to white actors. One of her early roles was in Lois Weber's film, *The Marriage Clause*.

Just like white Hollywood was building grand hotels and theaters, the Black community in Los Angeles was, as well. The Hotel Somerville (soon renamed the Dunbar Hotel) was located in what today is the Historic South Central neighborhood. Designed in a gorgeous Art Deco style, the Dunbar Hotel quickly became the center of Black entertainment in Hollywood. Count Basie, Langston Hughes, Billie Holiday, Duke Ellington, Louis Armstrong, and Lena Horne all stayed and performed there. The hotel opened in 1928[126] and hosted the first ever national convention for the NAACP. Financed by members of the local Black community, and created by Black workers and craftspeople, for a long time, the Dunbar was the only major hotel in the city where Black guests could stay.

Over at the studios, the restructuring sparked by Irving Thalberg was paying off. Movie companies began to be listed on the

126 The Dunbar was built by historical power couple Vada and John Somerville. Vada was the first Black woman in California to become a doctor of dental surgery at USC, a university from which John was the first Black person to graduate.

stock exchange. By 1926, it was the fifth-largest industry in the United States. Filmmaking was officially a big business.

Thalberg's methods were now standard, and formulaic movies were churned out to maximize their overhead. Every single film followed the same flowchart. A story came out of the scenario department and was approved by the producer. The producer assigned a budget to the story, and decided who would make up the cast and crew. If they were famous, the director might be allowed to fiddle with the screenplay. The producer then gave the screenplay to all the various departments, sets, costumes, props, etc. Once all the elements were ready, usually in a few weeks, the movie went into production.

This was when continuity clerks or, as we call them today, script supervisors, were born. The continuity clerk was a key part of the crew and monitored each scene to make sure everything in the screenplay was being captured on camera. Producers didn't want improvisation, changes, or new ideas.

Directors were now sought after for their ability to dominate, a quality that Cecil B. DeMille thought "rare in men and almost absent in women." In fact, despite female directors like Weber and Blaché who innovated many groundbreaking camera techniques, *who were his contemporaries*, DeMille believed that the technical and mechanical parts of directing a movie were "outside a woman's mind."

Once the film was shot, it went through the postproduction timeline, which involved editing the footage and adding intertitles. The finished product, once approved by the producer, was sent to the distributor. Prints were made and sent out to all the theaters owned by that studio. One huge assembly line, from start to finish.

Some studios, like Famous Players–Lasky, even hired Wall Street advisors to assess their business for maximum profits. Bankers and investors sent representatives to oversee operations and make sure films were being made in the most efficient (and profitable) manner possible.

The only departments where you could still find women were writing, editing, and costume design. Of all of them, it was the female screenwriters who hung on the longest. Historian Karen Ward Maher believes it was because writing was "often paid poorly and was chronically disrespected."

This might be why, when Weber tried to mount a comeback in 1925, Carl Laemmle put her in charge of the story department at Universal. Remember, Weber used to run one of the most successful production units at his studio. The next year, she was finally able to convince Laemmle to let her direct again, but it was a short-lived victory. Within a year, Weber was reversing the advice she gave to girls earlier in her career. She now told young women to avoid getting into filmmaking. She thought it was a waste of their time and effort.

For Grace Cunard, who used to make some of the most popular films in the world, she never directed again after 1921. Soon, even lead acting offers dried up and she was bumped down to supporting, then background and uncredited roles until she gave up and retired. One of the last films she made herself was a short called *The Man Hater*, about a woman who is sick of men and decides to go live in a cabin in the woods as a hermit. This is how most female filmmakers were feeling right about now.

Helen Holmes continued making films for a little while, trying to utilize her fame. But since no one wanted to watch censor-friendly serials, eventually, she gave up, too. The serial queen retired in 1926 and opened a dog training business.

The next year, 1927, Mabel Normand made her last film. The queen of slapstick and the woman who launched Charlie Chaplin's career was forced to retire in her early thirties.

Some women continued to hold on. Mary Pickford opened up her own studio space with Douglas Fairbanks (who was now her husband) and with United Artists, she still produced and starred in her own successful movies, some of which were written by Frances Marion.

But while some female filmmakers were battling to stay in Hollywood, there were no newcomers to bolster their ranks. Women of all ages were still traveling to Los Angeles, but the opportunities had dried up. The only options left were acting, designing or sewing costumes, and maybe writing or editing if they were lucky.

With the old filmmaking system, women could help other women and bring them into the fold. Frances Marion started out as Lois Weber's assistant, Mabel Normand got Helen Holmes her first job. Now, with stringent divisions, even if a woman became a costumer or a writing assistant, it was almost impossible for her to move into any other department, especially not to a position of power.

Every female filmmaker that gave up was a light that went out. These women had witnessed Hollywood grow from an orchard into a metropolis. They had gone from empresses ruling the city to bloody shield maidens fighting for their lives. And the year Helen returned to Los Angeles, one last blow was about to cut them off at the knees.

When Helen's circus contract expired, she decided not to renew it. In the fall of 1926, she encountered a traveling show outside of Boston made up of Native American performers, members of the Hopi nation in Arizona. They had just appeared before Congress to protest a law that forbade tribes from performing native rituals and dances. To drum up support, the group decided to get on the local vaudeville circuit and give performances to Americans in Massachusetts.

For whatever reason, they decided to hire Helen Gibson. From advertisements of the show, it seems like the group wanted Helen to introduce them and speak to the crowds about their mission. Maybe the group hoped that her fame might help convince audiences that these rituals and dances did not pose any harm. Helen happily accepted. She'd march out on stage in front of a packed theater in her two-gallon hat, boots, and fringed leather skirt, and regale everyone with a history of the Hopi people before the group came on to perform.

After a few months, however, Helen felt like she was ready to return to Hollywood. Fortified by three years of rodeos, traveling, and speaking to adoring crowds, it was time to try and get her career back.

Since its inception in the early 1900s, movies had advanced so much. Longer runtimes, better cameras, more interesting stories and shooting techniques. Film was still a silent medium, however.

Until someone had a wild idea: Why not add sound?

In the 1910s, wireless telegraphs existed, although they weren't exactly household technology. Soon, manageable (and affordable) transmitters and receivers were created, and radio stations started popping up all over the United States.

Once you got a radio, it was an endless supply of free entertainment (plus some ads, of course). You could listen to a live concert, live theater, live news, even live play-by-play sports. By 1925, 19 percent of the country owned one. Turns out, Americans really loved sound.

It was only a matter of time before a studio capitalized on the new trend. In 1926, Warner Brothers began working with a team to create a new system of sound-on-disc, where a wax record filled with a recording of sound effects, music, and dialogue could be synchronized with the film projector. That year, they released a romantic adventure film called *Don Juan*, directed by Alan Crosland and written by Bess Meredyth, with the new technology that Warner Brothers called Vitaphone.

Despite skepticism from critics, other studios, and prominent filmmakers, *Don Juan* was a huge hit. It made almost 1.7 million dollars and was easily the biggest film Warner Brothers, which was a smaller studio at the time, had ever made.

Even with the success, many in Hollywood thought it was a fluke. Mary Pickford was famous for saying that "adding sound to movies would be like putting lipstick on the *Venus de Milo*." Louella Parsons thought it would be a one-off, and Irving Thalberg thought it was a cheap gimmick that would be forgotten.

The folks at Warner Brothers knew that they were onto something, though. The next year, they made *The Jazz Singer*, directed again by Alan Crosland and written by Alfred A. Cohn. The film starred the hugely popular Jewish singer Al Jolson, which should be your first indication that something was amiss. Jazz music was already being widely appropriated by white singers and musicians. The story follows a man who defies the wishes of his religious family to become a jazz singer...and performs in blackface.[127]

The Jazz Singer was the first major feature film to incorporate dialogue as part of the action and it was an instantaneous, megasuccess. It made nearly double the money that *Don Juan* did, vaulted Warner Brothers to major studio status, and more importantly, started a revolution in the film industry. The future of film was clear: sound was here to stay.

Every other studio had to scramble to get sound or risk falling behind. The only problem was that no one fully realized that the addition of sound would change almost everything about how movies were made and screened. Jolson's now famous line from *The Jazz Singer*, "You ain't heard nothing yet" was the perfect harbinger of how the film industry was about to be turned upside down.

For a sound film, writers needed to create dialogue, not just lines here and there for the title cards. This totally altered the way films were written. Although women were being booted out

---

127 Jolson became famous by imitating traditionally Black styles of music, like blues and jazz, for white audiences.

the door, there were still some female screenwriters, and a few of them were hugely influential on these new types of screenplays.

At a time when slapstick and physical comedy were under attack from censors, comedic actors could now make audiences laugh with their words, not just their actions. Anita Loos, who would become colossally famous later in life for both the book and the film *Gentlemen Prefer Blondes*, was one of the smartest comedy screenwriters during this era. She's known as the inventor of the wisecrack.[128]

> Have you got the nerve to tell me you don't want to marry my son for his money?
> It's true.
> Then what do you want to marry him for?
> I want to marry him for YOUR money.

Aside from their writers, studios had to completely reevaluate their pool of acting talent. Thick accent? Fired. Unpleasant voice? Fired.

Some actors couldn't transition. Huge stars like Norma Talmadge, Lillian Gish, and Gloria Swanson were all forced into early retirement. Of course, it was no coincidence that this came at a time when studios were happy to get rid of stars who didn't want to follow orders.

Because early microphones had to be stationary and hidden in furniture or plants, actors were forced to stay close to them to get their voices recorded. Any big gestures would mess with the sound, which majorly restricted their movements. Actors had to change from an acting style where all emotion was conveyed through movement to an acting style where they could not move much at all.

---

128 Her films, which often featured whip smart female protagonists, were sometimes co-written with her friend Frances Marion.

Silence was now essential on set, and doors were often locked to keep people out. With all the hot lights, no air conditioning or fans (too much noise), and the Los Angeles heat, indoors shoots were now stuffy and uncomfortable.

Background actors, who previously could chat and whistle and do almost whatever they wanted, had to stay quiet. Crowd scenes were tricky to organize, especially if the producers wanted to pick up the noise of the crowd but not drown out the noise of the leads. Carl Laemmle's studio tours were ruined until he figured out how to either keep the public quiet or away from active sets.

Most film equipment at this time was rather loud. Cameras especially had to be dampened. Technicians rushed to redesign them, along with lights and other equipment, to be completely silent.

Sound even shook up movie theaters. For one thing, all the musicians who worked in the orchestra pit were out of a job. For another, movie patrons, who previously could hold quiet conversations with their friends, had to pipe down or miss the plot.

Even though audiences had to keep quiet, they couldn't get enough of the "talkies." Within a year of the release of *The Jazz Singer*, three hundred theaters across the country were wired for sound. By 1930, that number had grown to ten thousand.

Movie attendance skyrocketed. In the mid-1920s, about fifty million people went to the movies every week. By the end, it was one hundred and ten million.

And in the middle of all of this, Helen Gibson was trying to get her career back.

She returned to Los Angeles a few months before the release of *The Jazz Singer*, so she had a little bit of time to get settled in before everything went haywire. After getting a small place in Burbank, Helen started reaching out to friends and old colleagues to try and drum up some work. Thanks to the years on the rodeo circuit, she was in fantastic shape and ready to take on anything. Thrillers, Westerns, this former serial queen was willing to do it all.

The only problem was that no roles were offered.

At thirty-six years old, she wasn't the kind of baby-faced ingénue that studios were looking for. Most female characters in action movies got romanced and rescued, or the other way around. They were no longer allowed to beat up bad guys or put themselves in harm's way. The sort of stunt-heavy work she was famous for simply didn't exist anymore.

Most of her friends and colleagues were gone. The rise of sound films completely killed off Lois Weber's attempt at a comeback. Frances Marion had gotten her a job at United Artists, rewriting and punching up scripts, but that didn't last long. She made her last picture in 1934, and then opened a garden center.[129] Helen Holmes left the dog training business and started running a small antique shop out of her home. Mabel Normand was forced to retire, and got tuberculosis a few years later at the age of thirty-six. Mary Pickford tried to fit into the new world of sound films, but even she, one of the great titans, only made four sound films before she retired from acting.

Helen still had her skills, and didn't really want to open an antique shop or a garden center. She wasn't ready to give up just yet. So, she did her best to do what so many others couldn't.

Helen Gibson adapted, and became the one thing she always swore she didn't need.

---

129 She died, completely broke, of a stomach ulcer in 1939.

15

The Golden Age of Hollywood

So, here we are with the studio system, vertical integration, central producers, the seven-year contract, and almost every female filmmaker pushed out of the industry.

Welcome to the Golden Age of Hollywood.

This really is the moment that film historians mark as the beginning of American film's "Golden Age." Seems pretty grim when you're looking at it from a different point of view, huh?

Why is it called the Golden Age? Because this is when many classic Hollywood movies were made with iconic stars. Here was the age of *Gone with the Wind* and *The Wizard of Oz*, of Clark Gable and Cary Grant, Greta Garbo and Shirley Temple.

By this point, studios had almost total control of the industry. The "Big Five" were Metro-Goldwyn-Meyer, Paramount, RKO, Warner Brothers, and Fox, which would soon merge with Twentieth Century Pictures to become Twentieth Century Fox as we know it today. The "Little Three" were Universal, Columbia, and United Artists. What separated the Big

from the Little was vertical integration and the seven-year contract. Columbia, for example, produced films, but didn't own
a line of theaters. MGM, the biggest of them all, was a massive
empire that owned every part of the filmmaking process, from
the scripts all the way to the theater seats.

Every studio lot was its own kingdom. Following in Carl
Laemmle's footsteps, studios became little cities, with barbers and
doctors and stores and schools. For safety, most had their own firefighters and security.

With their star actors fully controlled, studios could comfort-
ably bolster and exploit their fame without worrying about them
becoming too powerful and leaving to create their own companies. Each of the Big Five had their own stable. Sometimes,
they rented out stars to smaller studios for a fee.

MGM, as the biggest and most powerful, also had the most
impressive roster. Clark Gable, Jean Harlow, Laurel and Hardy,
Spencer Tracy, Lon Chaney, Judy Garland, Joan Crawford, Greta
Garbo, and Buster Keaton, just to name a few. At their peak,
MGM shot sixteen to eighteen movies at a time on six differ-
ent lots, with a total of forty cameras.

Their biggest rival was Twentieth Century Fox, which had a
smaller stable of stars (including Shirley Temple and Betty Gra-
ble), but had a deal with Rogers and Hammerstein to make film
versions of their Broadway hits.

Warner Brothers had a smaller, but still impressive stable that
included Humphrey Bogart, Errol Flynn, Barbara Stanwyck,
and Bette Davis. However, their highest-earning star couldn't
even talk. Rin Tin Tin, a German shepherd who was found
and rescued on a battlefield by an American soldier, and trained
for movies, made more money than anyone. He ended up starring in twenty-seven adventure films, and helped make Warner
Brothers a continued success.[130]

---

130 He is also the reason why German shepherds became a popular breed in the
       United States.

Along with a new type of comedy, whole new genres came about with the advent of sound, musicals being the most prominent. Warner Brothers became known for them, which paved the way for them to produce animated musical films, like *Merry Melodies* and eventually *Looney Tunes*.

American animated films, however, were just beginning to appear on the scene. The grand majority of films were live action, and for that, the studios wanted the brightest stars.

Talent scouts roamed the country, from major cities to small towns. Theater productions were popular scouting grounds, along with nightclubs and beauty contests. Lana Turner was famously discovered at her job as a clerk in a lingerie shop. If a scout spotted someone they thought had the looks or the talent to merit consideration, that person got an invitation to come to Los Angeles, all expenses paid, for a screen test.

It would end up being two tests. The first was just a silent test for looks, and then a second for their voice. If they looked and sounded good, that's when the whirlwind really began.

The actor would be offered a contract, probably of the seven-year variety, and upon signing, the transformation would begin. No matter what gender someone was, the studio decided what their hair looked like, how they dressed, what their teeth looked like, how much they should weigh. Clark Gable had to get all his teeth replaced before he was given any roles. Like the Cowardly Lion in *The Wizard of Oz*, stars got primped and prodded and shaped and dyed until the executives were happy.

Sometimes, studios even involved themselves in stars' social lives, deciding who they were seen with and who they dated. If a studio didn't like who your partner was, you couldn't marry them. Sometimes phony romances were set up between stars for publicity. If a studio didn't want you to have a baby, and you got pregnant, it was time for a secret, fully funded abortion. There are legends of studios monitoring the menstrual cycles of actors to make sure they weren't getting pregnant.

If you had a health issue that the studio didn't want becoming public, they would find a way to hide it. If you committed a crime, say drunk driving or a fight at a bar, people from the studio rushed in to cover it up. If the problem was big enough, or the star caused too much trouble in public, or refused to take the offered roles, that's when suspensions came in. The seven-year contract had a "justifiable cause" clause, which meant that studios were both judge and jury when it came to stars' behavior. If you were suspended, not only could you not act in that studio's films, but you couldn't act in any films. In fact, you couldn't work at all. You weren't even allowed to become a waitress or a sales clerk. There was no actors union yet, and with so much competition from thousands of hopefuls pouring into the city every day, many actors took what they were offered without argument.

Besides the depressing reality of what was happening behind the scenes, the Golden Age of Hollywood truly was a glamorous time. All the glitz that those words evoke: draping furs and flowing silk, strings of pearls and curls of smoke drifting up from cigarette holders, top hats and shining waves of hair, martini glasses, and convertible coupes.

And the city itself had finally caught up to the glamor of its stars. Roads were being paved, electric lights were being installed everywhere, and the boulevards started to fill with one of the most iconic symbols of Los Angeles, the palm tree.

Since palm trees were associated with exoticism and dreamy trips to otherworldly places (everything Hollywood now stood for), the local government thought they'd be perfect to plant all around town. An unemployment relief program was created in the 1930s, and four hundred unemployed men planted forty thousand Mexican fan palms across one hundred and fifty miles of streets. The gently waving fronds helped sell the illusion of Hollywood, the fantasy land. Journalist Jen Carlon wrote "The History of How Los Angeles Became A City of Palm Trees" for

LAist in 2016 and said, "The city is one gigantic backlot, and the palm tree its most convincing prop."

The way Los Angeles looked in 1927 was closer to what it looks like today, almost a century later, than the way it looked just twenty years before.[131] For Helen, it was a strange, new world, with strange, new rules.

"My hopes of a comeback in railroad melodrama or Westerns were not fulfilled..." Helen wrote later in life. "When I returned to Hollywood, I found most of my friends and former stars working as extras and bit players. I just stuck my pride in my pocket and did the same thing." The former serial queen decided to take "character parts and extra work, and in fact took anything I could get." It was time for her to return to being a stunt double.

For years prior, film audiences complained about stunt doubles because they wanted to see "real" actors "really" doing the scenes. This didn't stop filmmakers from using them, though. Many actors did not possess those kinds of skills, and even if they did, studios certainly didn't want their stars getting injured. So, stunt doubles were kept a secret. For a long time, they weren't even credited. This long-held prejudice is the biggest reason why there isn't a category for Best Stunt Work at the Academy Awards, because many studios don't want to advertise that the actors aren't actually doing the stunts.

However, as Helen knew quite well, stunt work is artwork. The skill it takes to not just do the jump or the fall, but to do it in a safe yet cinematic way, is simply incredible. The acting talent, the physicality, the strength, the creativity. Whole genres of film, like action adventure and Westerns, simply would not exist without stunt people.

In the early, early days of film, some directors tried using

---

131 The last big Hollywood landmark, the Walk of Fame, didn't get added until 1953.

dummies instead of people for dangerous stunts, and it immediately became apparent that unless you're going for comedy, you can't use a dummy. Even in the 1910s, audiences could tell that the floppy shape flying across the screen wasn't a real person.

So began Helen's long, second career as a stunt double. She landed bit parts and small speaking roles here and there, but stunts became the meat and potatoes for the rest of her professional life. She stunted for all sorts of female stars, for just about every studio, and almost every genre. Helen was in indie films and huge studio movies. Her skills were undeniable, and she ended up doubling for lots of actors, especially comedians and character actors like Marie Dressler, Louise Fazenda, and Edna May Oliver.

Whenever she went through a dry patch, it wasn't because no one wanted to hire Helen. It was because there were no roles. In this new version of Hollywood, there just wasn't much action and physical comedy for women to play. And when there was, sometimes producers felt more comfortable dressing up a man in a wig and dress to do the stunt instead, even though there were available stuntwomen.[132]

Stuntmen made typically twenty to thirty dollars a day, with stuntwomen making a bit less than that. It was a far cry from the four hundred and fifty a week that Helen had been offered before, but it certainly beat waitressing. Stunt people didn't usually get contracts. Instead, they worked on a picture to picture basis. Stunts was, however, a tight community, and good stunt people (the men, at least) got steady work. Many had a specialization, either fights or horses or falls, and then as cars began to be incorporated into movies more and more, chases and crashes.

When she couldn't land a studio gig, Helen often did work for a small production company called Republic Pictures. It was the

---

132 The earliest tally I can find is from the July 1938 issue of *Silver Screen* magazine, which contains an article by stuntwoman Frances Miles, who says she has about thirty-six colleagues in Hollywood.

merger of several tiny indies—Liberty, Monogram, and Mascot, to name a few—with a central office in the San Fernando Valley north of Los Angeles. They cranked out low-budget genre films like mysteries and Westerns with a small crew. At the bottom of the ladder, their stable of talents was mainly actors and stunt people who had been working since the days of silent film.

When the crew at Republic prepared for a shoot, a stunt coordinator looked over the script and planned how to do all the stunts. At this time, this was always a man, since women were not allowed to work up to this position. Many stunt coordinators were (and are still) stunt people who are getting too damn old to do stunt work. This meant that stuntmen had a longer career path than women did. When stuntwomen got too old, too bad. Take up gardening, maybe.

Once production started, it was usually split into two units. The first unit had all the principal actors, and shot all the main scenes and dialogue. The director was in charge of this unit. The second unit was all the landscape photography, stunt scenes, and anything that didn't involve the lead actors. The second unit usually had a smaller crew, fewer cameras, and a separate director who answered to the main director. (This is still true today.) It was the second unit that Helen usually worked with.

In film, costs are either above or below the line. Those above the line are involved in the creative development of the movie, like directors, producers, and stars. Those below the line are the ones responsible for actually making the movie, as well as pre- and postproduction. This is sort of an ugly distinction that diminishes the essential contributions of those who are below the line, but it's standard industry speak.

Helen had crossed back over into a different world, from above to below the line.

So many female filmmaking titans were gone, and only a handful still battled to stay. Sure, there were lots of megawatt female stars, but few of them had any real power. The ground had been taken.

Mary Pickford was still producing films at United Artists, even though she had retired from acting. Frances Marion had a lucrative contract at MGM for a while, but left eventually (and independently wealthy) to write plays and novels. Anita Loos also worked at MGM in the 1930s, but followed Marion to write plays and memoirs. Loos said, of the early era of Hollywood, "In those days we made movies for fun and when it stopped being fun, I just got out."

Around this time, rumors of unions started floating around. So much money was being made by the motion picture industry, and very little of it was going into the pockets of the laborers who made the movies possible. To get ahead of the movement, Louis B. Mayer, co-founder and producer at MGM, decided to create an organization that would "recognize and uphold excellence in the motion picture arts and sciences"...but really, its purpose was to solve labor disputes without unions. And so the Academy of Motion Picture Arts and Sciences was born. Of the thirty-six filmmakers who made up the founding members, only three were women: Mary Pickford, Bess Meredyth, and Jeanie MacPherson.

Soon, the members started discussing the idea of handing out awards for various aspects of filmmaking, like directing and writing and acting. On May 16, 1929, the first ever Academy Awards ceremony, aka the Oscars, was held at the Roosevelt Hotel in Hollywood. Errol Flynn served bootleg liquor to guests in a back room.

There were fewer categories back then, only Outstanding Picture, Best Unique and Artistic Picture, Best Directing (Comedy), Best Directing (Drama), Best Actor, Best Actress, Best Writing (Original), Best Writing (Adaptation), Best Art Director, Best Cinematography, Best Engineering Effects, and Best

Title Writing (there were still some silent films being released). Not a single woman was nominated, except for Best Actress.[133]

The only exception in this barren, female-filmmaker-less wasteland was Dorothy Arzner. Aside from Lois Weber's ill-fated comeback attempt, Arzner was the sole female director working in Hollywood in the 1930s and early 1940s. She was an out lesbian[134] with short hair and tailored trousers. Even though Arzner was a wildly talented director, the reason why she was allowed into the boy's club is a mystery. Maybe they just saw someone in a pair of pants and got confused.

Arzner snuck into Hollywood right as the gates were closing. She started out as an assistant at Paramount Studios in 1919, trying out a job as a set dresser before she got work in the script department. She then moved to editing, and finally realized that what she wanted to do was become a director.

Paramount liked her work as an editor, so they let her try reshooting some scenes for the 1922 film *Blood and Sand* that weren't working. Arzner took her new footage, cut it together with stock footage, and ended up saving the studio a whole lot of money.

Her work on *Blood and Sand* attracted the eye of Paramount director James Cruze, who asked her to join his team, and write and edit for him. After a few years of this, Arzner realized it was time to step up. She told the executives at Paramount that if they didn't let her try her hand at directing again, she'd move to a different studio. They relented and in 1927, she directed her first feature, *Fashions for Women*.

Arzner's films are particularly special because they are mostly about unconventional romances. Love triangles, affairs, and most importantly, lots and lots of female sexual agency. Her 1932 film,

---

133 So yes, the Oscars have always been a little depressing.

134 Although she ended up in a forty-year relationship with film choreographer Marion Morgan, Arzner is rumored to have dated stars like Joan Crawford and Katharine Hepburn. This isn't historically relevant, but it is impressive.

Merrily We Go to Hell, features an open marriage. As film writer So Mayer says in her 2015 piece for the British Film Institute, "Dorothy Arzner: Queen of Hollywood," Arzner wanted to make films where women became "their own people, rather than beautiful possessions." Many of her movies showed the benefits of "rejecting the heterosexual contract because of the miserable dependency on men," as writer Jane Gaines says in her 1992 piece "Dorothy Arzner's Trousers" for *Jump Cut* magazine. In the era of the studio system, the fact that Arzner was making these movies at a major studio is nothing short of a miracle.

She even directed Paramount's first talkie, *The Wild Party*, making her the first woman to direct a sound film in Hollywood. Arzner was also the first to join the Directors Guild as a full member (although it would be quite a long time before another woman joined her). Adept at nurturing talent, she helped launch the careers of both Katharine Hepburn and Lucille Ball.

Aside from the incredible, baffling exception of Dorothy Arzner, however, things were pretty grim for women in Hollywood. Then, another disaster struck. In October 1929, a few months after the inaugural Academy Awards ceremony, the stock market crashed.

For the past decade, the United States had been enjoying a huge postwar economic boom. Within a span of two months, however, the roaring twenties came to an abrupt halt. The prices on the New York Stock Exchange popped like a party balloon. Soon, everything collapsed and the entire American banking structure crumbled in on itself.

By the end of the year, foreclosures were everywhere. Banks failed. Businesses closed. The stock market crash of 1929 was the catalyst needed to kick off what became known as the Great Depression.

At first, the Great Depression was devastating for Hollywood. Studios were still in the process of converting all their stages and theaters and production facilities over to sound, and most had invested huge sums of money into the process. And on a consumer level, in the initial fallout of the crash, everyone was afraid to spend money on anything nonessential, like movie tickets. Box office numbers plummeted.

Eventually, the studios couldn't pay anyone. It seemed like the glittering castle of Hollywood would fall. The major studio executives got together with the Academy to figure out what to do, since one of the core functions of the Academy is to "act as a mediator in disputes among various groups involved in film production." With studio heads still living in mansions and many of their laborers not receiving payments, this certainly counted as a "dispute."

The, ahem, "solution" they came to was that all studio employees take a 50 percent cut to their salaries for a few months. With so many millions of Americans out of a job, they figured it would be better to keep the industry going on a shoestring budget than let it collapse completely. Actors had to take a pay cut, as well. But none of the executives were included. Huh, weird!

Anyway, the studios promised their staff that they would receive the other 50 percent of their money when the economy was better. Yep, just keep working and we're definitely, absolutely going to pay you. Uh-huh.

Not a single studio kept this promise.

The only good thing that came of this was it made a lot of workers, both actors and craftspeople involved in film production, very, very angry. Angry enough to start forming unions and guilds. By 1933, the Screenwriters Guild (which would eventually become two guilds, the Writers Guild of America West and the Writers Guild of America East) was formed, and two months later was followed by the Screen Actors Guild. The first labor organization to wrest recognition from the major studios was the International Alliance of Theatrical and Stage Employees, known as IATSE, which included electricians, camerapeople, painters, and carpenters. (And still does.)

The formation of a union is almost never a bad thing, but in Hollywood it became another closed door for women. The spread of unions and guilds made it even easier to bar them from certain parts of the industry. If women were not allowed to join a particular union or guild, and studios agreed to only hire members of those unions or guilds...you see the problem here.

Eventually, box office sales began to rise again. Americans, broke and depressed, turned to film to lift their spirits. People cannot be without a form of escape for long, and movie tickets were still the cheapest method. Cinema became essential to the nation's mental health. President Roosevelt said, "During this Depression, when the spirit of the people is lower than any other time, it is a splendid thing that for just fifteen cents, an American can go to a movie and look at the smiling face of a baby and forget his troubles."

This is when the practice of selling popcorn, candy, and soda began in movie theaters. These cheap (for the theaters to buy, anyway) refreshments greatly increased theater profits. Next time you pay approximately two hundred dollars for a popcorn and a Coke, you can thank the Great Depression.

Western films survived the silent/sound changeover, and became extremely popular during this time. People longed for the "good old days" when the United States was glorious and well, not in the middle of an economic collapse.

Ol' Hoot was doing well for himself, having also survived the transition into sound, and was still making Westerns for Universal. He got divorced in 1929, because the new Helen Gibson charged him with "desertion," claiming that he had not been home with her and their five-year-daughter in over a year. Hoot didn't contest it, and claimed that he had stopped coming home because of fights over his busy filming schedule. Make that two Helen Gibsons who were happily divorced from Hoot.[135]

---

135 Hoot got married for a third time the next year, to another actor named Sally Eilers. He was thirty-six, and she was twenty-one. Stay classy, Hoot.

★ ★ ★

So, it seemed like almost all the forces that pushed women out of the film industry had won. Financial conservatism, rigidity of structure, the formation of sexist unions and guilds. Now it was time for censorship to have its final victory.

In 1927, the MPPDA approved Will H. Hays's request to move his public relations office closer to the action. He wanted it right on Hollywood Boulevard so he could keep a closer eye on the movies being shot in the area and offer advice to the producers. If he thought they were shooting scenes that might upset the censorship boards, he'd consult with them to find an alternative.

The producers were not particularly happy to see a Goody-Two-shoes like Hays creep up on their film sets, and mostly ignored his advice. The thing was, Hays didn't actually have the authority to make any changes. All he could do was shake his finger and tell producers that the censorship boards would get them. As the public relations officer, it was his job to placate the censors, but the censors were the ones with all the power. Hays wasn't wrong, of course. The censors did often flag those scenes, and studios ended up spending millions every year in wasted film and review costs.

When the stock market crashed, and the surviving banks came in to bail the studios out, they wanted to protect their investments. They didn't want to see millions of dollars being wasted, or their products being boycotted by conservative groups. The studio executives now needed to mollify both the bankers and the censors, so they decided to give Hays some power.

A committee of men from his public relations department drafted a list of "general principles" that films had to abide by. It stated that "no picture shall be produced which will lower the moral standards of those who see it" and that the "sympathy of the audience should never be thrown to the side of crime, wrongdoing, evil, or sin." A list of subjects not allowed to be shown on screen included:

Surgical operations

Lustful embraces

Excessive or lustful kissing

Sexual dances

Suggestive gestures

White slavery (but other types of slavery were A-OK)

Sex between races

Childbirth

Obscenity, even by suggestion

Profanity

Complete nudity

Ridicule of any religion

Disrespect of the American flag

And the "treatment of bedrooms must be governed by good taste and delicacy" because even the sight of a bed was too much. "Scenes of passion" must be essential to the plot.

The MPPDA looked at this ridiculous list and said, "Yeah, sounds good." On February 17, 1930, they unanimously voted to adopt the "Code to Govern the Making of Talking, Synchronized and Silent Motion Pictures." This mouthful was eventually shortened to simply the Code, or the Hays Code. Within two months, all the studios were submitting their movies to the MPPDA for approval.

The problem was that the censorship boards were not accurate representatives for most Americans. It was the Great Depression and people were goddamn depressed. They didn't want wholesome, bland films. They wanted exciting, provocative, fun movies that pushed boundaries. MGM released the rather spicy film *The Divorcee* that year to enormous success. It starred Norma Shearer as a woman who, upon finding out her husband has cheated on her, decides to "balance the accounts." They end up divorcing, with the famous words, "From now on, you're the only man in the world that my door is closed to."

So began the "pre-Code" era, the four years between the

creation of the Code and the creation of the Production Code Administration, which had the power to force studios to comply.[136] It's rather misnamed, since technically the entire history of American cinema up to this point was the pre-Code era. But the term "pre-Code" specifically refers to movies in this four-year period, when the studios came up with interesting ways to get around the Code and attract audiences to their films.

Which is when the magnificent Mae West reigned.

West came from the theater world and didn't try her hand in Hollywood until 1932, when she was thirty-nine. With the advent of sound, many studios were turning to the stage to recruit talent, and Paramount was quite happy to scoop up the curvy, blonde beauty with the husky voice. She was known for her controversial plays that dealt with sex, feminism, and gay rights. Her 1926 play *Sex* caused her and the entire cast to be arrested. She ended up being the perfect figure (pun intended) to bring sexuality to pre-Code Hollywood.

West's film debut was a supporting role in the drama *Night after Night*, which she only agreed to because the producer let her rewrite her dialogue. Her new lines made her an instant scene stealer. In one part, a young woman at a coat check counter is admiring West's jewelry and exclaims, "Goodness, what beautiful diamonds!" West quickly replies, "Goodness had nothing to do with it, dearie." Throughout her career, West was known for her hilarious and sexy one-liners.

An instant hit at Paramount, the studio immediately put her in a starring role. Her next film was *She Done Him Wrong*, based on one of her plays about a sultry barroom singer who gets caught up in a crime ring.[137] With West's censorship-proof innuendos and powerful screen presence, the film became a colossal suc-

---

136 Much is made of the "saucy" pre-Code era, but truly, the films that were being made in the silent era were in some ways much saucier. No one was showing boobs in pre-Code films.

137 Hollywood legend says that West launched Cary Grant's career with this movie by insisting that he be one of her co-stars.

cess, and *She Done Him Wrong* ended up saving the studio from bankruptcy.[138] Now Mae West was an American sex symbol.

Audiences simply couldn't get enough of her. Within a year of her starting in Hollywood, West was one of the biggest draws in the industry. By 1935, she was the highest-paid woman in the country.

If she'd been working in the late 1910s, Mae West would have been able to create her own production company and be entirely in charge of all her films. But now, she had to be content to write them. She quickly figured out ways around the censors and put outrageously sexual lines in her screenplays, knowing that they would be cut out of the final film, while other, slightly less sexual lines were left alone. West was the writer of many famous quotes, including, "It isn't the men in your life, but the life in your men."

Her films were always about bold, sexual women getting what they wanted out of life, usually sex and diamonds. She said, "No guy was going to get the best of me. That's what I wrote all my scripts about." But eventually, much to the dismay and disappointment of audiences all over, one man did get the best of her.

In 1934, the MPPDA formed the Production Code Administration. The PCA was tasked with the enforcement of the Code and doling out fines to theaters that screened films that broke it. A man named Joseph Breen, a strict Catholic, was hired to run the organization. He declared that "The vulgar, the cheap, and the tawdry is out. There is no room on the screen at any time for pictures which offend against common decency." All films released after July 1, 1934 had to comply with the Code.

West's films contained heaps of lustful kissing, heated embraces, sexual dances, and suggestive gestures. They were her bread and butter, and fans ate it right up. But soon, with the fear of the PCA on their minds, studios, including West's bosses

---

138 There is a lot at Paramount named after her because of this.

at Paramount, started reining in their films. Her bawdy humor and sexual characters were just not possible under the Code. By 1943, she had given up and left Hollywood for a very successful career performing in theaters and nightclubs.

Despite the best efforts by some to mount a comeback, the powerful women of Hollywood had been defeated.

The year before, twenty-four-year-old actor Peg Entwhistle jumped from the *H* in the HOLLYWOODLAND sign to her death. As film historian Bruce T. Torrence writes in his book *Hollywood: The First 100 Years*, "To many Hollywood signified the highest hopes, the ultimate attainment," but to Entwhistle "it spelled only shattered hopes, defeat, despair." Entwhistle had come to the industry as a lauded stage actor and hoped, but was unable to, repeat her successes.

Of all the great serial queens, the only one still working was Helen Gibson. In 1932, she turned forty years old, the great (and unnecessary) age divide for actresses. In some ways, it was lucky that she was working mostly in stunt roles, because the stunt coordinators didn't care how old she was, just as long as she could do the stunts.

Although she wasn't ready to quit film, Helen decided it was time to say goodbye to the rodeo. At the end of the year, she made her last appearance, as a featured rider in a small show north of Los Angeles. Afterward, the legendary champion hung up her gear for the very last time. It had been twenty-three years since a teenaged Helen had hung over the fence at a rodeo in Cleveland to watch the riders gallop around the ring, sparking a desire that shaped the course of her entire life.

This retirement came at an apt time. By now, with the counter swing of conservatism in America that followed the wild and roaring twenties, bold and brave cowgirls were being replaced by beautiful "rodeo queens" at events across the country. Cowgirls were not considered "womanly enough" to be featured in most shows.

Helen decided to focus the working years she had left on Hollywood. Full of her signature grit, Helen Gibson had outlasted almost all of her colleagues and friends. As a stuntwoman, in some ways, she was still delivering her beloved thrills. But it was a pale imitation of what once was. After a long fight, the serial queen had given up on reclaiming her career and her stardom. She just wanted to keep paying her bills, and settle down.

That included getting married again. Third time's the charm.

In August 1935, right before her forty-fourth birthday, Helen said "I do" to a man named Clifton Johnson. We don't know how she met a handsome boatswain, or how long they dated, but we do know that Helen really loved him. He was ex-navy, and worked on an oil tanker that traveled along the Pacific Coast. They must have met while he was on shore leave in Los Angeles.

The wedding was held at her home in Burbank, near the Los Angeles river, in a quiet leafy neighborhood. Helen and Clifton had an evening ceremony, surrounded by a small group of friends.

Working on an oil tanker, Clifton was used to being away for weeks at a time for work, so Helen's erratic work schedule didn't faze him. They had to delay their honeymoon by a month or so because they would both be away for work. The newlyweds ended up driving down to San Diego, then up to San Francisco.

The year before, Helen had returned alone to Cleveland to attend the funeral of her mother. In all those years, she never talked publicly about her relationship with her sisters or her mother. We'll never know what she thought of them, or them of her. Helen had chosen to shape and define her life in ways outside of family and children.

Speaking of, at forty-three years old, it was clear that she and Clifton weren't going to be having kids. There's a possibility that with all her career injuries (especially the scary battle with peritonitis) that she wasn't able to. There's also a possibility that she just didn't want children. Maybe the fact that she didn't have children and never talked about having them is enough of a statement on the matter.

Luckily, Prohibition had just ended, so at least she could have a stiff drink to dampen the emotions of returning to her hometown after her star in Hollywood had fallen.

The next decades passed like Helen was a ghost, haunting her own career. She was in the village scenes in *The Bride of Frankenstein*. Her stunt work was used in Westerns with popular cowboy performers like Gene Autry and Roy Rogers. She had a bit part in *Winds of the Wastelands*, with rising star John Wayne. Helen was in the same places, doing the same things, but now, she was barely seen.

In one of Wayne's biggest films, *Stagecoach*, considered the best Western ever made, you can see her in the saloon. Helen's wearing a similar costume to her character in *No Man's Woman*, except this time, she's not saving anyone. She's just a patron, adding atmosphere to the scene.

SCREENCAP FROM STAGECOACH.

Paramount, Universal, Columbia, MGM, RKO, Fox—Helen worked at them all, bearing witness to the great "Golden Age," where the reign of women-made women and the city of girls was already being forgotten.

In 1938, a syndicated film column mentioned her stunt work in the prison drama *Condemned Women*.[139] Helen plays a warden, and in one scene, she falls down a flight of stairs after being shot.

The article stated, "That's Helen Gibson—a stunt woman at forty-four....Miss Gibson says she is getting a bit brittle...a little tired of trying to break her neck."

---

139 The female lead was played, coincidentally, by Sally Eilers, who had just become the newest member of the Hoot Gibson Ex-Wife Club. Thank goodness she wasn't named Helen. I'm sure the two women had lots of interesting conversations between takes.

16

A Crack in the System

What can you do in the face of such overwhelming inequity? How can you stop something so huge, something systemic? What do you do when the power has been stripped from you?

You can give up, of course. No one would blame you. But you can also hold on, hunker down. Become a cockroach, a barnacle, a persistent little creature of resistance. You can refuse to go away. Sometimes, that's enough.

Remember back in the 1910s, when Mary Pickford forced studios to stop block booking her films with low-quality ones? Well, once the stars lost all their power, studios could block book until the cows came home and the actors and directors couldn't do a damn thing about it. Paramount, in particular, was known for it. So, they became the focus of a federal investigation into the legality of the practice in the late 1930s. The Federal Trade Commission decided that block booking needed to stop, and in 1938, the Department of Justice began a very long battle against the big studios.

When the case was finally settled two years later, studios were told they could no longer block book short films with features, could not block book more than five features together, and could no longer force theater owners to "blind buy," which meant owners had to buy the films without getting to see them first. Studios and distributors now had to set up trade showings so owners could review what they were going to screen in their theaters.

The studios unwisely decided not to comply with this ruling, and the Department of Justice sued them again in 1945. The first court actually ruled in favor of the studios, but the federal government decided to escalate the case to the Supreme Court. This ended up being terrible for the studios and good for, well, everyone else in the country. The Supreme Court decided in a seven to one ruling that not only was block booking unconstitutional, but also that vertically integrated studios were an oligopoly. Now the studios were also forced to get rid of their theater chains.

This kick-started the rise of more independent movie theaters *and* independent movie studios. Without having to buy films in a block, indie theaters could curate films the way they wanted to, usually meaning they could buy only the films they knew they could make money on. And now that studio-owned theater chains no longer existed, there was less competition. With an influx of indie theaters, indie studios could make movies and get them seen by audiences. To top it all off, foreign films now had a shot of being seen by American audiences. Wins all around, really.

A crack in the studio system had formed.

During the early 1940s, Olivia de Havilland was one of Hollywood's biggest stars. She had played Maid Marion in *The Adventures of Robin Hood*, and Melanie Hamilton in *Gone with the Wind*. A beautiful petite brunette, de Havilland was beloved by American audiences.

After these successful roles, de Havilland started to be a little more choosy with the movies she made. Her seven-year contract was with Warner Brothers, and she felt that the films they were offering were too formulaic. She wanted meatier, more complex female characters to embody.

The Warner brothers (the studio was still run by them) began to get annoyed. Whenever Havilland turned down a movie, they suspended her without pay, and added that time onto the end of her contract. By 1943, her contract was supposed to be up. De Havilland had signed with Warner Brothers in 1936 as a nineteen-year-old and was more than ready to leave. Thanks to her suspensions, however, they told her that no, she still had six months left.

De Havilland decided that enough was enough.

She consulted a prominent film industry lawyer named Martin Gang, who told her that she should sue Warner Brothers. He found an old, mostly forgotten California state law that forbade any employer from "enforcing a personal services contract for more than seven years."

It was a David and Goliath case, with the five-foot-three de Havilland going up against one of the biggest movie studios in the world, and things got nasty quickly. The Warner brothers were furious. They told the court that it was the studio that had made her career and "brought her from obscurity to prominence." But, according to California law, what the Warner brothers were doing was clearly illegal. The case went all the way up to the California Supreme Court. Olivia de Havilland won and freed herself from the clutches of her seven-year contract.

Warner Brothers immediately blacklisted her, and she didn't work for about two years. Soon, however, other stars started using "the de Havilland rule" to get out of their own contracts. For all the stars that enlisted during WWII, the studios had tacked that time onto the ends of their seven-year contracts. Thank you for your service, indeed. When they returned to

Hollywood and discovered this, both Jimmy Stewart and Clark Gable used the ruling to get out and go freelance.

Other studios finally began to offer Olivia de Havilland roles and she eventually won two Academy Awards, one for *To Each His Own* in 1946, and one for *The Heiress* in 1949. It was a great triumph for her to stand on that stage, Oscar in hand, and know that she had taken on the studio system and won. De Havilland said that the best part of her victory was the overwhelming amount of gratitude she received from her fellow stars. After the ruling, she received heaps of flowers and letters from other actors who were finally able to be free of their studio contracts.

The crack began to widen.

Just like motion pictures crept up on theater and vaudeville, a new entertainment medium was sneaking up on motion pictures: TV.

The first television broadcast was actually all the way back in 1927,[140] but it took quite a long time to develop the technology to the point where it was available for the public. By 1937, the Summer Olympics in Berlin was broadcast all around the world, and soon there were eighteen television stations around the United States. In 1939, the Radio Corporation of America unveiled the first publicly accessible television broadcast at the World's Fair. TV sets went on sale to the public the next day. In 1941, the FCC authorized commercial broadcasting, and later that year, Pearl Harbor became the first major news story to break on TV.

During the post-WWII boom, sales of TV sets grew and grew. By July 1947, there were three hundred and fifty thousand television sets in homes across the country. By 1951, that number had exploded to thirteen million.

The studios were starting to sweat a little.

They were still in the process of divesting themselves of their theater chains just as television started picking away at their audiences. Without the backing of the studios, many of the grand

---

140 It was simply an image of a straight line.

picture palaces closed. As networks like NBC developed more and more television shows, like sitcoms, dramas, and mysteries, Americans could now enjoy motion pictures at home, for free (after they bought the TV set).

It was a similar situation to the advent of streaming services. Turns out, sometimes people just want to stay home in their pajamas, with their own snacks that don't cost seventy-five dollars.

With the opulent picture palaces gone, going to the movies was no longer a special event. If there was no draw other than the film itself, it became easier and easier for television to lure people away from theaters.

There was also a decline in foreign sales. After the war, European countries were able to get their bearings and protect their local film climates from the overwhelming force of the American film industry. Many imposed a quota on the number of films that could be imported from the United States.

New films in color were a draw for a while. 1939's *The Wizard of Oz*, although certainly not the first color feature film,[141] was the first color film most Americans saw. By the 1950s, most studios had started shooting films in color. But color TV wasn't too far behind. Studios were even forced to start licensing their films for television, which some critics likened to rich families "selling the silverware to survive."

Even the censorship boards were losing their power. In 1949, a film distributor named Joseph Burstyn imported a short Italian film called *The Miracle*, directed by Roberto Rossellini. The film featured sexual assault and childbirth, among other things, which censors were normally on the lookout for. It was screened in New York the next year for a total of twelve days before the local censorship board caught wind of the film. The theater was

---

141 Color film was actually possible as early as the 1910s, but it was incredibly expensive. The first feature-length narrative film was *The World, The Flesh, and The Devil*, which you can probably tell from the title was not made in the studio system days. It came out in 1914, but it used Kinemacolor, which didn't represent the full color spectrum, only reds and greens.

ordered to immediately halt all screenings of *The Miracle*. The New York board called it "sacrilegious" and by the next year, it was banned outright.

But Burstyn decided to challenge the ruling in court. The case went all the way up to the Supreme Court in 1952, who sided with Burstyn, and decided to reverse the 1915 ruling that films were not protected by the First Amendment. The court declared that "It cannot be doubted that motion pictures are a significant medium for the communication of ideas. Their importance as an organ of public opinion is not lessened by the fact that they are designed to entertain as well as inform."

And just like that, film was now entitled to free speech protections.

They didn't immediately disappear, but censorship boards across the United States began to shut down. With movies protected by the First Amendment, it was difficult for censors to keep their power.

Even Hollywood itself was struggling. In 1953, the chamber of commerce added the Walk of Fame to Hollywood Boulevard, to "maintain the glory of a community whose name means glamor and excitement in the four corners of the world," also known as, "Dear god, we know you all love TV now, but please, at least come to Hollywood on vacation."[142]

The cracks had finally reached all the way down to the foundations, and the great and terrible studio system began to crumble.

The seven-year contract system petered out in the mid-1950s. RKO shut down in 1957. By 1958, after trying budget cuts and theater gimmicks, studios were forced to scale back production

---

142 The parks commission actually wanted to tear down the HOLLYWOOD-LAND sign at this time, which had fallen into disrepair. Maintenance had long been discontinued, and all the bulbs had been stolen during the Great Depression. The Hollywood Chamber of Commerce was allowed to repair the sign instead. They removed "LAND" and the HOLLYWOOD sign was finally in its iconic form.

and make fewer movies. More and more films were made by independent producers, and the central producer system also fell apart.

The vast flow of money that had sustained the studios was gone. Many sold or fired some of the elements that had made them magical in the first place, like live orchestras to score films. MGM, among other studios, found themselves paying bills by renting out their soundstages to TV commercials. In the same place where stars like Greta Garbo and Judy Garland had stood, crews were now filming advertisements for dog food and diapers.

The Golden Age was over. The classic Hollywood glamor, the furs, the cigarette holders, the soft lighting illuminating floor-length drapes of silk, all swept away, like confetti after a parade.

Many film historians say that the last film of the "great" studio era was *The Man Who Shot Liberty Valance*, which starred John Wayne, James Stewart, Vera Miles, and way in the background…Helen Gibson.

All those years, Helen had continued stunt and background work, fashioning a quiet life for herself.[143]

Her husband, Clifton, a former gunner in the navy, volunteered for active duty in WWII. While he was serving, Helen stayed behind, making movies to keep the nation's mind off wartime fear. When the war ended in 1945, Clifton made it safely home, and she got him a job as a film electrician.

In 1950, Helen got a call that Helen Holmes had fallen ill. She rushed to the San Fernando Valley to be with her. Holmes had been supporting herself by selling her old film memorabilia. Her daughter helped with the sale of photos, props, posters at "bargain prices," according to Helen. Helen had visited her old friend regularly, and wrote later in life that Holmes was "very lonely."

When Helen arrived at Holmes's home, she discovered that

---

143 Aside from a brief period of three years when she and Clifton moved to Northern California to try their hands at real estate. Helen said it was not "her forte." Probably too boring for her.

the woman who had launched her career had suffered a heart attack. Holmes died with Helen by her side.

Ruth Roland, Pearl White, and Helen Holmes had all passed away. Helen Gibson was now the last living great serial queen.

The next year, she was invited to star in *The Hollywood Story* alongside several silent film actors. The movie was based on the murder of William Desmond Taylor, one of the big, early Hollywood scandals. The chamber of commerce threw a glamorous huge gala for all the silent stars of *The Hollywood Story* at the Academy Award Theater, and presented them all with plaques for their "outstanding contribution to the art and science of motion pictures, for the pleasure you have brought to millions over the world, and for your help in making Hollywood the film capital of the world."

At fifty-nine years old, rocking silver curls, Helen looked stunning.

After years of working in the background, Helen was delighted at the recognition. She wrote that it was a night she was
"not apt to forget for a long time."

The recognition, however, didn't lead to any offers for more
substantial roles. Helen continued as a stuntwoman and background actor for another decade.

In 1961, Helen Gibson was nothing short of a marvel. She
was *sixty-nine* years old and still making her living by galloping
on horseback and leaping off moving vehicles. But she was really starting to feel her fifty long years in the film industry. She
told a reporter, "I have to laugh when I see the stuntmen today
loaded up with harnesses and pads. I did all my stunts the hard
way. Of course, I'm paying for it today."

Helen had been in hundreds and hundreds of movies in her
career (an accurate number is almost impossible to guess) and
it was finally time for her last role. She went out the way she
came in, as a background actor in a Western.

The Man Who Shot Liberty Valance was made by Paramount
that year. Directed by John Ford, it starred some of the biggest
names of the day. Ford shot the film in black-and-white partly
on Paramount soundstages and partly in Wildwood Park, north
of Los Angeles. The costumes for the film were designed by
Edith Head, the most awarded woman in Oscar history.[144]

Ford and Wayne did not get along, which often caused the
atmosphere on set to be tense, and sometimes a little miserable.
It didn't bother Helen too much, though. She was way too old
for bullshit.

Cast as a townswoman, Helen was given thirty-five dollars a
day, and her role involved driving a team of horses. If you watch
the film very, very closely, you can see her.

For "the most daring actress in pictures," her final role was

---

144 A record eight wins!

an easy one. It was rare that she got to sit down, instead of leaping, running, dangling, or punching. Helen deserved the break.

The Man Who Shot Liberty Valance was released in April of 1962, and became the highest-grossing film of the year.[145] It was an enormous critical and financial success, and is still considered one of the best Westerns ever made.

The movie is also significant because many film historians use *The Man Who Shot Liberty Valance* to mark the end of an era. The great studio age of Hollywood, after four decades, was finally over.

Through the rise and fall of women in Hollywood, the rise and fall of the studio system, and the rise and fall of Hollywood itself, Helen Gibson was there. She made it through the advent of feature films, of sound, of color, of television.

Even with everything thrown at her, no one ever managed to get rid of Helen. The "girl of grit," the "queen of the rails," the "girl who tames trains" outlasted them all. Now it was time for some rest.

---

145 Later that year, Helen had another victory. She got word that Hoot, at age seventy, had died of cancer. After a successful run as a Western star, he retired from film in 1944. Helen did not attend the funeral.

17

A Matter of Guts

Now that Helen had finally performed her last stunt, she had to figure out what she wanted to do with the rest of her life. Even at seventy, the "Kalem madcap" wasn't very good at staying still. So, about a year after the release of *The Man Who Shot Liberty Valance*, Helen and Clifton decided to sell their house and move up north to Oregon.

When she first traveled to Pendleton for her rodeo tour, Helen had fallen in love with the natural beauty of the state. For her, it was the perfect place to retire.

Before she left, the *Los Angeles Examiner* published an article about her career. "The Hazards of Helen are somewhat more sedate today" it said, "than they were 40 years ago when movie villains tied her to the railroad tracks." Helen told the reporter that she was still figuring out her retirement. "I don't know what to do with myself. I don't go to bars or places like that." Her biggest annoyance, she said, was that the post office still mixed her up with Hoot's second wife, the other Helen Gibson. "I'm still forwarding her mail..."

"HAZARDS OF HELEN" SERIAL QUEEN RECALLS EARLY FILM DAYS
Helen Gibson Johnson holds book of mementos and photo proof of daring skills

LOS ANGELES HERALD-EXAMINER, SEPTEMBER 9, 1962.

Perhaps that's why she started using Clifton's last name. Born Rose Wenger, now Helen Rose Gibson Johnson. Her name was a scrapbook of her life, a map of her long journey and all the people she had been. A girl in Cleveland, a young rodeo rider, a Hollywood star, a legendary stunt woman.

Clifton and Helen took the money from the sale of their house and bought a small house on a leafy street in Roseberg. Helen could look out her front door and get a view of rolling green hills. The couple spent a lot of time relaxing and fishing, and Helen fostered a newfound appreciation for being out in the quiet of nature.

Even decades away from the peak of her career, Helen still

attracted attention. As soon as they moved, a local reporter came to talk to the "retired movie queen." She told them that she was glad to be out of Hollywood. "I don't miss it at all. I thought I might, but I don't. Of course, I still think I hear the phone ringing. When you get involved in the movie business, they have you on the phone 24 hours a day." She decided not to buy a phone for the new house.

Helen had finally learned to live on a budget and kept a simple, unpretentious home. A niece of Clifton's told film historian Larry Telles later in life that Helen "wasn't a housewife" and Clifton was the one who did all the cooking.

The only indulgence she allowed herself was her car. Clifton's niece told Telles that they "bought a new Cadillac every two years" and paid for high-performance tires. Even in retirement, Helen liked to speed. A gasoline shortage in the early 1970s infuriated her because it caused the Oregon highway speed limits to be decreased to fifty-five miles an hour. Helen was eighty-two at the time, and told Clifton's niece that she liked to drive *at least* seventy miles an hour and that her Cadillac "wasn't made to go fifty-five." Her days of riding horses and standing on top of speeding trains were over, but Helen still liked to feel the wind in her hair.

Clifton's niece described her to Telles as an independent person, who wasn't "flashy" and had a "great sense of humor." Helen seemed, to her, "happy with who she was."

On October 10, 1977, after fifteen years of retirement and breaking the speed limit in Oregon, Helen passed away from heart failure. She was eighty-six years old, and full of spirit until the very end.

She gave an interview with the local paper near the end of her life, which was titled, "From Hollywood to Roseburg...a Long Journey."

*THE NEWS-REVIEW, ROSEBURG, OREGON.
MAY 15, 1975.*

When asked again if she missed Hollywood, the article notes her response: "'Movies are too much of a racket now,' she says. 'They are just factories,' she adds, a bit wistfully."

Death had finally caught the "girl with nine lives," the last living serial queen. For fifty years, Helen had performed all over the country and in hundreds and hundreds of films. She showed the world, and most importantly, a generation of girls, exactly what women could do. Out of sheer grit and determination, Rose Wenger built Helen Gibson into an icon.

Authors Arthur Wise and Derek Ware talk about Helen in their book, *Stunting in the Cinema*, and pinpoint exactly what it was about Helen that made her so successful.

What one sees her doing on the screen, she did in reality. Success depended entirely on her physical ability, her highly developed sense of timing, and her absolute conviction that the stunt, for her at least, was possible.

KALEM KALENDAR, DECEMBER 1916.

Helen jumped because she trusted in herself. She knew what she wanted was possible. And she inspired so many women to think about what was possible for them, too. Helen's heyday was an age when most American women were not able to record their thoughts, write down their ideas. We don't have their firsthand impressions of how serials affected their lives. We do, however, have their ticket sales, and we know that, for at least a little while, millions of them turned out every week to see Helen and her fellow serial queens fight the bad guys, thwart danger, and most importantly, save themselves. Helen gave these women excitement, encouragement, and hope. She told a reporter after retirement that for her, "Screen acting was a matter of guts."

The life and work of Helen Gibson shows us what things could have been, had this era of possibility continued. It also shows us what we lost, and how far we still have to go.

But what happened after she left?

The film industry is, in almost every possible way, completely different now. The studio system had fallen. Could female filmmakers regain the power they once had? Could they rip the gates off their hinges and create a Hollywood where everyone, no matter who they are, has a chance to tell their own stories on screen?

"I refuse to stop making movies."

—*Kathryn Bigelow*

Epilogue

Strong Female Protagonist 2:
Electric Boogaloo

It took a few years after Helen's retirement, but in the late 1960s, women finally began to return to Hollywood.

When the studio system ended, the American film landscape was a really strange place. The industry had grown up around the studio system like a plant grown around a trellis, and when that was removed, the entire structure just sort of collapsed. Box office numbers were down, thanks to a postwar slump and competition from television. Social movements were igniting all across the country for gay rights, feminism, Mexican Americans, civil rights, environmentalism, not to mention protests against the Vietnam War. Many people didn't want bland, cookie-cutter musicals and formulaic movies anymore. They wanted films with substance.

By 1968, the Hays Code had collapsed, as well. The MPPDA (which became the Motion Picture Association) realized that it was essentially useless at that point, and abandoned the code in favor of a new and voluntary ratings system.

328   Mallory O'Meara

It originally consisted of only four ratings:

Rated G: Suggested for general audiences.
Rated M: Suggested for mature audiences—parental discretion advised.
Rated R: Restricted—Persons under sixteen not admitted, unless accompanied by parent or adult guardian.
Rated X: Persons under sixteen not admitted.

This eventually changed into what it is today:

Rated G: General audiences—all ages admitted.
Rated PG: Parental guidance suggested—some material may not be suitable for children.
Rated PG-13: Parents strongly cautioned—some material may be inappropriate for children under thirteen.[146]
Rated R: Restricted—Under seventeen requires accompanying parent or adult guardian.
Rated NC-17: Adults Only—No one seventeen and under admitted.

This rating criteria meant a curtain call for censors around the United States. By the late 1970s, states began to sign "sunset laws" to shut down censorship boards. Since films were no longer required to get approval, fewer and fewer studios and production companies wasted the money on the process, and the boards cost money to run.

The very last censorship board in the entire country was in Maryland. It held on until 1981, sixty-five years after it was first established. The three censors on the board were absolutely

---

146 For a while, it went from PG to R, but PG-13 was added in 1984 because parents complained that some of the blockbuster films of the 1980s, like *Indiana Jones*, were rated PG but contained lots of violence and gore. I guess thirteen is the appropriate age to see a Nazi get his face melted off.

devastated. The retired white women threw themselves a farewell party after a screening of the last movie they reviewed, *The Great Muppet Caper*. The group baked cookies and exchanged gifts for the occasion.

Ben A. Franklin, a reporter from the *New York Times* traveled down to interview them that June. Mary Avara, the senior censor of the board at seventy-one years old, was known as the "Joan of Arc of antipornography"[147] and acted as the board's "most vigorous" defender. She had appeared before the Maryland State Congress to plead against the board's removal, and told the representatives that she was an "expert witness" to the importance of censorship, that she had "looked at more naked bodies than 50,000 doctors." The grandmother of nine told the *New York Times* reporter that she would "serve free," giving up her forty-five hundred dollar stipend if only someone would introduce legislation to reinstate her beloved board.[148]

The other two members of the board "issued dire forecasts for what will happen to the morals of Maryland and indeed the nation" when their guard against "cable television and video cassette pornography" was gone.[149] One censor, Martha S. Wright said that the country was now "degraded" and had taken yet another doomed step toward becoming a land of "lovers of pleasure rather than lovers of our fellow man."

Their retirement had almost no effect on the great state of Maryland. Hopefully those ladies found something equally fulfilling to do with their time, like yelling at store managers and writing stern letters to their local homeowners association.

Anyway, now that studios didn't have to worry about people

---

147 It's unknown whether or not she gave herself this title.

148 Please, oh *please* let me keep looking at those naked bodies! Oh, how I simply live to censor art!

149 Which was already available to purchase in many stores around the state.

like Mary Avara and Martha S. Wright censoring their films, they were much more open to taking a chance on new directors and new genres. As film historian and head of the UCLA Film & Television Archive Research and Study Center Maya Montañez Smukler says in her book, *Liberating Hollywood*, now that the studio system was dead, "movies came back to life."

The new rating system allowed not just sex and violence back up on the screen, but it brought the dawn of the age of the exploitation film, the sexploitation film, the grind house flick, the weird art house film, the wild low-budget indie. Drive-ins were hungry for these movies. The rise of these genres in the 1970s opened the door for stuntwomen and stuntpeople of color to get in the game.

Up until this point, the Stuntmen's Association of Motion Pictures controlled almost all of the stunt jobs in Hollywood. It only admitted, by invitation, white male stuntmen, stunt coordinators, or second unit directors who made at least ten thousand dollars a year. They were reluctant to admit women because, as film historian Mollie Gregory says in her book, *Stuntwomen: The Untold Hollywood Story*, they were "afraid women would create sexual problems" because they'd want to "hook up with people." And non-white men were not admitted at all. These stuntmen still, into the 1970s, doubled for women and worked in blackface. Racism was so ingrained in Hollywood at this point that studios, Gregory writes, "were sometimes called plantations."

When the Black Stuntmen's Association was formed in 1967, they welcomed women of all races to train with them on the weekend and taught them how to do fights, jumps, and falls. This was a huge boon for Black stuntwomen, who rarely got jobs. Besides the fact that members of the Stuntmen's Association of Motion Pictures were out there wearing blackface, there just weren't many action roles for Black performers in the 1960s.

The Screen Actors Guild technically had a nondiscrimination policy, but it was never enforced. If anyone who was non-male or non-white or both complained, they'd suddenly find that stunt coordinators were not interested in hiring them.

"Blaxploitation" films were great for Black filmmakers to break into the industry because they were low budget and there was a huge market for them. They were great for Black stunt-people because they created a swell of jobs. Soon, the Black Stuntmen's Association had a hundred members, and ten of them were women, including Peaches Jones, who did stunts in *Foxy Brown*, Evelyne Cuffee, who did stunts in *Disco 9000*, and Jadie David, who did stunts in *Dr. Black, Mr. Hyde*. David became the first Black stunt woman making a living in the film industry.

A new wave of television programming shifted the landscape further, creating new opportunities for stuntwomen. Female-led action shows like *Charlie's Angels, Wonder Woman*, and *The Bionic Woman* were massively popular, especially with girls and young women. Lynda Carter, Wonder Woman herself, was particularly open with her praise of her stunt double, Jeannie Epper. Soon, there were more and more stuntwomen, and they even began to get hired as stunt coordinators.

The rise in skimpy outfits for female action heroes was both a blessing and a curse. On one hand, it was much more difficult to do jumps and fight scenes in heels and short shorts. Ginger Rogers did everything Fred Astaire did, but backward and in heels. Well, stuntwomen were doing it backward and in biki-nis. On the other hand, the tiny outfits also meant that it was much harder for stuntmen to take the place of stuntwomen. So much shaving!

What about behind the camera?

Female directors started to find more success in the 1980s and 1990s, when they saw a 150 percent increase in their number from the previous decade, with forty different women direct-ing nearly ninety commercially distributed movies.

Some made films at the big studios, like Amy Heckling's *Fast*

Times at Ridgemont High, Barbra Streisand's *Yentl*, and Penny Marshall's *Big*. Some female directors of color found success as well, like Euzhan Palcy, whose *A Dry White Season* with MGM in 1989 made her the first Black woman director to have a film produced by a major Hollywood studio, and Julie Dash, whose *Daughters of the Dust* in 1991 became the first feature directed by a Black woman to get a wide theatrical release. Indie filmmakers had more and more opportunities as well, such as Kathryn Bigelow's *The Loveless*, Mira Mair's *Salaam Bombay!*, and Donna Deitch's *Desert Hearts*.[150]

There was also an increase in female executives. In 1980, Sherry Lansing became the first woman to be the head of production for Twentieth Century Fox. In 1987, Dawn Steel became the president of Columbia Pictures.

Having women in executive roles at studios was great because it meant, theoretically, that female directors and screenwriters would have an easier time getting their feet in the door. But sometimes, it backfired. Some women girlbossed their way to the top and didn't send the ladder back down. Dawn Steel did not greenlight many female-directed films during her tenure at Columbia, for example. As Maya Montañez Smukler says in her book, many female executives "didn't want to seem like they were hiring women just because they were women" and didn't want to seem "like they couldn't work with men." Wouldn't it be hilarious if you asked a male studio head if he was greenlighting a movie just because it had a male director? It helped somewhat to have visible women in power in Hollywood, but it's always temporary if they aren't holding the door open.

The situation slowly continued to improve, and a select few female directors were finally able to make a career and create a body of work. The improvement wasn't coming fast enough,

---

150 This is known as the first mainstream feature film about a lesbian love story that portrays it in an unproblematic, non-creepy way.

though. Films were still largely made by non-marginalized men, despite the fact that most people were not. You'd think that after all these successful films, women would have an easier time getting meetings with studios and production companies and investors. But for most women, every project felt like reinventing the wheel. Director Patty Jenkins is a great example. After her 2003 film *Monster*, which won star Charlize Theron an Oscar, she worked in television for over a decade before she was offered another substantial directing job with 2017's *Wonder Woman*.

Things continued to languish this way for years. Much better than they were in the 1950s, but not nearly where they should be. Then, two online movements changed the game.

It's slightly painful to attribute any positive life changes to Twitter, but between 2015 and 2018, two women launched social media hashtags that drastically changed the American media landscape.

First, in 2015, after seeing the Academy award Best Actor nominations go to an all-white slate, writer April Reign started #OscarsSoWhite. The hashtag was meant to call attention to inequality in Hollywood, and there was an immediate frenzy on Twitter and other forms of social media, pointing out the overwhelming whiteness in the film industry.

Then, in 2017, #MeToo began after Alyssa Milano tweeted, "If you've been sexually harassed or assaulted write 'me too' as a reply to this tweet." The hashtag was originally created by activist Tarana Burke in 2006. #MeToo went viral, and sparked another media storm. The center of it all was the trial of film producer Harvey Weinstein, an industry titan (and now convicted sexual predator) accused of sexual harassment, abuse, and assault by eighty women, many of which work or worked in film.

Both of these colossal online movements forced major film organizations and studios to make promises to change and make the industry more inclusive. They also highlight the fact that no matter how many "nice" guys there are, they still have had the power to make changes and open the door for female filmmakers for *a hundred years* and never did. Sure, there are always exceptions. But the real shift was from women saying, "Fuck this."

And afterward...*some* change came.

The next year, Best Supporting Actor winner Mahershala Ali became only the second Black actor in history to win multiple acting awards. Best Costume Design winner Ruth E. Carter and Best Production Design co-winner Hannah Beachler were the first Black winners in their respective categories and the first Black women to win in a nonacting category since 1983. But all the Best Director nominees that year were male, as they were the year after.[151]

In 2020, *two whole women* were nominated for Best Director, and when she won, Chloé Zhao became the first woman of color to win Best Director and the second woman overall after Kathryn Bigelow won in 2010. Best Supporting Actress winner Youn Yuh-jung became the first Korean actor and second Asian woman to win an acting Oscar.

These are all wonderful, but they're still just small steps if they don't reflect wider, systemic changes in the film landscape. Social media fervor has mostly died down around these hashtags. The truth is, despite what entitled men online will tell you about how "hard" it is to be a non-marginalized man in Hollywood, we're not even close to where we need to be.

In 2022, female protagonists only made up 33 percent of the top one hundred domestic films, and only 37 percent of all speaking roles. Eighty percent of movies had more male than female characters. In movies with female directors and/or screenwriters, however, women made up 56 percent of protagonists. In movies with male directors and/or screenwriters, women

---

151 Although for 2019, Bong Joon-ho absolutely deserved to win. I just wish some women were nominated.

accounted for 23 percent of protagonists. In 2022, of the two hundred and fifty top-grossing movies, women comprised 24 percent of directors, writers, producers, editors, and cinematographers. This is *down* 1 percent from 2021.

Film historian Anthony Slide said in *Early Women Directors* that "during the silent era, women might be said to have virtually controlled the film industry." Then, the pendulum swung so far in the other direction that it's taken over a century to even begin to pull it back.

I'm finishing this book in 2023, after a successful WGA strike, and during one for SAG. It's clear that the way things are only works for a tiny percentage of people, while many others struggle to pay their bills, and many more struggle to break in at all.

How do we get to a place where even the most marginalized among us have the opportunity to make movies? Is this even possible in our current filmmaking industry? Does the whole system need to be broken and remade?

In 2022, I interviewed historian Cari Beauchamp to ask her this very question. Beauchamp, along with Karen Ward Mahar, Ally Acker, and others, was part of a groundbreaking group in the 1990s who started taking a closer look at film history and unearthed the story of when female stars ruled Hollywood.

The women they wrote about invented, created, influenced, changed, and rearranged the very foundation of American film, as directors, actors, writers, producers, and even as audiences. Between 1912 and 1919, eleven different women directed *one hundred and seventy* films at Universal Studios alone. A hundred years later, from 2012 to 2019, the number of American films directed by women *total*, from *every studio combined*, was only about sixty.

Titans like Lois Weber, Mabel Normand, and Grace Cunard were not just shaping the film industry. The movies they made shaped American culture. Mabel Normand's *Mickey* was the highest grossing film of 1918. Their films were seen by millions and millions of people. Until historians like Beauchamp, Acker, and Mahar began to change the narrative in the 1990s, these female filmmakers were *purposely written out of history*.

Beauchamp told me that she started out of curiosity and frustration that there wasn't more available material on the early female filmmakers. She started reading the credits for silent films, increasingly amazed at the amount of women she found. "It was all women and Jews back then," she told me, two groups of people "not accepted in professions that were respected." Once Wall Street came in and "made it respectable," men came in and got jobs simply "because they took them."

She says nowadays, there is absolutely no excuse for studios not to be hiring women. I asked her how we get back to those days, where women were empowered in Hollywood. "The keyword is still persistence. That hasn't changed," she told me, and to "send the ladder down…it's crucial."

Of course, these problems are systemic. For real, lasting change, we need enormous shifts, or an entirely new system.

In the meantime, what can you do?

Support them. Support women, support marginalized films, support independent films. Holy shit, you would not believe how hard these filmmakers are trying.

Reflect on the movies you see. How many are made by people of color? How many female-directed movies have you seen this year? If you can use Google to find the best pad thai in your area, you can use it to find a new movie made by a woman.

In American history, it feels weird to take inspiration from the way things used to be done. But we can look at the conditions that fostered the early days of women-led Hollywood and get ideas. It can be difficult to feel hope, but it's possible to create the world that could have, and should have, been. Where production companies run by marginalized filmmakers, and the movies they make, thrive.

★ ★ ★

I also spoke to La Faye Baker, stuntwoman, stunt coordinator, and co-founder of the Action Icon Awards with stunt legend Jadie David. The awards recognize the achievements of stunt women, and benefit Baker's organization Diamond in the RAW, "devoted to empowering and transforming the lives of foster care and at-risk teen girls" through the arts and STEM education.

Baker is a legend herself as the first Black female stunt coordinator to head a big budget project (*Introducing Dorothy Dandrige* starring Halle Berry), and has doubled for icons like Angela Bassett and Regina King. She started the awards in 2008 to "bring awareness to stuntwomen." Because the Academy Awards still do not honor the hard work and artistry of stunt people, Baker wanted to give these women "a chance to walk the red carpet."

One of the awards, the one for stuntwomen who have over thirty years in the industry, is the Helen Gibson Award. Past recipients include Debbie Evans, who has been in over three hundred films, and Melissa Stubbs, who started doing stunts in 1989 and whose most recent credit is supervising stunt coordinator and second unit director on Elizabeth Banks's *Cocaine Bear*.

There are so many things I wish Helen Gibson could have lived to see. I wish she could have been there when millions cheered for Furiosa in *Mad Max: Fury Road*. I wish she could have felt what female audiences felt when Harley Quinn handed Dinah a hair tie in the middle of a fight scene in *Birds of Prey*. But I really wish she could have been around for this, for legendary stunt women being honored in her name, a name that belongs in the pantheon of Hollywood action stars.

Helen didn't set out to make her mark on the world. She just wanted to make her mark on her own life, to be in charge of her own destiny. Her courage opened an escape from a life where she wasn't in control.

Helen Gibson didn't risk life and limb because she had a death wish. She did it because she wanted to see how far she could jump, how fast she could ride, how far she could go.

★ ★ ★ ★ ★

Acknowledgments

If books take a village to make, history books take a whole city. Luckily, I have one of the best.

I have to start by thanking my agent, Amy Bishop-Wycisk. To me, you are an angel. A beautiful angel with a giant sword. Thank you for rescuing my confidence in my work, for immediately responding with enthusiasm when I first emailed about Helen, and for generally making sure my brain doesn't explode. I am grateful for you every single day.

Unending thanks to my editor, Peter Joseph, who has been dealing with my weird footnotes and jokes for years now. Peter, it's truly such a pleasure to work with you, and I feel so lucky to do so. Grace Towery, you're simply brilliant, and it was an honor to have your sharp eye on this book. I don't know how the two of you make me look forward to getting an edit letter, but you do.

My entire team at Hanover Square Press is just a dream, including Tracy Wilson, Eden Railsback, and all the wonderful folks who make my books possible. Laura Gianino, my indomitable publicist, you are the reason I have not yet walked into the sea. I appreciate you more than I will ever be able to say.

It would be impossible for me to write books without the help of the library, particularly the Los Angeles Public Library and the Riverside Public Library system. Librarians, you make my world go round.

Ned Comstock, at this point, I don't know how I would write a film history without your help. The resources and wisdom you gave me for this book were invaluable.

There are so many archivists who helped get this book off the ground. Particular thanks goes to Elizabeth Youle at the Margaret Herrick Library for spending so much time helping me, and Lulu Zilinskas at the National Cowboy and Western Heritage Museum. Lizzy, I owe you a drink! Matt Severson, director of the Margaret Herrick Library, thank you so much for befriending that weird girl at the gym. I'm so, so grateful for your help on this.

My writing stands on the shoulders of history giants like Cari Beauchamp, Ally Acker, and Karen Ward Mahar. This book would have been possible without your work, but it would have really sucked. To me, you're all superheroes. Cari, thank you so much for taking the time to talk to me.

Speaking of, a massive thanks to Larry Telles for his work on Helen Gibson, which gave me a vital springboard to leap from.

To all the film pals who helped me out with this one, I love you all. Scott Wampler, you sent so many request emails for me and listened to so much of my panicking, despite my relentless bullying and regular threats on your life. I'm so grateful for you, and I will forever carry you in my heart.

To all the friends who kept me sane during this one, so many thanks and so many cocktails: Charles Meyer, Rich DeStefano,

Ify Nwadiwe, Pete Brett, Meg Ellison, Diana Biller, and especially Emily Louise.

Brea Grant, there are about a zillion reasons to thank you. Your constant support with, well, everything is deeply appreciated. I need to find you the world's biggest chocolate bar. Frank Woodward, without whom I would never have gotten into film, your friendship and wisdom is essential for me.

To all the *Reading Glasses* listeners who support my writing, please know how much I adore you. You're truly the best bookish community I could ever ask for.

And of course, my magnificent therapist, Chris, you are as essential to my work as notebooks, or Google Docs, or bourbon.

To Jeremy Lambert, a titanic amount of gratitude for taking care of me while I wrote this, especially when long COVID was kicking my ass and I thought I would have to change careers. There are not enough cheesy gordita crunches in the world to show my love for you.

Thank you to the fountain pen community for being my mental safe haven. The first draft of this book was written entirely with fountain pens, mainly a Kaweco Liliput, a LAMY 2000, a TWSBI Eco, and a Nahvalur Original Plus (all broad nibs).

I must mention my cat, Lula Fortune, because I strongly suspect you know how to read. Despite your tireless efforts to stop me, I somehow manage to keep writing books. Even though I hopefully will never stop, I do appreciate your companionship, even when you try to chew on my pens. You are my heart.

Finally, thank you to all the women in film who have never given up. You are miracles to me, Amazons, wonders. I draw constant inspiration from you, and I look forward to the day when things are better in this goddamn industry. When that day comes, it will be because you did not stop.

Sources

Archives:

Margaret Herrick Library
National Cowboy and Western Heritage Museum
USC Cinematic Arts Library
Women Film Pioneers Project

Articles:

"Ageless Anita Loos Talks of Herself and Hollywood" by Jim Watters, August 5, 1974, *People*

"Dirty Secrets of Stunt Work—a Job with a 100% Injury Rate" by Kirk Cauoette, June 14, 2021, *Moviemaker*

"Dorothy Arzner: Queen of Hollywood" by So Mayer, March 7, 2015, *British Film Institute*

"Dorothy Arzner's Trousers" by Jane Gaines, July 1992, *Jump Cut*

"The History of How Los Angeles Became a City of Palm Trees" by Jen Carlson, April 6, 2016, *The LAist*

"Hollywood's Glass Ceiling Remains in Place: Infinitesimal Increase in Movies with Female Protagonists" by Brent Lang, March 7, 2023, *Variety*

"Introducing Florence Lawrence, Hollywood's Forgotten First Movie Star" by Margaret Heindry, May 25, 2018, *Vanity Fair*

"'It's Not for Wimps': 8 Stuntwomen Reflect on Their Careers" by Amisha Padnani and Daniel E. Slotnik, January 20, 2017, *New York Times*

"Last State Board of Censors Fades Away after 65 Years" by Ben A. Franklin, June 29, 1981, *New York Times*

"The Lost Years: Skating and the Great War" by Ryan Stevens, August 23, 2018, *Skate Guard*

"Rolled Over: Why Did Married Couples Stop Sleeping in Twin Beds?" by Alison Flood, August 16, 2019, *The Guardian*

Books:

101 Ranch Wild West by Ellsworth Collings and Alma Miller England
University of Oklahoma Press, 1973

Bright Boulevards, Bold Dreams: The Story of Black Hollywood by Donald Bogle
One World, 2006

Catching the Big Fish by David Lynch
TarcherPerigee, 2006

Chinese in Hollywood by Jenny Cho
Arcadia Publishing, 2013

Comic Venus: Women and Comedy in American Silent Film by Kristen Anderson Wagner
Wayne State University Press, 2018

Complicated Women: Sex and Power in Pre-Code Hollywood by Mick LaSalle
St. Martin's Griffin, 2001

Continued Next Week: A History of the Moving Picture Serial by Kalton C. Lahue
University of Oklahoma Press, 1964

The Cowgirls by Joyce Gibson Ranch
Texas A&M University Press, 1990

Death of the Moguls by Winston Dixon
Rutgers University Press, 2012

Earning Power: Women and Work in Los Angeles, 1880-1930 by Eileen V. Wallis
University of Nevada Press, 2010

An Evening's Entertainment: The Age of the Silent Feature Picture
by Richard Koszarski
University of California Press, 1994

A Feminist Reader in Early Cinema edited by Jennifer M. Bean
and Diane Negra
Duke University Press, 2002

From Reverence to Rape: The Treatment of Women in the Movies by
Molly Haskell
University of Chicago Press, 1973

The Glamour Factory: Inside Hollywood's Big Studio System by
Ronald L. Davis
Southern Methodist University Press, 1993

The Golden Age of Cinema: Hollywood, 1929-1945 by Richard
B. Jewell
Blackwell Publishing, 2007

Go West, Young Women! The Rise of Early Hollywood by Hilary
A. Hallet
University of California Press, 2013

*Helen Gibson: Silent Serial Queen Who Became Hollywood's First
Professional Stunt Woman* by Larry Telles
Bitterroot Mountain Publishing, 2013

The Hollywood Action and Adventure Film by Yvonne Tasker
Wiley, 2015

Hollywood at the Intersection of Race and Identity edited by Delia
Malia Caparoso Konzett
Rutgers University Press, 2019

Hollywood: The First 100 Years by Bruce Torrence
Hollywood Chamber of Commerce, 1979

The Hollywood West: Lives of Film Legends Who Shaped It edited
by Richard W. Etulain and Glenda Riley
Fulcrum Publishing, 2001

Ladies of Labor, Girls of Adventure by Nan Enstad
Columbia University Press, 1999

*Liberating Hollywood: Women Directors and the Feminist Reform of
1970s American Cinema* by Maya Montañez Smukler
Rutgers University Press, 2018

*Los Angeles before Hollywood: Journalism and American Film Culture,
1905 to 1915* by Jan Olsson
Wallflower Press, 2009

Mary Pickford: Hollywood and the New Woman by Kathleen A.
Feeley
Westview Press, 2016

Mediocre: The Dangerous Legacy of White Male America by Ijeoma
Oluo
Seal Press, 2020

Melodrama and Modernity: Early Sensational Cinema and Its Context by Ben Singer
Columbia University Press, 2001

Movie-Struck Girls: Women and Motion Picture Culture after the Nickelodeon by Shelley Stamp
Princeton University Press, 2000

Off with Their Heads! A Serio-Comic Tale of Hollywood by Frances Marion
MacMillan, 1972

Pre-Code Hollywood: Sex, Immorality, and Insurreciton in American Cinema 1930–1934 by Thomas Doherty
Columbia University Press, 1999

Reclaiming the Archive: Feminism and Film History edited by Vicki Callahan
Wayne State University Press, 2010

Reel Women: Pioneers of the Cinema 1896 to the Present by Ally Acker
Continuum International Publishing Group, 1993

Ride, Boldly Ride: The Evolution of the American Western by Mary Lea Bandy and Kevin Stoehr
University of California Press, 2012

Riding Pretty: Rodeo Royalty in the American West by Renee M. Laegreid
University of Nebraska Press, 2006

The Sagebrush Trail: Western Movies and Twentieth-Century America by Richard Aquila
University of Arizona Press, 2015

Silent Magic: Rediscovering the Silent Film Era by Ivan Butler
Bookthrift Co., 1988

Sin in Soft Focus: Pre-Code Hollywood by Mark A. Vieira
Harry N. Abrams, 1999

The Story of Hollywood by Barry Norman
Plume, 1989

The Story of Hollywood: An Illustrated History by Gregory Paul Williams
BL Press, 2011

Stunt Related Injuries in the Motion Picture and Film Industry: A Literature Review by Billy Quirke
University of British Columbia, 2012

Stuntwomen: The Untold Story by Mollie Gregory
University of Kentucky Press, 2018

Thick: And Other Essays by Tressie McMillan Cottom
The New Press, 2019

Universal Women: Filmmaking and Institutional Change in Early Hollywood by Mark Garret Cooper
University of Illinois Press, 2010

When Women Wrote Hollywood: Essays on Female Screenwriters in the Early Film Industry edited by Rosanne Welch
McFarland and Company, 2018

Wild West Shows by Paul Reddin
University of Illinois Press, 1999

Women Filmmakers in Early Hollywood by Karen Ward Mahar
Johns Hopkins University Press, 2008

Films:

Beth Stelling: Girl Daddy (2020)
The Cigarette (1919)
Gentlemen Prefer Blondes (1953)
I'm No Angel (1933)
Mabel's Strange Predicament (1914)
Merrily We Go to Hell (1932)
She Done Him Wrong (1933)
Stagecoach (1939)
Stuntwomen: The Untold Hollywood Story (2020)

Interviews:

Cari Beauchamp, April 6, 2022
La Faye Baker, March 20, 2022

Magazine Archives:

Films in Review
Motion Picture Magazine
Motion Picture News

Moving Picture Weekly
Moving Picture World
Outing magazine
Saturday Evening Post
Silver Screen

Newspaper Archives:

Cleveland Plain Dealer
Herald Examiner
Los Angeles Daily News
Los Angeles Evening Express
Los Angeles Times
News-Review Roseburg Oregon
Ogden Standard-Examiner

Index

Italicized pages are illustrations.